Des Lynam

I should have been at work!

HarperCollins*Entertainment*

An Imprint of HarperCollins*Publishers*

All photographs courtesy of the author with the exception of the following:

Army Public Relations Photo Section/Klaus Marche 13(t);
Bente Fasmer 9(t); BBC Photo Library 9(b), 14, 16, 23(b), 24(t), 25(b), 28(b);
Empics 11(b), 23(t), 26(b), 29(b); Snowdon/Radio Times 27(t); Rex 32;
Reuters 19(t), 27(b).

First published in Great Britain by
HarperCollins*Publishers*
77–85 Fulham Palace Road,
Hammersmith, London W6 8JB

Published by HarperCollins*Publishers* 2005

3

Extract from '*Another date with Nigella*' by Victor Lewis-Smith.
© Evening Standard Newspaper, 2005

Extract from '*More gush than guts*' by Victor Lewis-Smith.
© Evening Standard Newspaper, 2005

A catalogue record for this book
is available from the British Library

ISBN 0 00 720544 9

Printed and bound in Great Britain by
Clays Ltd, St Ives plc

For Rose and Patrick

CONTENTS

ACKNOWLEDGEMENTS

Writing this book has been a cathartic experience. I have had to be honest with myself about certain incidents in my life that I had put at the back of my memory; but I have had to touch on them, and it has been somewhat painful to do, but this would have been an incomplete book had I not done so. Generally, though, I hope this is a happy book that will give the reader plenty to smile about.

I could not have done it without the support of my lovely Rose, who has stuck by me through thick and thin. We have shed a tear or two over some of the more difficult reminders of my past.

Jane Morgan, my closest of friends, inadequately described as my agent, has been nothing but supportive and has lifted me through occasional troughs of despair at whether I was doing a decent job.

The main problem I faced was that, for the most part, I have not kept meaningful diaries, so my thanks go to Jonathan Martin, Martin Hopkins, Rick Waumsley, Brian Barwick, Penny Wood,

Phil King, Paul McNamara, John Graham, Audrey Adams and many other old colleagues and friends for their help in prompting my sometimes sketchy memory.

Thanks too to Trevor Dolby and all at HarperCollins for their belief and support for this old worrier.

INTRODUCTION

It was the second of August 1999. It would be the most momentous day in my broadcasting life. That evening I would be all over the television news, the following day's front pages and be the subject of columnists' opinions for weeks. What was I doing to attract so much attention?

I was changing jobs. I was shocking myself in the process and obviously, to my amazement, a lot of other people too.

I had made my decision, although my partner, Rose, had been very circumspect about the move. She knew how much I had loved the BBC; how I had worked hard to get to the position I occupied, aided by a good share of luck; how I had fought battles to defend the organisation when it was under attack from outside, and often waged war when the sports department was being battered from inside the Corporation itself. But now I would fight those battles no longer. As I went up to the office of my agent, Jane Morgan, in Regent Street, I kept wondering if I was making the biggest mistake of my working life. I had one of the best jobs in broadcasting. The

BBC had always looked after me. I was never going to get rich working for them, but they were family. I worked with a great number of wonderful and talented people, and I knew for the most part that I was popular with them. There were laughs every day. I had been given awards for doing my job, which I loved. Now I was about to throw it all in.

Had I lost my sanity? The day before, in the back garden of my house in West London, I had shaken hands with ITV's Controller of Programmes, David Liddiment, their Head of Sport, Brian Barwick, and their lawyer, Simon Johnson. I had confirmed I would be joining them. The deal was that I would not accept any counter-offer from the BBC to stay. ITV now needed confirmation that I had resigned.

'There's the phone,' said Jane. 'Take a deep breath and the best of luck.'

1

DADDY WHO?

I was born on 17 September 1942, in the new hospital in the town of Ennis in County Clare, Ireland. For the privilege of being born in the country of my heritage, I am indebted to Adolf Hitler.

My mother and father had both left their homeland before the Second World War to forge careers in nursing in England, where they had met. Unemployment was rife in Ireland at the time, and would continue to be so for many years until the economic boom brought about by Ireland's membership of the European Community in the Eighties. Like many before and after them, my parents had become economic migrants when still in their teenage years. Both, and entirely independent of each other, had been close to making their new lives in America but had been prevailed upon by their families to stay within reasonable reach of home.

They had begun their training in Bournemouth but had moved to Brighton in Sussex, where my father had become a senior mental health nurse at the Brighton General Hospital and my mother a nursing sister. But in 1941 my father was called up by the British Army to do his duty on behalf of his adopted country and joined the Royal Army Medical Corps. Initially, he was posted to Northern Ireland, and so my mother decided to go back to the bosom of her family in Ennis so that they could continue to see each other from time to time.

Shortly after my mother found out that she was expecting yours truly, Dad was posted to the Far East. I would not meet him until I was nearly four years old.

Mother, Gertrude Veronica, was from a large family, eight children in all, of whom she was the youngest. Her father and my grandfather, Packo Malone, was a famous local sportsman when a young man, excelling in particular at the Gaelic sports of football and hurling, representing the county at both, and playing in an all-Ireland final before the First World War. He was well over six feet tall and as strong as an ox. Of all his grandchildren, I am the only one to match him in terms of height, and I also seem to have inherited his rather large conk as well. When he was young, he had enjoyed a few drinks, but on his fortieth birthday he had suffered an almighty hangover, subsequently 'took the pledge', and never did a drop of alcohol pass his lips for the next half-century.

My maternal grandmother Hannah, known as Annie, was a beauty when young and in later life devoted herself to the family and to the Roman Catholic Church. She rose early to go to Mass every day of the week. Packo went to church on Sundays, but each night of his life he could be seen kneeling on a chair in the living room of the tiny house in which he brought up his large family to say his prayers – his 'duty', he called it. They had absolute faith in the Catholic Church and their God and gave enormous respect to the local clergy, several of whom, including the bishop, became Packo's close friends on his weekend hunting or fishing expeditions.

The house did not boast a bathroom: a tin bath was kept for the purpose of the occasional full-body ablution, with the water boiled in large kettles on the turf-fired 'range'. The toilet was outside in the back yard. There was no refrigerator, food was bought fresh each day, and of course there was no telephone. My grandfather conducted his business by 'message'. People would arrive at the door, to book their horse in for a 'shoeing', or simply turn up, in hope, at the forge that was a short walk from the house.

My grandfather was a farrier, a blacksmith, with his own business, like his father and grandfather before him. In the Forties and Fifties, the west of Ireland had not changed much since the turn of the century, and people continued to be largely dependent on the horse for transport. Deliveries were made by horse and cart; the pony and trap was still used by many for their personal journeys and donkey carts were prevalent too. Business was brisk for my grandfather, and only the hours in the day limited the amount of work available.

The story goes that Packo and his father had decided not to get involved in those newfangled motor cars, probably thinking them a passing fancy. Henry Ford's Irish grandfather, a farrier from County Cork, had made a different decision, and the family had done rather well as a result.

My Uncle Frank, a dab hand with car mechanics, had been persuaded to assist his father as a farrier and eventually took the business over; but of course he saw its decline into a virtual tourists' showpiece as the motor car began to dominate our lives.

My earliest years were spent in a home full of warmth, fun and security. The house was in the town centre, opposite the

Friary Church, handy for my grandmother. There were always visitors – aunts, uncles, cousins, neighbours – calling. Sometimes, on a Sunday, we would take the pony and trap out to visit a relative's farm a few miles from town. I can still hear the clip-clop of the little animal's hooves and smell the leather upholstery of the highly polished trap. One of my earliest memories is of being allowed to hold the reins of the pony.

I was too young to be aware of the horrors happening all over Europe – the bombing, the Holocaust, the terrible suffering. Ireland was a haven of tranquillity, having declared its neutrality under President de Valera.

My mother kept mentioning this fantasy figure called 'Daddy'. I could not quite imagine who or what he was. This mysterious person had actually written to me from India, telling me to be a good boy and look after Mummy while he was away. This letter was read to me, as I was only three years old. I can imagine it not meaning too much to me.

Then, one day, a good-looking man in a grey pin-striped suit and a trilby hat arrived at the door, picked me up in his arms, and kissed me on the cheek. This was an invasion of privacy – and he was paying a rather undue amount of attention to my mother as well. I cried my eyes out.

Eventually, I must have warmed to this intruder; but, not so long after, there was another interloper, and I was no longer the focal point of everyone's attention. My sister Ann was born. Of course, she had been delivered by an angel to my mother in hospital, a story I must have bought without further question. All I knew was that this new person was taking up a vast amount of my mother's time and interest, and for the first time in my young life I felt the pangs of jealousy. My grandmother had to take me to one side and explain that Mummy certainly loved me the best but, because Ann was so small, she needed to be specially looked after.

But the 'looking after' wasn't enough to save her young life. Within six or seven weeks of her birth, she died of meningitis.

While I remember my baby sister arriving, I have no clear memory of her death or that it affected me very much at the time. I suppose I was shielded from it, and my grandparents would have explained it all as 'the will of God'. I have often wondered what sort of person Ann would have grown into and what effect she would have had on my life.

Obviously my mother and father were distraught at the loss. Soon afterwards they decided to take up their jobs in England again, and I found myself on the train to Limerick and Dublin and then the mail boat crossing from Dun Laoghaire to Holyhead in North Wales, a journey I was to experience almost every year during my childhood as we went 'home' for the summer holidays.

My parents had rented a flat in Brighton before the war but now needed a new home. At first we became lodgers in the house of one of Dad's work colleagues, who had two sons, both older than me. I didn't take to them, and the feeling was entirely mutual. They continually mocked me when I spoke. I could not understand why, but of course I had a broad County Clare accent and they couldn't make out a word I said, and neither could their parents.

Pretty soon we moved to a brand new council house, the building of which was virtually going on around us. Amongst the labourers were German prisoners of war, yet to be repatriated. I learned, much later, that they were treated badly by some of our new neighbours, but my Dad showed them respect. His view was that they were probably family men like him whose lives, like his, had been disrupted for five years through no fault of their own. Soon they disappeared back to their homeland, and I was disappearing off to school.

St John the Baptist Roman Catholic Primary School was a pretty dismal-looking place in a poor part of the town run by a combination of nuns and lay teachers. Most of the kids were from Irish or Italian Catholic families, but I was the only one nobody could understand, for a while at least. My earliest memory of school is of being asked to draw a line. I drew a funny little animal with four legs. For me a line, with my Irish accent, was a tiger without the stripes. The teacher thought I was mucking about. My parents told me that within a few months, the Irish accent had disappeared and I became like the other kids in my speech patterns, unlike my parents, who retained their Irish accents all their lives.

Once I could make myself understood I became accepted by my infant peers and I began to enjoy going to school. I worked out pretty soon too that I wasn't the dullest in the class by a long way. Within a year, though, I was to be out of school for nearly three months. I had been complaining of stomach ache and a local doctor had diagnosed indigestion, told my mother not to let me eat apples, prescribed some milk of magnesia, and said I would be alright in a day or two. Over the next few days, I gave them great cause for worry. I developed spots, which my father immediately knew was measles, and the stomach pains were getting worse. Dad telephoned another doctor, Dr John O'Hara, who saved my life and whom I met again thirty years later when he was on the council of the Football Association. Dr John immediately diagnosed a septic appendix: I was in a fever with the measles, and now needed an urgent operation as well. My parents, having lost Ann a short time before, were

6

now close to losing me. The appendix was taken out – probably in a hurry. The scar is still prominent all these years later. After the operation, I was removed to an isolation hospital, where I would remain for some weeks. When I eventually returned home, I must have looked a very poor specimen indeed. I could scarcely walk, having been bedridden for so long, and for weeks my mother had to take me to a clinic for physiotherapy to help me get the use of my legs again.

I didn't like this place called England. First they mocked the way you speak, and then you got hit with not one, but two serious illnesses at once. I wanted to go back to Ireland, and said so in no uncertain terms. But, in time, I settled into the rhythm of my new life in Brighton. In those days, everyone who had been given a council house seemed to be inordinately proud of it. Gardens were tended with great enthusiasm – my father won several prizes for his garden; doors were regularly re-painted, and windows sparkled. We had a refrigerator, which was unusual for working-class people in the late Forties and early Fifties. Few of our neighbours had a car. If they did it was usually a pre-war model. My Dad cycled the four or five miles to the hospital where he worked, but after a time was able to afford a modest motorcycle combination. The bike was a 500 cc BSA with a Watsonian sidecar capable of seating my mother, with me behind her. It was a very fragile piece of equipment and seemed to be made largely of plywood, covered with a black lining. These 'combinations' were very popular in those days, being cheaper to run than cars. You rarely see one now. Sometimes, when the weather was good, I was allowed to sit on the pillion seat behind Dad. This was long before crash helmets were deemed compulsory, or indeed necessary. We often went up to London to see relatives by this mode of transport and once went all the way to Ireland, singing at the tops of our voices as we meandered through the country roads of Wales to the boat train at Fishguard. That sort of happiness should be bottled.

At school I was progressing from cowboys and indians to football and cricket. I also sang in the school choir – our rendition of 'Panis Angelicus' won us first prize in the Sussex schools' competition. My best pal was Micky Weller and I was in love with a pretty girl called Janice Prossor. I usually showed my passion for her by chasing her round the playground. It was unrequited love, but I did manage to kiss her once. Sheer bliss. It gave me a wonderful tingling feeling of which I have never tired.

In class, I was doing well under the guidance of Miss Thornton and Mr Beech, but being a Catholic school we were consumed with religious instruction that took up around an hour of each day. I kept hearing about the Immaculate Conception many years before I knew what immaculate or conception meant, never mind the two of them together. It was a wonder we had time for the academic stuff.

I got into a few fights in the playground, won a couple, lost a couple. Steeled myself not to cry when I lost, but the emotions usually got the better of me when I won. In summer evenings I would gather in the local park with a few other boys and we would play cricket till dark.

Although we had little money, my parents loved to go to the local variety theatre, when the housekeeping budget allowed, to see some of the great comics of the day, and I went with them. They had heard Frankie Howerd, Jimmy Edwards, Max Bygraves and Max Miller on radio; and in those pre-television days, or at least before most people had TVs, this was the way to see your favourites. The Brighton Hippodrome was usually packed when a big name came to town, which happened regularly. The theatre was a 'number one'; that is to say, the top-line acts would appear there. As well as those mentioned above, I remember seeing Tony Hancock, Vic Oliver, and even Laurel and Hardy live on stage. And of course we never missed a pantomime. To this day I can smell the red velour seats and remember the anticipation as the orchestra struck up their introduction to the evening or matinee.

But each year, Mum and Dad and I would set out for 'home'. This was a trip back to Ireland for two or three weeks. While my pals were enjoying Brighton beach, I would be spending my time with the family, either in Ennis or at my Dad's village, Boris in Ossery, in the county of Laois in the midlands of Ireland. I would usually return to Brighton, pale as death in contrast to my sun-tanned pals, having suffered from the wet Hibernian climate.

When in Ennis, I would go to my grandfather's forge and spend hours pulling the bellows to heat up the fire for smelting the horseshoes. There, I would listen to stories and jokes as the men got about their work. I learned not to be afraid of horses, but never to stand behind them. The forge seemed to be the meeting place for many boys after school or on Saturdays, and I remember a great atmosphere of camaraderie. I was now occasionally ribbed for my English accent. What a turnaround.

On Sundays it was off to Mass, then lunch and either a trip to the country or, more likely, down to Cusack Park to watch a hurling or Gaelic football match. My grandfather was known to everyone and his former sporting prowess earned him a good deal of respect. He proudly introduced me to people, and being 'Packo's' grandson seemed to give me some reflected glory. I learned how to use a hurly stick and, a lifetime later, I was walking in Richmond Park one day when I came across two

Irish boys smacking a ball between them with hurlies. 'Can I have a go?' I asked. They were amazed that I could pick up the ball with the stick, control it at speed, and fire it to them accurately.

I loved being in Ennis, but would also spend a while at the home of my paternal grandparents, Joseph and Bridget Lynam. Joe was a signalman on the railway, a task he combined with running a small farm. Between them they produced no fewer than fifteen children, most of whom survived into old age, a couple of them into their late nineties.

Once, when I was about fourteen, I cheekily suggested to my Dad that grandfather must have been a sex maniac. Dad, rather amused, reckoned that his father might only have had sex fifteen times. Can you imagine bringing up that many children in a small farmhouse, with no modern conveniences, on low pay and no benefits? Well they all ate well, all went to school, all ended up with responsible jobs, and the only case of lawbreaking in the family was when Uncle Gerald was had up for a bit of poaching. My grandparents set standards for their children that were adhered to throughout their lives.

I was always frightened in the house at night. My parents, with my grandmother (who liked a Guinness) and other family members and friends, would go off to one of the many pubs in the village. I would be left in the house with my teetotal grandfather. I was always given a room that had a picture of Jesus Christ on the Cross wearing the crown of thorns; his eyes always seemed to be staring right at me. Whichever way I turned in the bed, the eyes never left me. I never slept a wink until daybreak. Then I could never get up.

Bridget and Joe Lynam were as different as chalk and cheese, underlining the old adage that opposites attract. Joe was

10

straightforward, hardworking, and very literate. He could quote Shakespeare readily, and enjoyed most of the plays. He particularly liked George Bernard Shaw, a man of his own vintage. Bridget was somewhat capricious, with a ready wit. She liked a drink and whenever a visitor with similar tastes arrived at the house, she would ensconce herself in the 'parlour' to pour the guest a glass of Guinness. Then she would liberally imbibe herself. The theory was that Joe knew nothing of this habit, but of course he wasn't that stupid and left her to her own devices.

To this day I remember some of Granny's sayings. About someone always complaining about their aches and pains, she would say, 'He's never without an arse or an elbow'. If she saw an odd looking couple, she would remark that 'Every old shoe meets an old sock'; or on seeing someone strange she might say, 'It's amazing what you see when you haven't got a gun.'

She told stories about the village cheapskate, a lady who, when it was her round, would describe the Guinness as having got 'very bitter' until it was someone else's round. Her favourite one was when someone came up with something she had missed. 'You're an eejit but you're right,' she'd say. Bridget was quite a lady, a lady who had endured being pregnant over nineteen summers of her life.

But it was back in England that I remember enjoying one of the best days of my life. I was ten years of age and it was Christmas morning. I had received a great array of presents, everything I could have wished for, when Dad called me from the kitchen. 'There's something here in a big parcel,' he said. 'What can this be?'

I ran in, and there underneath the cardboard wrappings was a brand new Raleigh bicycle. I don't think at any time in my life since have I exceeded the happiness of that moment.

11

But that morning, a boy who lived across the road learned that his mother, who was probably only in her early thirties, had suddenly died – on Christmas Day. I could see his pale face looking through the window of his house, tears streaming down. I took my bike several streets away to ride it. I didn't want to display my happiness in front of his abject misery.

As I went through my years at junior school, it became clear that I had a good chance of passing the Eleven-Plus examination. In every test I usually came top or near the top of the class. When the examination came round, Dad promised me a cricket bat if I passed, which I did. I still have the bat, with the signature of the then famous England captain Len Hutton inscribed on it. Years later when I interviewed Len, who had long been retired, he asked me to sign an autograph for him, for his grandchild. How could I have imagined at eleven years of age such a turn of events? Dad told me later that the bat would have been mine even if I had not passed the exam. 'You would have had it for trying your best,' he said.

Janice Prossor was also successful. My pal Micky Weller was not. He was distraught and deemed to be a failure at that tender age. Whenever I hear arguments in favour of that life-changing test, I think of Micky's tears.

And so, in September 1954, I was off to Varndean Grammar School for Boys along with Pat Dale, Ron Cavadeschi and Geoff Macklin, who had also picked up enough information at St John the Baptist – in addition to the catechism and the doctrine of the Immaculate Conception – to win places to Varndean.

I was now the proud possessor of a red blazer with black piping and a 'Just William' style cap, similarly decorated. The blazer was a bit on the large side. It had to last. I found myself studying subjects like Latin and Chemistry and Physics, playing sports on Thursday afternoons on the spacious playing fields, and being introduced to the marvellous game of chess, which I enjoy to this day.

For a time I was a member of the Army section of the Combined Cadet Force, which was compulsory for a year. I learned how to fire a rifle and a Bren gun and march up and down. On our first day a boy called Douglas Pitt, later a university professor, volunteered to show us how to march at the request of the officer in charge. He did so with his left arm and left leg in unison rather than right arm, left leg. We were hysterical with laughter, and so was the officer/master in charge of us. Another cadet, Eric Cager, when asked what he thought camouflage meant, replied, 'Is it when we put trees on our heads, sir?' I enjoyed all that; but what I hated was getting on the school bus on 'Cadet's Day' in my army gaiters and heavy boots and being the subject of much ridicule as the local 'secondary moderns' spent the ride saluting and making wisecracks. I made some great new friends at the school, in particular Doug Hillman, with whom I still play tennis nearly half a century later, and Charlie Trinder, whom I visit in America, and many others.

And I discovered Brighton and Hove Albion.

I had of course heard a great deal about the local professional team and knew the names of the players, but I had never been to the famous old Goldstone Ground in Hove until a neighbour, Bob Seymour, invited me along with his two daughters. They were of a similar age to me, and I was desperately in love with both of them, though they treated me with considerable disdain. I had been looking forward to the experience for weeks. We arrived, me in particular in a high state of excitement, and found ourselves, standing of course, behind the goal in the north enclosure. Being small, we were helped to the front.

These were the days when football crowds were sporting and friendly, long before hooliganism took its ugly hold on the game. In the kick-in before the match started, a Brighton player called Des Tenant (my favourite because he shared my Christian name) fired the ball past the goal and flush into the face of one of Bob's daughters, who had not been quick enough to get out of the way. She was knocked down and out. Off we went to casualty, where she was revived and checked over for any serious head injury. I described the incident years later as my first experience of a woman's headache getting in the way of a lot of fun. My enthusiasm for the club was undimmed by this experience, however, and I have been a lifelong fan during their ups and downs, of which there have been many.

I played football for the school and took up tennis instead of cricket, although I continued to play the latter in the park on summer evenings. And I found myself shooting up from about five foot three to six feet tall. Suddenly I was gangly, and very self-conscious of it. Luckily, my mother told me to stop stooping and be proud of my height.

My first form master at the grammar school was Michael Wylie, known as 'Bubble' for his rounded features and frame, under whose care and guidance I soon began to excel in class, especially at English, Maths and Latin, and I was marked out as having university potential. I took part in a couple of 'house' plays but was never ambitious enough to go the whole hog and try for a part in the school's annual Shakespearian production.

Meanwhile, my mother, who was a good dancer, persuaded me to enrol for ballroom dancing lessons at the Court School of Dancing. 'You don't want to be an eejit all your life, with two left feet,' she said, and so, rather sulkily, off I went, to be clutched to the bosom of some old lady of about twenty-eight years of age as she tried to instil in me the basic moves of the quick step, the foxtrot and the waltz. I was much more interested in her bosom and found myself sexually aroused as she held me tightly. I think she was having some fun at my expense as she nodded and winked to her fellow instructress whenever I took to the floor with her. On Saturday nights there would be a free dance night when all the pupils and guests would turn up to show off their limited skills. It was full of pretty girls outnumbering the men and boys by about three to one. I had a whale of a time.

Back at school, my academic ambitions waned, and although I managed a good crop of exam results I could not envisage putting my parents through three extra years of struggle to keep me studying, and so I left without going on to university. My father, who might have been a doctor had he had the chance to further his schooling, had thoughts that I might be able to move in that direction; but having absolutely no ability whatsoever in science subjects, that hope went out of the window. I wanted to be a journalist, or, as I saw it, a newspaper man. We read the *Daily Mirror* at home and I was a big fan of their chief sportswriter, Peter Wilson, whom I got to know many years later. His by-line described him as 'The Man They Can't Gag'. I also avidly read William Connor, the columnist who wrote under the pseudonym of 'Cassandra', the prophetess of doom, and who extraordinarily lost a libel case to the American showman Liberace after describing him as effeminate. Try as I might, though, and I must have written scores of letters to various publications, I had no luck in that direction, and so I joined a bank. My headmaster, who was highly critical of my leaving school without going on to college, having been unable to persuade me to stay on, wrote a letter of introduction to a contact of his who was the general manager of the Bank of London and South America. I went off to Threadneedle Street in the City of London for an interview and was offered a job. It would entail six months' training and I would then be posted to Buenos Aires. 'We'll never see you,' said my mother on hearing about it. So I joined a bank a little closer to home, in Brighton. I hated every waking minute of it.

I had had a couple of dates with girls at this time. The thrill of simply holding hands in the cinema was almost overwhelming. I had got into a little trouble on one trip to Ireland when I had taken a beautiful local girl from Ennis to the pictures. Her name was Maura Gorman, and I had given her a kiss in the back row. I had been spotted and was marched off to see my Uncle Frank, who took me to one side: 'We don't do that sort of thing in public,' he said. I was mortified, feeling that I'd let the family down. Mind you, Maura had enjoyed it as much as I had.

Then, back in Brighton, I had bumped into Susan, who with her blonde hair and good looks was making the social side of life very bearable indeed. Sue was still at the girls' grammar school and looked good even in her navy blazer. Her parents were nice people but a bit suspicious of this boy from the council estate. Over the next ten years, they would get to know me pretty well.

2

NOT A COMPLETE BANKER

After a couple of years in banking, and with Part 1 of the Institute of Bankers' exams passed in double-quick time, I decided I couldn't stand the job any longer and left. For a couple of months I worked as a trainee salesman, which involved me moving away from Brighton and staying in digs.

My landlady, some ten years my senior, took a liking to me and was quite keen to introduce me to the comforts of her bedroom. Had her husband, who was a man mountain, returned home from his job (which involved unsocial hours), I would not now be alive to write about it; but I managed to stay pure despite her constant provocation, which did occasionally lead to a bit of slap and tickle, but nothing more.

Both the landlady and the job were very temporary experiences and I soon returned to Brighton to seek further employment and begin doing a little freelance writing. This clearly would not pay many bills and so I took another temporary job driving a fish delivery van. That lasted a few weeks in the summer. It involved getting up at 5 a.m. to pick up the 'locally caught' produce (which had come down from Hull or Grimsby) at the railway station, take it to the shop for filleting, and then off to deliver it to the local hotels and other outlets. The head chef of one hotel would take the baskets of fish, returning them empty to me, save for the fillet steak and a mountain of groceries that I would then deliver to his girlfriend's flat. There would be a steak in it for me as payment. This was plainly dishonest, but at the time I convinced myself that the chef was doing the stealing. I was merely the 'mule'.

Soon I had to get a proper job again and found myself in the world of insurance, and started to climb the career ladder. It wasn't very stimulating but it would give me some sort of future if that was the way my life was going to pan out.

Then I got married to Sue and off we went in her mother's coffee-coloured Triumph Herald convertible to the Isle of Wight on honeymoon. We were young, I was 23, Sue not yet 22, but we had already known each other for five or six years.

Having enjoyed good health since my early brush with illness as a small boy, I was now to experience another nasty shock.

I had suffered a pretty severe headache one day while at the Farnborough Air Show and, like a fool, had taken a couple of aspirin washed down with a pint of lager. I felt decidedly unwell on the journey home and that night woke and was sick. Frighteningly, I was vomiting blood. Sue called the doctor, who inspected the residue of my insides and decided it was hospital for me.

On arriving at the Royal Sussex County Hospital, I was wheeled into the reception area, where I was asked for my date of birth, next of kin, etc. Then, the woman instructed the ambulance men: 'He's for death list.' So that was it. Twenty-three years of age and it was all over. I hadn't had a life. I had achieved nothing. I gripped Sue's hand and a tear slid down my face. All I could think of to say to her was 'sorry'.

And so I was taken to Defflis Ward, named after a former mayor of the town. Thankfully they eventually changed it; apparently I was not the only one who, over the years, thought they were on the way out instead of up to the third floor.

I was diagnosed with a slight scarring of the duodenum, an indication that I had had an ulcer at some time. But I soon recovered and was back on my feet, but banned from ever taking aspirin again.

It was the middle of the Sixties. I was in my early twenties with a wife, a mortgage and a career in insurance. I had passed the examinations of the professional body, which made up some way for my not going to university. I had reached the heady heights of inspector, the company had supplied me with a car – a shining new pale green Ford Anglia – and I spent my days racing around Sussex, calling on insurance brokers, assessing risks of burglary or fire or anything else insurable and, in the main, was having a pretty good time of it. Up till now the Sixties had hardly swung for me, but I was on a fast track to promotion to branch manager, and would probably be one by the time I hit thirty. I would have earned a reasonable salary for the rest of my life

But was I happy? Hell, no. I constantly felt there was more to life. More to me. I felt that I had made some wrong decisions and was now paying for them. It looked as though I would be stuck in this world of business for the next thirty-five years – fine for some, but not for me. My private life was pretty good, and I had an excellent group of friends; but there was a burning dissatisfaction within me.

But my thoughts about the future, and how I might escape

19

from my routine, slipped way down my list of priorities one day in early 1968. My mother, who had scarcely had a day's illness in her life, suddenly suffered a brain haemorrhage and was rushed to hospital, where she was operated on. The prognosis was not good. If she made any recovery at all, she would almost certainly have been severely disabled. Day after day for a month, my Dad and I, often with my wife Susan, journeyed the thirty or so miles there and back to visit her in hospital. Day after day we would imagine improvements in her condition: 'I'm sure I saw a flicker of a smile' – 'I thought she moved her fingers ever so slightly'. We were trying desperately to give each other some comfort, some hope. After a month my darling mother passed away at the tragically early age of fifty-four. She had been my rock. I loved her very dearly. She was a sensible, funny and charming woman. A looker in her day who rode motorcycles when young and was the life and soul of any party. And dance! How she loved to dance, twirling round the floor on a fine pair of legs. She was the youngest of eight children, but the first to die apart from a brother who had suffered from tuberculosis before the War. Her other brothers and sisters lived on to healthy old age. I and my father were distraught. I had never seen my Dad cry before. We wept together and could find no consolation. I thought my life had come to an end too. I had recently discovered W. H. Auden's poem 'Funeral Blues', made more famous years later in the film *Four Weddings and a Funeral*. At the time, I certainly felt as though the clocks had all been stopped. Nothing else would worry me ever again. Nothing could be this bad. We hadn't had a chance to say goodbye. I worried that she was going into the unknown without our support. She would be scared. I wouldn't, at that stage, have minded paving the way for her.

As the weeks went by, I was even surer that security didn't matter a tinker's cuss. I needed to grab life by the throat and wring some meaning out of it. I felt I could write something, but what? I had been unable to get my break into journalism, and as time went by the chances were becoming slimmer. Why would any paper take on someone who worked in insurance? I had offered the odd article to the local papers and to football magazines. Sport was my interest, so I contacted a few sportsmen and asked if I could write a profile on them, without being able to guarantee that the article would ever see the light of day.

Amazingly, several agreed. Even more amazingly, one or two were published.

Seeing my by-line in print had given me a thrill and I began to imagine that sooner or later I would get my break.

And it came, not from print journalism, but from radio.

In those days, to get into the BBC was well-nigh impossible, unless you had either exemplary qualifications or connections. I had neither and it hadn't even occurred to me to try to breach the citadel at Broadcasting House.

But then I saw a notice in the local paper that the BBC was opening up local stations around the country and that one of the first would be Radio Brighton. It registered with me and a little later, when the station was under way, they began advertising for people who might have an interest in broadcasting to get in touch. I didn't know anything about broadcasting but I rang them up and, to my utter astonishment, I was invited to come and have a look at the station and try my hand, or rather my voice, in front of the microphone.

A gentleman called David Waine, who was probably no older than me but whose face I recognised from regional television, gave me what transpired to be my audition. Years later, David was to become a very senior figure at the BBC but, at this time, he had given up his television job to embark on a new radio adventure.

'You have a good voice,' he said. 'Very fluent.' He told me that he would get in touch. He knew of my interest in sport.

I now began to think that my dear mother was pulling some strings for me. The feeling was strong. I was gaining some confidence from the thought, or the fantasy, whichever it was, that I was throwing off my shackles of self-doubt, of concern for the future. Not long after, I found myself in the studio on a Saturday afternoon reading football results and other sports news. It was great fun, entirely unpaid.

In no time at all, under the experienced (he had been in the business for weeks) eye of an amiable chap called John Henty, I was presenting the Saturday night sports desk. Soon I was writing a weekly review of the local press, which involved arriving at the studio at 6.30 in the morning; reading through the three local weekly papers and writing, by hand, a three-minute piece to be voiced live just after the 8 a.m. news bulletin. I was amazed that I could do it at all; but I was also apparently making it interesting and funny and getting a terrific response. The local newspaper editors began paying attention to it, occasionally complaining if they thought I was being harsh on them. I was using their copy for flights of fancy into areas that had little to do with the content in their papers. In short, I was using them as an excuse to write a weekly radio essay. Then I branched into comedy – or at least I and my writing partners thought it was comedy.

Together with Ivan Howlett, still a radio broadcaster, the aforementioned John Henty, Peter Vincent (who went on to be a top comedy writer for The Two Ronnies and others), and a girl singer called Amaryllis, I began putting together and performing in a Sunday half-hour show called *How Lunchtime It Is* – there was a TV series called *How Late It Is* that had prompted the idea for the title.

I could do passable imitations of the two leading politicians of the time, Harold Wilson and Edward Heath. Actually they were impersonations of Mike Yarwood doing Harold Wilson and Edward Heath, and 'they' appeared in every show. Incidentally, years later I was invited to lunch at Edward Heath's majestic home in Salisbury. On entering, Ted wondered if I 'could abide champagne' – a curious way of posing the question, but I answered 'Yes, and plenty of it.' I asked him who had been the most impressive leader he had met down the years. Unhesitatingly, he said, 'Mao-Tse-Tung.' 'But he was a mass murderer,' I ventured. 'You're typically falling into the trap of misunderstanding his position,' said Ted, an acknowledged Sinophile.

I loved being involved in *How Lunchtime It Is*. We went into the studio on Sunday mornings to record our offerings, having roped our friends in to be the audience. They laughed more at our attempts at being satirists than at the quality of the content, but these were some of the happiest days of my life. I was becoming fulfilled at last. I was a broadcaster. Unpaid, but I was a broadcaster. My hobby was now interfering with my career.

So, naturally enough, I gave up my career.

Sue and I had rented a small terraced house owned by her father, a local funeral director. He knew I was not overly enthusiastic about my job in insurance and one day he had sat me down and offered me a junior partnership in his business. I think he was mostly thinking about his daughter's future quality of life, but it was a very generous offer to make. But 'Des the Funeral Director' was never going to be, and I politely refused, with much gratitude for his consideration.

Soon after this, I bought my first house for £3,750 (the vast majority of it paid for by mortgage). For that I got a four-bedroom Victorian terraced property with a garden in an old but decent part of town. My move into insurance had been yet another career change, but it was only postponing the inevitable and the shocking death of my mother made me realise that there was no longer anything left to lose. Her passing spurred me on to leave the conventions of a nine-to-five profession. I had been helped in my decision by a veteran local journalist and friend, Jack Arlidge. 'Fortune favours the brave, Des,' he had said to me. And so it seemed that everything was telling me to pursue my dream of becoming a journalist.

I discussed it with Sue. I wanted to give up the security of my job, my company car, my preferential mortgage deal and my pension rights, not to mention my income, for a tilt at the windmill of broadcasting. Sue, good girl that she was, was all for it. 'Time to have a go,' she said.

It was a brilliant response, and so I gave in my notice, bought a twelve-year-old Volkswagen Beetle from my new colleague, John Henty, for £140 and turned up each day at my new job at Radio Brighton. I got paid per item in guineas. After a few months, my income had slumped to about a tenth of what it had been. Sue was now paying most of the bills from her job as a librarian.

Soon I was expecting reasonable broadcasting standards of myself and others around me. One day, a colleague, fed up with my criticism of the poor quality of a sports item, turned on me: 'Who do you bloody well think you are, David Coleman?' he bellowed. 'No, but the listeners have a right to expect professionalism from any broadcaster they have tuned in to hear or watch,' I pompously replied. I was crossed off this chap's Christmas card list straight away, but I knew I was right. What I could not have envisaged was that one day I would take over from David Coleman as the main presenter of *Grandstand*, a decision about which he was none too pleased.

In the early Eighties I began sharing the programme with Coleman. His period on the show coincided with most of the major events, like the Five Nations Rugby Championship (as it then was), the Grand National and the FA Cup Final. Then I would take over, allowing him to commentate on the athletics championships, his speciality. I had mentioned once or twice that I wouldn't mind trying one or two of the major outside broadcast events. I had made no firm requests or stipulations. However, after the 1984 Olympics, it was decided that I should be the number one presenter. Coleman remained the athletics commentator and presented *A Question of Sport*.

But all that was a long time in the future. For the time being I was happy just simply being in local radio. After a couple of months I had managed to get one or two reports sent up to the network in London and they had been well received. Soon after that, I spotted an advert in the BBC in-house magazine. The sports department in London were seeking 'Sports News Assistants'. Despite my limited experience, I applied. It would be the last job I ever applied for at the BBC.

3

TAKING THE MIKE

It was one morning in the late autumn of 1969 that I caught the train from Brighton to Victoria Station in London, hopped on the tube to Oxford Circus, and duly presented myself at the reception desk at Broadcasting House as requested. I was excited and nervous. I sensed that a few very important hours lay ahead.

Somebody took me up the three floors to the offices of the radio sports news department, and there I was introduced to a slim dapper man with a thin moustache and slicked-back grey hair. I thought he was pretty old. He was about fifty-eight years of age. He greeted me with a firm handshake and a smile.

'So you want to come and join the big boys,' he said. His speech pattern and Scots accent seemed to produce a slight menace in the words as he said them. He was Angus McKay, a legend in BBC Radio. Shortly after the Second World War he had begun a programme called *Sports Report*, the five o'clock show that is still going today on Radio 5 Live and which is the longest running sports programme in the world. Its familiar signature tune, 'Out of the Blue', remains to this day as well. Angus had started with Raymond Glendenning, the most famous sports commentator of his day before television got into its stride, as his presenter, but soon found a young Irishman with a mid-Atlantic style of speech whom he would mould into a star. That young man was Eamonn Andrews, who of course went on to television fame with *This is Your Life*.

I noticed that Angus worked from an easy chair and in front of him was just a low coffee table. I learned later that he didn't like desks. 'If you have a desk, people put bits of paper on it,' he would say. For Angus, everything was dealt with there and then.

He had heard one or two of my reports from Radio Brighton and apparently thought that my voice was OK and that if he put me through my paces I might make the grade. 'First though,' he said, 'you're a bit old to join the department [I was just twenty-seven]. We normally catch them younger. I want to make sure you know your sport, so we have worked out a little quiz for you.'

I was put in the hands of his number two, Vincent Duggelby, and asked to fill in the answers to a list of thirty-six sports questions. I got thirty-five right. I must have been a bit of an anorak. Anyway, things went pretty well and I was allowed to apply formally for one of the vacancies as a sports news assistant. The job might involve some broadcasting or production work or writing, or most likely all three. Some weeks went by before I was back at Broadcasting House for a voice test conducted by Bob Burrows, who in due course would take over as boss of the radio sports news department. I passed that test as well, and now came the appointments board. There were four people on the board, but I had figured out that Angus would be making the decisions and was the man to work to. I knew I had hit it off with him because I made him laugh, not the easiest of tasks. Bob Burrows told me later that Angus thought he might make something of me. He told Burrows he had found a new *Sports Report* presenter. Having been a military man, he had also liked the fact that I was neatly dressed and my shoes were polished. Angus was to change my life.

In a short space of time, I had gone from being an insurance inspector, to a freelance local radio broadcaster, to a member of the staff in national broadcasting at the BBC on a starting salary of £2,030 per annum.

I could not have been happier. Three other hopefuls were appointed with me: Chris Martin-Jenkins, the cricket writer and *Test Match Special* commentator; Bill Hamilton, who went on to be a television news man; and Dick Scales, who left broadcasting after a few years for jobs with Coca-Cola, Adidas and other businesses connected with sport. Dick and I hit it off straight away. He had a great sense of humour, an eye for the ladies, and was tough as you like – he had spent a few years in the military police before entering journalism. In fact, all of us new boys became good friends. Among those already in the department were Peter Jones, the then presenter of *Sports Report* and an outstanding football commentator; Bryon Butler, a man with a deep baritone voice and a clever wordsmith; and John Motson, who was younger than all of us.

After my first morning in the department I went off to lunch with Roger McDonald, one of my new colleagues, in the BBC canteen on the top floor at Broadcasting House. After lunch we got separated and I made my way down in the lift back to the office. I duly sat at the desk I thought I had left an hour or so before. After a while a chap came over to me and asked if he could help in any way.

'No thanks,' I said. 'I'm just waiting to see how the afternoon sports desk is put together.'

'Then perhaps you should go down one more floor,' he said. 'That's where the sports department lives. At the moment you're in documentary features.'

Wrong floor. Idiot.

After a couple of days I was asked to read the racing results live on air. Although I had done a good amount of far more difficult tasks in local radio, I was actually quite nervous imagining the enormity of the national audience at 6.45 in the evening.

Soon I was writing and presenting the fifteen-minute sports desk on some evenings, or else I was producing the programme, putting the recorded or live pieces together, briefing whoever was the presenter of the day, and getting the timing spot on so as not to trample all over the news at 7 o'clock. I was also occasionally producing the department's half-hour weekly sports programme for the World Service called *Sports Review*. I found the voice work much easier than the production and gradually that part of my role fell into the hands of others who were more adept at it.

Just after I joined the department Angus told us that a new slot was to be our responsibility. The *Today* programme, the early morning current affairs show on Radio 4, was about to introduce a sports section that would go out live twice every morning – it is still part of the programme today. It would entail a reporter from Angus' department coming in the night before to put the broadcasts together and then present them live the following morning. If you could grab a few hours sleep, a room was provided at the Langham Building, across the road from Broadcasting House.

Angus had selected me to do the very first one. 'Vitally important you get it right, old son,' he said. 'Big audience. Don't let
me down.'

So on Grand National day 1970, the late Jack de Manio
linked over to yours truly to look ahead to the nation's big race.

After my second broadcast of that morning, Angus telephoned me.

'An outstanding start,' he said. 'You have maintained the
reputation of my department as top-notch.' I thought my chest
would burst with pride.

A few months later, after another early morning broadcast,
Angus phoned me again. 'I want you in my office in an hour,'
he said. 'And you'd better have a very good reason for me not
to sack you.'

I had transgressed simply by using in one of my pieces a
journalist who was on Angus' 'black list'. Apparently he had
warned me never to use this individual. I had either forgotten or
not listened properly, and Angus was fuming with anger that
this person should have made his way, at my invitation, on to
one of 'his' programmes. After wiping the floor with me, he
forgave this mortal sin of mine and I continued to be one of his
boys. Angus put the fear of God into all of us who worked for
him; but he disciplined us, taught us how to be proper broadcasters, and we had the utmost respect for him.

One of the problems with grabbing a few hours' sleep in the
Langham was that you had to remember to wake up. It was the
job of the security man to call you at the appropriate time, but
not all of them were reliable. One morning there was no call
and I woke up at 7.15 – ten minutes before I was due to broadcast. I threw on a shirt and trousers, dashed across the road to
Broadcasting House, grabbed my unfinished script from the

sports room, and ran down the corridor to the *Today* studio.

'Ah, here he comes', said the presenter. 'Desmond Lynam with the sports news.' I could hardly breathe. I read my first line or two, stopped, and tried to catch my breath. 'What's the matter?' enquired the presenter. 'Well, I've just come from the bedroom,' I replied.

The other problem for some staying at the Langham was the ghost. Eminent broadcasters like the late Ray Moore and James Alexander Gordon would not stay in a certain room there for all the money in the world. The story went that an old actor-manager had thrown himself from the window of this room when the Langham had been a hotel before the war (it has now reverted to being a five-star hotel). I stayed in the said room several times and had no spiritual experiences, but Ray and James were adamant that they had seen the ghost and that it had frightened them out of their wits.

In amongst all of this, in August of that year, my son Patrick was born. My wife Sue had an easy and uneventful pregnancy and had looked her most beautiful during this time. What a year we were having! New career, new baby, it was all going too swimmingly.

After just a few months, and by the time the football season was getting under way again, Angus decided I was ready to have a go at presenting *Sports Report*. Peter Jones, who wanted to spend more of his time commentating, would be a hard act to follow. He had a wonderful lilting voice, with just a slight trace of his Welshness, and had considerable style on air. Also, his pedigree was light years better than mine. He was a Cambridge graduate, a soccer blue, a fluent linguist in French and Spanish, and hugely literate. Robert Hudson, the Head of Outside Broadcasts and a rather dour traditionalist, was very much against my quick promotion. He felt I did not have the appropriate experience. He was right, but Angus saw my potential and was all for throwing me in at the deep end. Angus won the day and I did a few programmes not too badly, after one of which, Angus told me that I had appeared disingenuous during one interview. I had to look the word up.

Normally in broadcasting, the editor will be in the gallery or booth outside the actual studio. This wouldn't do for Angus, who insisted on sitting next to his presenter and whispering instructions in his ear, often while the presenter was talking to the nation. Instruction through a talkback system is commonplace in broadcasting and it becomes second nature to react while still speaking, but it was most disconcerting to have Angus' lips in contact with your earhole, and if you didn't react immediately to his instruction, for the very valid reason that you couldn't actually hear it, he would become apoplectic with rage.

Before one such programme, he and I were sitting in the office putting the final touches to the script for the evening show. At the time, a well-known *Daily Mail* journalist called J. L. ('Jim') Manning used to come in to the show on Saturday nights and do his 'final word' piece. Jim was quite a contentious individual and his three minutes were worth listening to.

The phone rang and it was for Angus. I obviously only heard his end of the conversation, the abridged version of which went like this.

'Hello, Amy [Manning's wife]. Oh no. A heart attack. In the small hours. Intensive care. Our love goes out to you, Amy. We'll be thinking of Jim. Call you later.'

Then Angus turned to his number two, Bob Burrows. 'Bob,' he said, 'we've got a problem. Manning's fucking let us down.'

A couple of years after I joined the department, a young Alan

Parry came for an interview. If he was lucky enough to get the job, Angus asked him, what did he think his ultimate ambition in broadcasting would be? Alan thought for a moment and, probably struggling for a response, said: 'I suppose, in the long term, I would like to have a go at television.' There was a long silence and then much sucking in of air and glances round the room. 'Don't you think, Alan, that if television was important Mr Burrows [his assistant] and I would be in television?'

That was Angus: a man with little self-doubt and possessing a consummate belief in his standing in the great world of radio. Alan, of course, has gone on to forge a highly successful career in television.

If I wasn't doing *Sports Report*, then I usually presented *Sports Session*, which went out at 6.30 in the evening on Radio 4. Chris Martin-Jenkins sometimes filled this role as well. One evening, I had finished a stint on Angus' programme and was listening to 'Jenko' doing his bit on *Sports Session*. It was a half-hour show. At about 6.50 I heard him say, 'That's all for this week. Good night.' We couldn't believe it. There followed about a minute of nothing, then much shuffling of papers, and then came Jenko's voice again. 'I'm afraid that wasn't the end of *Sports Session*. And now the rugby.' One producer had got his timings a bit wrong. We were hysterical with laughter and gave the future much-respected cricket correspondent plenty of stick when he appeared in the office later.

A fairly regular guest on *Sports Report* at the time was Eric Morecambe who was a director of Luton Town Football Club. I interviewed him several times at their Kenilworth Road ground and once at the BBC Television Centre where he and Ernie Wise were in rehearsals for one of their shows. He always gave his time, no matter how busy he was.

On one occasion I was presenting the programme from London and was talking to him 'down the line' during one of Luton's games.

'By the way,' he said, 'We've got a penalty. Whey hey!'

'Tell us about it then,' I said and Eric proceeded to do a perfect commentary on the build up, the spot kick and the celebrations. It's a much replayed piece of radio history. Eric was such a huge star at the time, I couldn't believe how down to earth and how kind he was to this unknown radio reporter.

My first really big adventure with BBC Radio came in the summer of 1972, when I learned that I had been selected for the team to cover the Munich Olympic Games.

Peter Jones had gone out to Germany early to do some preview reports and he phoned me in typically upbeat fashion. 'When you arrive on Thursday, old son,' he said, 'call me straight away. I have fixed up two beauties who are going to join us for dinner.' I was already greatly excited about going to the Games anyway. Now I had an extra incentive. I was of course married at the time, but I thought a little innocent flirtation would not go amiss.

When I arrived I met Jonesy for a drink and was told that the ladies in question would be joining us shortly. A few minutes later I looked up the long staircase adjoining the bar, and one of the most beautiful girls I had ever seen was descending in our direction. I nudged Jonesy. 'Have a look at that,' I said. 'Ah, that's Heidi,' he said. 'She's my partner for the evening.' Heidi turned out to be the daughter of a baron, twenty-four years of age, and a multi-linguist who would be working as a translator at the Games but who would not have looked out of place in a Miss World competition. Her friend arrived a few minutes later. I used to tell the story afterwards that Jonesy tucked me up and the friend was hideously ugly. In truth she wasn't a bad-looking girl and we had some fun for a few days before the Games began.

One day we hired a car so that 'Marguerite' could show me a little of the Bavarian countryside and its wonderful castles. I had forgotten to bring my driving licence, so the car had to be hired in her name and she had to be seen driving it away. Only then did she inform me that she had passed her driving test just a few weeks before. Result: first big roundabout, a Munich taxi hit our Ford Taunus amidships. Cue much screaming and yelling in a foreign tongue. Our car now had a mighty dent in it but was drivable and I took over, despite having no valid licence or insurance. The rest of the day went without mishap. In fact it turned out to be idyllic.

When Dick Scales arrived at the Games, he spent the first few days in Munich moaning about everything. He didn't like the place, hated the food and had been given an impossible task, etc. Then we went to the Games village and as we entered, a group of female interpreters approached. 'I think I may get to like it here after all,' said Scalesy. He certainly did. He married one of them a year or two later and I was his best man.

The story of the Munich Olympics is well documented. Mary Peters won her marvellous gold medal in what was then the women's pentathlon. I remember Alan Minter being cheated out of a potential gold medal in the boxing when he was on the receiving end of a dreadful decision in his semi-final; and of course these were the Games of Olga Korbut, who charmed the world with her gymnastics. Then there were the seven swimming gold medals of Mark Spitz. But, most of all, the Munich

Games will be remembered for the tragic killing of several members of the Israeli team by terrorists.

On the morning it happened I found myself the reporter on duty. In the course of that day I became a news correspondent, answering the questions of London-based presenters on the *Today* programme and *World at One*. Did I think the Black September movement was responsible? I was being asked by William Hardcastle, doyen of radio news presenters. It could have been the Green October movement for all I knew, but I waffled my way through and came to realise very quickly that it was more important to sound fluent than to produce any real facts. To this day I never put too much weight on those incessant two-ways by which television news programmes are mesmerised.

When I returned from the Games I was hauled before the Head of BBC Radio News. 'Listen,' he said, 'you handled the terrorist story pretty well in Munich. I think you should stop messing about with sport and join the news team as a reporter. In a couple of years we'll make you a correspondent and you'll be off round the world covering proper stories.'

'Like wars?' I asked.

'Well, that might be part of it,' he said.

'Thank you for the compliment,' I said. 'But I'm perfectly happy doing what I'm doing.'

'I think you're making a mistake,' he said. In the ensuing years, not for one moment have I ever thought he was correct.

Twenty-five years later I returned to Munich for a television programme and reported from the very apartment where the tragedy had taken place. It all came back and I shuddered at both the memory and at the rapid passage of time.

I telephoned home fairly regularly from the Games but there was one period lasting about a week when my home phone was not being answered. Whenever I rang, at whatever time of the day, there was no reply. This was worrying. I telephoned my wife's parents. What was going on, I wondered? I was told that Susan was just taking a little break and that they were looking after Patrick. This was most odd. Why had I not been told about this? When I got home I subsequently learned that Sue had fallen for someone else and was having an affair. I knew the person in question; he was an accountant. I had thought he was a friend. My marriage was over. It had lasted just seven years. Now I would be one of those 'visiting' fathers. Heartbreaking.

I had nobody else to blame but myself. I had been so absorbed with my new life and career, Sue and my new baby son had not received the attention they deserved. How many times have you heard of men throwing themselves into careers at a cost to their families?

I was especially guilty in Sue's case. After Patrick's birth in 1970, she had suffered a breakdown. It wasn't just post-natal depression. Sue was seriously ill: for a time she became a completely different personality and had to spend some time in hospital. Baby Patrick was without his mother for the first three months of his life. How I wish that my mother had been alive to look after him. As it was, my mother-in-law did a pretty good job, but it was a desperate time. When Sue recovered, she needed my arms around her and a great deal of loving attention, but I was intrigued with my new job. I was commuting, travelling abroad, working nights from time to time, and enjoying all the social invitations that went with it. Sue had to recover her health and deal with a demanding infant, mostly on her own. It should have been no real surprise that when an affectionate arm was offered, she took it. Nonetheless, it did come as a huge shock, and she made it clear there was no way back. We had met as kids, I had been at the local boys' grammar school, she at the girls' equivalent. We had had some good times and she gave me my wonderful son, who remains a delight in my life. No recriminations. Had she not strayed, it is almost certain that I would have done: there were so many temptations.

The most important thing to do now was to make absolutely sure I didn't lose touch with my son. Of course I had to pre-plan my visits to him, and for a time it was awkward. I missed seeing him grow up on a day-to-day basis; but as he got older we had marvellous times together and I know that to this day he remembers them as fondly as I do. We ate out together a great deal. Even as a four-year-old he was asking for parmesan cheese with his spaghetti. He had impeccable manners in restaurants and I was often complimented on his behaviour. We played table tennis and we swam.

Brighton was a great place for us to be together. We enjoyed the beach and the funfair and exploring. Like all small children, Patrick would ask those questions that stun adults. 'Why does the sea stop coming in, Daddy?' Pause for thought. 'Ahem, it's because the land stops going out.' Four-year-old accepts answer and moves on to jumping over cracks in pavement.

Meanwhile my BBC career was expanding into areas other than sport. I had been popping up on a Radio 2 programme called *Late Night Extra*, reporting on the day's sport. I had one close shave on the programme. I had adjourned to the bar after what I had thought to be my day's work done when, having consumed about four pints of lager, I was asked by a chap called Derek Thompson, now of Channel Four racing fame, if I could stand in for him on *Late Night Extra* as he felt decidedly ill. Well, I did; but I shouldn't have done and I slurred my way through the broadcast, much to the amusement of the presenter, David Hamilton.

Normally I did the job responsibly, and I seemed to interact well with whichever presenter was working on the show. Soon I was asked by the music department if I would like to introduce a new programme that would go out just after the seven o'clock news each night, appropriately called *After Seven*. I would do one night a week, while the likes of Michael Aspel, Michael Parkinson and the late Ray Moore would do other nights. I used to joke on air that I was the only person doing the show that I had never heard of, and soon under the guiding hand and ample bosom of a fearsome lady producer called Angela Bond, I established a new strand to my broadcasting life. It was basically a middle of the road music programme with some features included. I came up with an idea which we called 'Monday's Mimic'. Members of the public could win a prize for their impressions of famous figures, but they had to do it live down the telephone. Some were good, the odd professional was clearly ringing in, but we tried to avoid them because the deluded amateurs were hilarious. We had one poor chap whose 'James Cagney' and 'Mae West' were indistinguishable and we used to fall about in the studio.

In addition, having presented the sportsdesk on the *Today* programme I was asked if I fancied actually presenting the whole programme. I began doing this on the occasional Saturday by myself and then joined Jack de Manio, John Timpson and later Robert Robinson, as one of the weekday presenters of the show. All the while, I continued with my sports programmes. I was working flat out. Some weeks I was up at three in the morning to present the *Today* show, did *After Seven* on the Monday, plus a six-hour sports show on the Saturday. Bear in mind that I was now to all intents and purposes a 'single' man again. I was not exactly behaving like a monk, and the candles were being burnt

39

not just at both ends but in the middle too. Eventually I turned down the invitation to renew my agreement with *Today* and got my life back on a more even keel. But being on the programme taught me a huge lesson about how to work under pressure and write lucidly and concisely in a very limited space of time.

I retain undying admiration for the likes of John Humphrys, who, despite the ungodly hour his day begins, is as sharp as a tack on the current *Today* programme. He also has to deal constantly with heavyweight issues. In my time, although politics was very much part of the programme, overall it had a lighter feel to it. There was still time for the 'record egg-laying hen' type of story.

In fact one morning, when Jack de Manio was still doing the show, he had to conduct an interview with a chap who had bred an unusual type of mouse. The creatures had been brought into the studio in a small cage. Jack, rascal that he was, finished the interview and, as I began the next item, I could see out of the corner of my eye that he was heading towards me, small furry beast in hand. He promptly shoved it up the sleeve of my jacket. As it ran across my shoulder and down my back, I just kept ploughing through my link. Jack later told the listeners what he had done and was amazed I had kept going. In truth I was still a bit raw, and thought that was the thing to do.

While working on *Today* I had a few dates with a pretty secretary on the show. One evening I arrived at her flat in North London to take her out to the pictures. While I was enjoying one of her liberal gin and tonics, the door bell rang. She peered out of the window and very quickly ushered me into the back garden.

'Slight problem,' she said. From the safety of the pitch-black garden, I was able to see her problem. He was one of my occasional co-presenters on *Today*, famous both then and now, and seemed most put out when he was fairly hastily dealt with and shown the door. I was retrieved from my hiding place and it was explained to me by my date that he was just a friend and he had arrived on this occasion uninvited. Off we went to the cinema and the incident was never mentioned again, although for some time afterwards every time I saw him I was sorely tempted to ask him if he fancied the lady in question.

In my radio days I was sent up to Hampstead one morning to do an interview with Dudley Moore for the *Today* programme.

I was quite nervous about it. Dudley and Peter Cook were hugely famous at the time and I was a big fan. I had first seen them in their satirical hit 'Beyond the Fringe' at the Theatre Royal, Brighton, during their pre-London run.

Dr Jonathan Miller, one of the famous quartet – the fourth of course was Alan Bennett, once told me that the local theatre cognoscenti who came back-stage after a performance were of the opinion that while the show was attractive it had its limitations. Apparently one old, rather camp theatre regular told him 'whatever you do, don't even think about taking it to the West End.' Of course, it had a record-breaking run in London.

By the time I was to interview Dudley, he and Cook had been delighting television audiences with their shows and were at the peak of their popularity.

I arrived at Dudley's home and he came to the door himself. 'Welcome,' he said. For some reason his facial movement as he said the one word, made me laugh. 'I'll have to write a sketch around the word "welcome",' he said. 'It obviously works for you.'

I turned on my tape-recorder and Dudley went through a comedy routine for me, interspersed with a few delightful

41

examples of his genius on the grand piano. I ended up with a brilliant interview, which had precious little to do with me. Dudley had just performed.

As I was about to leave, he asked me where I was heading. 'I'm going back to the West End,' I said. 'Back to Broadcasting House.'

'I'll give you a lift,' said Dudley. 'I've got to go down that way myself.' And so in a few minutes I found myself a passenger in Dudley Moore's blue Mini, being driven by the star himself.

It was another example of how my life had changed in a few short years. I was mixing with the stars. Well, if not exactly mixing, at least having the opportunity to meet them.

I bumped into Dudley again some ten years later, by which time he had become a hit in Hollywood. He seemed as down to earth and personable as ever but thereafter his life became complicated and ended horribly when he contracted a disease of the nervous system.

Another star I met during those radio days was Fenella Fielding, she of the sultry voice and the fluttering eyelashes who appeared in numerous British comedy films.

Again with my trusty tape-recorder in tow, I had made arrangements to interview Fenella at her flat in Knightsbridge.

When she opened the door, I was astonished to find this glamorous lady attired only in a rather flimsy negligee. 'Oh darling, you're a little early. I hadn't quite finished getting ready,' she said. My eyes were now popping out of my head. And I was consumed also by the obviously expensive perfume she seemed to have bathed in.

Anyway we settled down to do the interview, Fenella going through her vamp routine, when for some reason I asked her why she had never married. This question touched a nerve and she burst into tears. I found myself trying to console her. 'Please don't cry, Miss Fielding,' I said. 'Let's ignore that question and move on.'

She recovered and off I went to Broadcasting House with my interview. Unfortunately, my colleagues got hold of the tape recording before I could edit it myself and the 'Please don't cry, Miss Fielding,' quote proved to be difficult to shake off for some considerable time.

I had a few nice times with a sparkling girl called Pam and then I met Jill, a lovely girl, just twenty-three years of age, but already a nursing sister. She was bright and pretty with a great figure, and she was also a beautiful and considerate lover. So what did I do? I messed her around, took a few other girls out, and eventually lost her. I was having my twenties in my thirties and I had a roving eye. Jill came back to help me in a time of need a couple of years later and is still a wonderful friend, living happily in rural France with her husband.

There were already so many strings to my professional bow when along came another. One of the sports in which I was particularly interested was boxing. I had always been a fight fan and took all the magazines connected with the sport. Before joining the BBC I had been to Henry Cooper's fights with Muhammad Ali, saw Brian London attempt to take on the great man, and took in a boxing show whenever I could afford it. As a schoolboy I had tried my hand at the sport but found it the greatest laxative known to man. In one bout I got knocked out: nearly half a century later I still dream about it. I'd done it because my Dad had encouraged me to learn to stand up for myself. But it wasn't for me, though my very brief experiences underlined for me how much courage and dedication are needed to have a successful ring career – or indeed to step into the ring at all. I continue to have great admiration for those who do.

So I began to report on boxing for the radio. One Saturday afternoon my guest on *Sports Report* was the famous fight promoter Harry Levene. Harry was not an easy man to interview. If you asked him what he considered to be a stupid question he would let you know. But after the broadcast he said to me: 'You know your boxing. Why don't you become a commentator? You've got a good voice and bigger fools than you have done it.'

I began to think about the possibility and asked if I could take a commentary test. I did reasonably well and when the Commonwealth Games came round in New Zealand in early 1974, I was selected as the boxing commentator. What a trip, and what a challenge … oh, and what a girl I met there.

4

NOT AS DUMB AS I LOOKED

I was off to the other side of the world, to Christchurch, on the South Island of New Zealand, for the 1974 Commonwealth Games. It was to be my first trip outside Europe.

First stop was Hong Kong. What a culture shock, and what a delight. The BBC had managed to do a special deal on flights, which meant we could stay over for a couple of nights to sample the wonders of this extraordinary outpost of the British Empire, as it then was. I was in the company of Jonesy once again, plus Bob Burrows, Dick Scales and a good all-round broadcaster who to this day can be heard commentating on television football, John Helm.

We had a ball, enjoying the food, the sights and the fantastic harbour. I fell in love with the place and have been lucky enough to revisit it several times down the years. Then it was on to Australia, where we were due to make just a refuelling stop. As it turned out we were there for a little longer than planned.

On the flight I had been sitting next to Dick, who, despite his physical toughness, was a very nervous air passenger. I had been having a little fun at his expense, for instance when the note of the engines changed. Then, as we were slowly taxiing to begin take-off, I looked out of the window and saw the wing-tip of our aircraft hit the wing-tip of another plane. The bit of our wing came off. Oddly, there was no great crash or noise inside the aircraft.

'Scalesy,' I said, 'a bit of our bloody wing has just fallen off.' At this point Dick had had enough of me.

He grabbed me round the throat.

'Lynam,' he said. 'If you don't stop taking the piss, I'm going to clock you one.'

But I wasn't fooling around this time. The plane was now out of service and we were stuck in Brisbane until a replacement aircraft was made available. The incident did nothing to help Dick's flying phobia.

Christchurch, New Zealand, in the Seventies reminded me of an English town in the early Fifties. Certainly many of the cars were of that vintage. Indeed there were even plenty of people driving around in pre-war British vehicles. Fords and Morrises and Austins of the Thirties were commonplace. It was something to do with a tax penalty the government imposed on imported cars, and so people just kept the old ones going.

I had three roles in Christchurch. Firstly, to present the Saturday editions of the *Today* programme from there. The first one occurred just a few hours after our arrival, with me full of jet-lag, but I managed to get through it. Michael Aspel was at the London end. Secondly, I had to present some of the Radio 2 sports programmes, and, thirdly, I was the boxing commentator, not just for the UK but also for the BBC's World Service.

I found myself mugging up on boxers from Uganda, Kenya, in fact from all corners of the Commonwealth. I loved every minute of it, and covered as many as fifteen bouts in a day. It was invaluable experience for what was to come.

During our first evening in Christchurch, I'd met a beautiful girl, one of the hotel receptionists. We started seeing a little of each other, on the few occasions I had time away from the microphone. Apart from her lovely looks and kind nature, this young lady had one other marvellous asset. She was the proud owner of a red Sunbeam Alpine sports car, rare in New Zealand at the time. My popularity with the other guys slumped every time they saw me hop into this red sports car with my gorgeous companion.

We got on very well, but of course the few weeks we were together flashed by. I was sorry to leave both New Zealand and my new friend. Of course I told her that, while it was unlikely that I would be returning to New Zealand in the near future, if she ever came to Europe I would be delighted to see her again. Our parting was emotional, and I thought that, in other circumstances, the relationship might have developed into something more meaningful.

While in New Zealand we had a chance to sample the marvellous beaches. One morning we went swimming and John Helm pointed to a lookout tower with a lifeguard perched on top. 'He's very high up,' remarked John. 'That's so he can see the sharks,' I said. Helmy left the water, never to return for the rest of our trip.

We came back from New Zealand via the West Coast of America and spent a couple of days in San Francisco, where I met up with an old school friend of mine, Charles Trinder, who had emigrated to the States.

A month or so after returning home, there was a call for me one morning in Broadcasting House. 'Hi, Dis. It's me,' said the voice from the other end. Unmistakable New Zealand accent. 'Wow. This is a good line,' I said to my Christchurch companion. 'I'm downstairs in reception,' she said. Shona had set out, as so many New Zealanders do, on her European tour. She had just decided to make it a little earlier than planned. Like about two years.

We saw each other a couple of times, but I think we both decided, without saying anything, that perhaps our blissful short relationship had its beginning and end in Christchurch. Off she went to see Paris and Rome and I never saw or heard from her again. I hope she has had a wonderful life.

It was the start of a busy year. I did my first commentary on a world title fight as John Conteh beat an Argentine boxer, Jorge Ahumada, to become the World light-heavyweight champion at Wembley; then I was off to Kinshasa in Zaire to cover the 'Rumble in the Jungle' – George Foreman, defending the World heavyweight title he had taken from Joe Frazier, against the former champ, the great Muhammad Ali.

I had been fortunate enough to have met Ali when he came to London a year or two earlier and he did a marvellous interview for me. Now I found myself in the company of Ali once again in a bungalow provided by President Mobutu, whose government had put up much of the money to bring this extraordinary sporting extravaganza to the heart of Africa. Also there were two or three British boxing writers. Ali was explaining to us how he was going to beat Foreman. None of us believed a word of it. Foreman was hot favourite, a colossus in the ring and one of the hardest-punching heavyweights of all time. I was sitting next to Ali while he was going through his routine because I had my trusty tape-recorder under his nose. Close to my nose was the Ali left fist as he explained how he was going to win the fight with his jab. He kept thrusting it towards my face and at first I flinched a few times. Then I thought, if Ali actually misjudges and makes my nose bleed, what a scoop that would be. So steadfastly I resolved not to move an inch backwards as he continued his tirade. In fact I edged forward ever so slightly. When he finished, he gave me that old Ali sideways glance and that big smile. 'You're not as dumb as you look,' he said. I was hugely complimented. Of course Ali's timing and judgement was so impeccable, the chances of him actually connecting with my hooter had been extremely slim.

He went on to shock the world by regaining the heavyweight crown, hardly throwing a jab in the process. With extraordinary courage and durability he allowed Foreman to punch himself out, and then went in for the kill.

Recently I spent some time with Big George in London, when he did a splendid interview with me for BBC Radio 5 Live. Just before Ali knocked him out all those years ago, he had whispered in George's ear, 'Awful bad time to get tired, isn't it George?'

Another of the former World heavyweight boxing champions I met was Floyd Patterson. A BBC producer, John Graham, had come up with the idea of a series of programmes on the history of boxing in the Olympic Games. Patterson had won the gold medal in the middleweight division at the 1952 Games in Helsinki, Finland. He had been involved in just twenty-two bouts before being selected for the American Olympic team.

He turned professional straight after his success and campaigned as a heavyweight, one of the smallest of modern times.

He became World heavyweight champion at just twenty-one years of age, then lost the title to Ingemar Johannson of Sweden before becoming the first man to regain it when he avenged the defeat.

So John and I found ourselves flying to a little airport in upper New York State to meet the man, now in his early sixties. There was a thin layer of snow on the ground as we drove to the small town of New Paltz and as we approached the Patterson household, there was the old champion himself, waving to us from his front garden.

Patterson was Chairman of the New York State Athletic Commission and at the time was a wonderful advert for the sport of boxing. Despite a gruelling career which involved two meetings with the fearsome Sonny Liston, Floyd looked at least ten years younger than his age. We filmed him shadow boxing and hitting the heavy bag which he did as a routine every day of his life in his own gymnasium. He still had rhythm and timing and looked spritely but there was an air of sadness about the man. For many great sportsmen, life after the competitive years goes cold. In his mind, Floyd was 'boxing on' because everything since paled in comparison.

But at least Patterson had retained a little wealth and was living in some style.

Jimmy Ellis, a contemporary of Muhammad Ali, having begun his boxing in Louisville, Kentucky alongside his young friend, the then Cassius Clay, was not so lucky.

Ellis, a wonderful ring craftsman, had held a version of the heavyweight crown too, but when I went to see him, still living in Louisville, he was wearing the green overalls of a worker in the city's Parks Department. Ellis had also lost the sight of one eye, from an old ring injury. Wealth had passed him by. Did he have any regrets? Not a bit of it. If he had his youth, he would do it all over again, he told me.

My time as the BBC Radio boxing commentator lasted nearly twenty years and overlapped with my television work. It gave me some great times and I made many friends; but one of the saddest days I ever had while I was covering boxing came in 1980 when, along with a BBC Television producer, Elaine Rose, I attended the funeral in Wales of Johnny Owen.

Johnny was known as the 'Merthyr Matchstick' and, together with Elaine, I had been to Merthyr some weeks before to film a television feature on him. He was a painfully shy young man who, despite his slender frame, expressed himself best in the boxing ring. And he was good. Our feature was to preview his challenge to Lupe Pintor for the World bantamweight title in Mexico. Tragically, Owen had been injured in the contest and seven weeks later died from those injuries.

I remember the entire population of Merthyr lining the hills of the town as the funeral cortège passed by. On that day some of the toughest men of British boxing cried their eyes out as they paid homage to a brave young boy whose great ambition had cost him his life.

During my time in boxing, I covered around forty world titles and numerous British and European championship fights. For most of them, the legendary Henry Cooper was my ringside summariser. No finer man to have with you and after a nervy beginning, he became a master at filling the minute between each round with his pearls of boxing wisdom. Once in a while Henry would find himself up a verbal cul-de-sac but always extricated himself. ''E's as big as a brick ... [pause] ... building.'

Once, when talking about the British heavyweight Richard

Dunn, Henry was praising him after one round when he said: 'He knew what he had to do and in that round Dunn … done it.' Strange syntax. Wonderful man.

I had met Henry several years before we became ringside colleagues. He used to come into *Sports Report* on the Saturday before his big fights, along with his manager, Jim Wicks. They considered coming into the programme as a lucky omen. Jim always used to talk in the first person plural. 'We landed a great punch'; 'He made our nose bleed', etc. He spoke as though he was actually in the ring with Henry, which he certainly was in spirit. He protected Cooper too. For example, he would never agree to Henry's fighting Sonny Liston, who had been considered unbeatable until Muhammad Ali (or Cassius Clay, as he was at the time) shocked him and the world.

Henry did meet Floyd Patterson and I think it was after that contest, in which Henry had been stopped, that he was driving home to south-east London with Wicks and his brother George in the car when he made a slight misjudgement at a traffic light that caused an old boy to stumble off his bike. Henry wound down the window to apologise when the elderly cockney threw him a punch to the face. 'I'd have you out the car except there are three of you,' said his elderly aggressor. Two defeats in the one night for 'our 'Enery'.

After the 'Rumble in the Jungle' I was off to Kuala Lumpur in Malaysia to see Britain's Joe Bugner have a tilt at Muhammad Ali's crown. I was there for two weeks, sending back interviews with the fighters. Ali was always readily available to pronounce in front of a BBC mike. I even got him to record the opening of *Sports Report*, and Bugner's wily manager Andy Smith would always talk, even if Bugner himself was sometimes reluctant to do so. Or I would simply do a straight report down the line on the condition and mood of the fighters and their associates. I did one piece in which I had worked out how many hangers-on there were in the Ali camp. It turned out he, or the promotion, were paying the air tickets and hotel bills for about fifty people, forty-five of whom he could have done without.

My producer in London was Dick Scales, who always called everybody 'son'. Each day I would go to the Malaysian Broadcasting Centre to send my contribution down the line. Scales would address me from the other end in his usual fashion. After a few days, the female Chinese sound assistant who was helping me remarked how nice it was for me to be working with 'honourable father' in London. It suddenly dawned on me what she was talking about. I didn't try to explain.

This was the life. There were at least a couple of hours each day spent by the pool, and then in the evenings, usually in the company of members of the British boxing writers, it was out to sample a little of the night life of Kuala Lumpur. One evening we were enjoying a few drinks when a group of very glamorous ladies asked to join us. We were very happy for them to do so. After a while we realised that these were no ladies; they looked the part, but they were in fact what they call in the Far East 'lady-boys' – and they were looking for business. We enjoyed their company and they stung us for some very expensive drinks, but in the time-honoured way of British journalists in such situations, we made our excuses and left.

I made no excuses when I bumped into an extremely attractive female photographer who was covering the build-up to the fight for a Malaysian magazine. I took her out a couple of times and then she invited me to have dinner at her parents' home. This was indeed an honour. On the evening in question, I took a taxi from my hotel, the directions to the lady's family home scribbled on a piece of paper. The taxi driver smiled at me rather strangely, I thought, and then hurtled us about ten miles out of the city until we were finally driving up an unmade track. I had visions of being on the end of a scam. Any minute now, I thought, out from this jungle will come a couple of heavies, and I'll become the story.

Oh me of little faith. Eventually the cab pulled into a clearing and there, waiting for me on the balcony of this neat timber bungalow, was my friend and her parents all decked out in their finery. I had a magical evening and got the distinct impression I was being looked over as potential marriage material. For some months afterwards I was in regular air-mail correspondence with Kuala Lumpur.

The fight itself lasted the full fifteen rounds, but Bugner was never likely to win it. Later, back at the hotel, he was found doing laps of the swimming pool. Ali, despite winning clearly, had gone to hospital with exhaustion, an indication of their respective approaches to the toughest game of all.

Just three months later, Ali was boxing in the Far East again, this time meeting Joe Frazier in the 'Thriller in Manila', perhaps the greatest heavyweight fight of all time, in which both of them experienced 'near-death'.

Later in the year I found myself in a bull ring in Mexico City watching the British welterweight John H. Stracey create a huge upset by beating the great Mexican José Napoles to become world champion. It was a rarity: a British fighter winning a world crown abroad. On the night, the preliminary bouts had all ended early and the Mexican promotion wanted to get on with the main attraction. Our air time was still an hour and a half away. Mickey Duff, part of Stracey's promotional team, almost had a heart attack persuading the Mexicans to delay things, and very nearly caused a riot in doing so; but he did the job for us. Terry Lawless, Stracey's manager, came on the show and insisted I do my 'Michael Caine' for the listeners (it was a bit of a party piece at the time) before he answered a single question. The listeners must have wondered what on earth I was doing.

Stracey eventually lost the title in London to a fighter from the USA called Carlos Palomino. He had been brought in as a challenger because he was not expected to be too tough an opponent. In fact, a few days before the fight, I asked an American journalist to mark my card about him. 'How big is he in the States?' I asked my man. 'Palomino,' he said, 'he's not even a household name in his own house.'

Phil King was on the trip as my producer. While we were there, I told him that we should enjoy a bit of Mexican culture as well as the hospitality and duly booked for a coach trip to the pyramids. Unfortunately, we had enjoyed a bit of a night out the evening before. At 6 a.m. the phone rang in the room and a voice said, 'Señor, the coach for the pyramids, she is leaving in ten minutes.' Phil says my reply down the phone certainly included the word 'off'. He might be accurate. In those times of budgetary restraint at the BBC, we were sharing a room.

He and I also shared a taxi on our first night in Mexico City. We had asked the concierge for the address of a nightclub where there might be a bit of fun and a few girls. The cab dropped us at this sombre-looking place and when we entered there was no action at all, just a bar with a couple of men sitting at it. Then suddenly a lift came down and out of it stepped a dozen or so girls and paraded in front of us. So much for a nightclub: we were in a brothel. It took some persuasion, and a bit of my Spanish, to get us out of there in one piece.

But, just as in Kuala Lumpur, I did bump into a very sweet girl, and for a short time afterwards I was back in the air-mail business. It's a wonder I found time to do the broadcasts.

The late Seventies and Eighties usually saw a dozen or so big boxing promotions each year in England, at the Royal Albert Hall or the Wembley Arena. They were either under the banner of Harry Levene or Barrett-Duff Promotions. Mike Barrett was a genial character, Mickey Duff a more rough and ready type who knew boxing inside out and who had once been a professional fighter himself. Levene was an old stager, grumpy as you like, but the man who had planted the thought in my mind about becoming a boxing commentator. They all got on with each other – sometimes. Once when Levene, now in old age, was ill, he telephoned Duff. 'Mickey,' he said, 'I'm leaving it all to you.' 'I don't want your money,' replied Duff. 'Not my money, you prick, the promotion,' came the response. There was not a top-line boxer in Britain at the time who didn't perform on their bills. They worked closely with Terry Lawless, who managed many of the champions of the time, and they had a virtual monopoly; but they put on great shows. In recent years, the sport has been largely lost to the average fight fan, with promotions in small halls and television coverage only on satellite channels. Sitting ringside in close proximity to the weight of the punches, the blood and the sweat constantly underlined the courage of the boxers. Mickey Duff, the old pro himself, with a face to prove it, once told me that if his son ever looked as if he wanted to become a professional boxer, he would be tempted to cut his arm off. He knew precisely how hard a game it was.

I had said on one of our programmes that the first live coverage of a world title fight would be 'Here, exclusively, on BBC Radio'. This was of course under instruction from the legendary Angus.

Arriving back at the office after the show I was told there was a phone call for me. I picked it up and a voice said, 'Mr Lynam, I have to tell you that you are a liar.' Who was making this preposterous statement? The voice introduced himself as Jarvis Astaire, of whom I had scarcely heard. It was his rather graceless way of telling me that our forthcoming broadcast would not be exclusive because his company were beaming the fight into a chain of cinemas. Strangely, the conversation ended with us on good terms, despite his inflammatory opening line. Later, on several occasions I hosted his closed-circuit shows. Down the years, whenever I have gone to a major sporting event, almost at any time and anywhere in the world, I have found Jarvis there. Oh, and he'll definitely have an opinion about it.

Before each big fight I was nearly always allowed in the dressing rooms, where I witnessed the pre-fight nerves of the boxers involved. I began to acquire a useful knack of spotting the winners and losers even before they entered the ring, and I consistently did well when placing a bet on the outcome of fights, in marked contrast to the lack of success I have had over the years when having a flutter on the horses.

I continued to travel round the world when British fighters were involved in major championship bouts abroad. In May 1976 I went to Munich to see another British fighter have a crack at Muhammad Ali. This time it was Richard Dunn, a tough former paratrooper from Yorkshire who had worked his way to the British title after some mediocre years. Dunn was nowhere near world class, but Duff and Barrett had engineered a big pay day and a probable beating for him.

For this fight Richard had acquired an addition to his usual retinue. Now he had a hypnotherapist with him who was boasting that not only would the British fighter enter the ring with absolutely no fear, but that he would actually create one of the all-time great upsets by beating Ali.

At the weigh-in for the fight, there was a near disaster when the ring collapsed with Ali in it. He could have been killed. As it was, he clambered out of the wreckage, unmoved by the untypical German inefficiency, and got on with the formalities.

In the fight, Dunn was indeed fearless and even caught the great man with a few decent punches; but you can't hypnotise someone to be more talented than they truly are, and the inevitable end came in round five with an Ali knock-out.

After the fight something strange occurred. Dunn, who had always had a stutter, did an absolutely fluent interview with me, speech impediment missing for the first time in his life. A couple of hours later, the old stutter was back. A punch to the jaw is obviously only a temporary cure.

I had travelled to Germany with a heavy heart. Just before I left home, I learned that my father had been diagnosed with colon cancer. A couple of months later he died, after a major operation. This warm, generous and humorous man, full of common sense and decency, would no longer be there to advise me and make me laugh with his wit and wisdom. I was devastated. He had spent his life caring for others but when he needed care, it seemed to me that the doctors showed less concern than they should have done. Despite many requests at the time, the surgeon who operated on my Dad was always 'too busy' to give me the benefit of his advice or expertise about my father's exact condition and I was continually palmed off with his juniors. I bitterly regret that I did not demand his attention more.

I felt alone and in despair. I needed a friend. I telephoned Jill, who had taken a job at a hospital in Holland. Jill had known and liked my father very much; so she came and held my hand

and made arrangements, looked after my relatives from Ireland, and got me through. I took a few weeks off work and we spent some lazy days on Brighton beach as I tried to get over my loss. Then, once again, I let her go.

I now immersed myself into work even more and was glad of the boxing trips abroad. And of course, like millions of other people, I was still intrigued by Muhammad Ali. But he was now getting well past his prime. Many people thought he should have retired with his faculties intact after the 'Thriller in Manila'. Certainly his doctor, Ferdie Pacheco, who had always been in his corner, strongly advised him to do so. By 1978, Ali was still very much active, but his speed of reflexes had deserted him and the wonderful footwork was a thing of the past. Now he was defending his title against Leon Spinks, a blown-up light heavyweight whom I had seen win the Olympic gold medal two years before in Montreal, the very title that Ali had won sixteen years earlier.

The fight was taking place in Las Vegas and, as usual, I got there about a week before to cover the build-up. On the day I arrived, my producer Phil King and I were having a bit of a disaster. Not only had the airline managed to send our luggage somewhere else, including all my pre-fight preparation, but the hotel in which we were supposed to be staying had no record of the booking. We were standing in the foyer bagless and roomless, and wondering what our next move was going to be, when the receptionist called my name. 'Ah, a room,' I thought. On the contrary, she just had a telephone call for me, on the other end of which was a BBC producer in London. 'Des,' he said, 'I've been trying to find you for ages. You're on live in thirty seconds.' On came the familiar voice of Tony Lewis, the *Sport on Four* presenter. 'Joining me now live from Las Vegas where he's been watching Ali train is Des Lynam. How is Ali looking, Des?' There are lies, damned lies, and reports from correspondents in difficult situations.

Eventually we got our hotel sorted out but now we had another problem. With his usual flair for publicity, Ali had a new gimmick. He reckoned that he had been talking too much and was going round with sticking plaster over his mouth. Well, this was jolly fun for the film and television crews and the newspapers, who would all have their pictures of the now wordless Ali; but for this radio commentator it was a total nuisance. Eventually, I managed to persuade him to remove the plaster for a radio interview and he made a big play of ripping it off, so that the microphone could pick up the sound. He always knew precisely what the media needed from him in any given situation.

Then the unthinkable happened. Ali fought his most lethargic contest to date and was on the losing end of a points decision over fifteen rounds. The new heavyweight champion of the world was Leon Spinks, who had only a few professional fights to his credit. Extraordinarily, his brother Michael, who also won an Olympic gold medal in Montreal, at middleweight, went on to win a version of the heavyweight title some years later too.

I always loved going to America for big fight occasions. I felt perfectly at home in the States. All those American movies of my boyhood had set the stage perfectly for me. The first time I went to New York, it seemed so familiar, as though I had been there all my life.

On that first trip there, I came out of my hotel and hailed one of the famous yellow cabs. 'I wonder if it would be possible to take me to the BBC offices on Fifth Avenue,' I said to the driver. 'What is possibility, you want to go there, get in the cab,' he replied. It taught me an early lesson to cut out the P. G. Wodehouse stuff.

5

A FACE FOR RADIO?

I had been broadcasting on national radio for less than three years when I got a call from someone in BBC Television inviting me to stand in for Frank Bough for four weeks, presenting the Sunday cricket on BBC 2. I explained that cricket was not a special interest of mine in a broadcasting sense. Although I had loved to play the game as a boy, I did not keep up to date with the details of the game in the way I did with many other sports. I was certainly not an expert.

I was told that the job would be simply to 'top and tail' the broadcasts and read the scores from other games. It seemed a simple enough task and I agreed to do it. It turned out to be pretty much of a disaster. It rained at all the matches I attended and I was a shuffling nervous wreck as I tried to get the words out to camera. I felt totally ill at ease.

The late, great John Arlott was involved in some of the broadcasts, and it has to be said that he was not overly welcoming. I didn't particularly blame him. He was hugely famous; I was a raw broadcasting newcomer in comparison. Not for me this television lark, I thought, and I scuttled back to the safety of my radio microphone and ventured nowhere near a television camera again for several years. I had actually received a nice letter from the producer, Bill Taylor, who thanked me for my efforts and thought I managed extremely well. I think he was just being kind.

As time went by, though, people in the business kept telling me I should have another go at television. I was happy doing *Sports Report*, and my boxing commentaries: by now I had covered the 'Rumble in the Jungle' in Zaire, the Olympic Games in Munich and the Commonwealth Games in New Zealand; presented the *Today* programme; and had my own Radio 2 weekly music show, *After Seven*. I was a busy and successful radio broadcaster. Nonetheless, other people's ambitions for me were beginning to sway me towards the possibility of doing television. I had put the cricket disasters to the back of my mind by now and had completed a short series of television quiz shows for BBC Northern Ireland. One day I found myself applying for a job with Southern Television (a forerunner to Meridian) to be their sports reporter. I duly sped off to their studios in Southampton, where I was interviewed and given an audition. A few days later I was notified that the job was mine. I would give three months' notice to the BBC and off I would go to become a regional TV 'face'.

I went to see Cliff Morgan, the legendary former Welsh rugby union star, who by this time had enjoyed a long career at the BBC and was the Head of BBC Radio Sport and Outside Broadcasts.

'Cliff,' I said, 'I have decided to take the plunge towards television and I think that working on a regional basis would give me the appropriate lower profile in which to learn something about the craft. Then I will find out if I could ever do the business at a national level, hopefully with the BBC. It's a gamble, but it's one I have decided to take.' I must have sounded a pretentious little twit.

'Lynam,' he said, 'you haven't got the sense you were born with. Here you are making a name for yourself in radio. You're having brilliant experience covering all the big events. You'll end up reporting Bournemouth and bloody Boscombe Athletic. I'll tell you when it's time for you to make your television move and it'll be national television, not piddling about on the Isle of Wight.' Cliff was not being disparaging about those charming areas of the South Coast; he was merely using his graphic language to dissuade me from my intentions.

He was a very persuasive boss, was Cliff, as well as being one of the major influences in my broadcasting life. He remains a dear friend and I am proud and privileged to have known him. Ironically, he now lives on the Isle of Wight, where, sadly, he has not been enjoying the best of health.

The outcome of our conversation was that I telephoned Southern Television and told them I wasn't taking the job. They were not best pleased with me. It would be another twenty-three years before I did make my move to ITV.

Some time later, Cliff, who had moved back to television, fixed me up with the chance to present two days' racing at the Grand National meeting, on the Thursday and Friday before the big day itself. Once again I felt less than comfortable. Nowadays I envy those young presenters on satellite television who get their break reading the sports news off an autocue in front of a minimal audience. At least they have the time to get used to a TV camera up their snout. I was out in the wind and rain of Aintree, notes blowing all over the place, desperately trying to remember where I was, who I was, and what the hell I was doing there. By the Friday night I had convinced myself that live television was not for me, and was tempted to write to Southern Television to tell them what a lucky escape they had had. Once again, though, I received a very kind note, this time from the Head of BBC Television Sport, Alan Hart. He thanked me for making what he thought had been 'a first-class contribution to the programmes' and wrote that it was the opinion of everyone in his department, not just his. He also mentioned that if I felt disposed to appear on the box again, I should ring him and arrange lunch. I didn't, and I didn't. I would not in my wildest dreams have thought then that I would have ended up presenting the Grand National broadcast, one of the most prestigious and difficult events that BBC Television covers, for fifteen years running.

I didn't call Alan but amazingly enough later in that year, 1977, he called me. He said he had been discussing me with Cliff and that he and I should meet, which we did at the Chelsea home of the racing commentator Julian Wilson. Over lunch, Alan spelled out that he thought – despite my fears and lack of confidence – that my future lay in television and that, once I really got the hang of it, the future could be rosy. I didn't believe a word he was saying, but a part of me wanted him to be right. I actually thought a bit of fame might not go amiss.

Eventually Alan made me an offer. It was for a three-year contract with BBC Television at nearly twice my then salary of just short of £7,000. That was the part of the deal that encouraged me to move. I thought, I'll have one more go. I can always go back to radio. I had to resign my comfortable staff job and now, apparently, I needed someone called an 'agent'.

An agent. I had never needed one before. I had simply taken

the salary offered me by the BBC and any increases they had felt like giving me in the eight or so years I had been a radio broadcaster. I had started on just over £2,000 a year at the end of 1969, and by 1977 I was earning the princely sum of close to £7,000 a year. I had been totally content with this compensation. I had a pleasant place to live, usually a nice sports car, and when I wanted to eat out or buy my friends a drink I could afford to do so. Money hadn't really entered the equation. I could have still been in the insurance business. I was mostly thanking my lucky stars, David Waine and Angus McKay, for changing my life.

But now the BBC wanted to double my money – unimaginable riches. So I took the plunge and decided to have a real go at television. I went with the blessing of Bob Burrows, an old Angus hand, who had taken over as the boss of radio sport, with Cliff moving back to be Head of Outside Broadcasts at Television. He promised me that, if it didn't work out, I could return to the fold, and anyway he wanted me to continue as the radio boxing commentator, which I did for many years, until the early Nineties.

But an agent. Why did I need an agent? Cliff explained that now I was a potential contractee, it would be necessary to re-negotiate my deal from time to time and that it would be much better to have an intermediary involved. They need have no shame in making any demands and, at the same time, the BBC could be honest and direct about the broadcaster's talents or deficiencies without being personal or hurtful.

I didn't know any agents, so Cliff recommended the most powerful one around, a gentleman called Bagenal Harvey. Bagenal's first client had been the outstanding English cricketer of his day, Denis Compton, who was also an Arsenal and

England footballer. Denis had not only been cavalier with his wonderful skills but had been much the same with his business opportunities. Bagenal had found that Denis had a pile of unanswered letters, which contained various lucrative offers for product endorsements. Bagenal asked if he could deal with them and take a cut. That's how Denis became the first 'Brylcreem boy' and how Bagenal Harvey started in the agency business. By now, though, he had numerous clients, many in broadcasting, including the two big hitters in television sports presentation at the time, David Coleman and Frank Bough. It occurred to me that I might be better off with an agent who was not representing the men in the jobs I aspired to, but I went to see Bagenal on Cliff's recommendation.

The meeting did not go well. I thought Bagenal Harvey was interviewing me in the manner that he might adopt when hiring an office boy. 'Mr Harvey,' I interjected, I suppose rather cockily in retrospect. 'I have not come here to be interviewed for a job. I have the job. I have come here to decide whether or not I want to hire you to work for me.' The meeting came to a fairly swift end. Later, I got a call from Cliff. 'What have you done to Bagenal Harvey? He's not very happy with you and he's a dangerous enemy.' I explained my position and I think secretly Cliff admired me for my stance.

But I still needed an agent, and so I rang my old friend John Motson, who had made a highly successful transition from radio to television a few years earlier. He was using as his agent a chap who was entirely new to the business, a chartered accountant by profession called John Hockey. I went to see John and we formed a pretty good partnership for the next thirteen years.

But now, what was my role to be in television? Coleman, Bough and Harry Carpenter were filling the main presentational roles, and there were people like David Vine and Tony Gubba, more than capable broadcasters, backing them up. Firstly, I took over a slot called *Sportswide*, a fifteen-minute programme tacked on the back of the early evening news and magazine programme, *Nationwide*. Frank Bough, busy man as he was in those days, was also doing the main show, as was Sue Lawley.

It was fairly seat of the pants stuff. My seat was usually vacated by Frank or Sue, or one of the other *Nationwide* presenters, a few seconds before I began my piece. The same applied to my producer and director, who almost had to fight their way into position in the gallery.

I had a couple of early disasters. We used autocue for the programme, unless we were at an outside broadcast, and the system in those pre-computer days was pretty basic. One was actually reading from a roll of paper rather like a narrow toilet roll; sometimes it became detached and one had to adjust quickly to the script on one's lap and/or hope you could remember the lines. On one occasion the operator had typed the same paragraph twice. I hadn't had a chance to spot it before going on air and was halfway through repeating myself, word for word, when I had the presence of mind to say, 'I'm sorry, I'm repeating myself' and got away with it.

Sometimes we would record part of the slot and I would link in and out of it 'live'. The recorded insert would include me in vision. On one occasion the make-up girl, seeing that my hair was too long before the live part of the programme, suggested 'tidying up my ends'. Like a fool I let her do it, and she went a bit over the top. The viewer at home saw me with short hair, then long hair, then short hair again, all in the same broadcast.

On another occasion somebody stopped the videotape machine for the recorded section of me in vision and the director cut back to me live. The viewer must have thought I'd had a stroke and then recovered. It was all great experience for bigger and, in a way, easier things to come.

Since my move from radio, I had also been doing a little stand-in presentation on *Grandstand*, as well as helping out when the first London Marathon took place in 1981. My role would be to run back and forth over Tower Bridge and interview some of the slower runners 'on the hoof'.

Of course it was the beginning of a fabulous event, the dream of Chris Brasher and John Disley, which has caught the public's imagination so dramatically. Now everybody could become a marathon runner, not just those supermen we watched in awe at the Olympic Games. On the day, I ran across the bridge and back maybe thirty times. I might as well have run in the event itself and bitterly regret that I didn't give it a go when my fitness was rather better than it is now.

Another year I was doing interviews with the finishers and posed one of the dumbest questions of all time. I asked Grete Waitz, the great Norwegian athlete, if she had been pleased with her time: she had just broken the world's best time for the event, but I didn't know. My monitor had been on the blink and somehow the director didn't get the information to me. To viewers, I must have seemed like a right dope.

Presenting a show like *Grandstand* is quite demanding, particularly so when the presentation is at an event, sometimes in the wind and rain, trying to listen to talkback instructions with a load of ambient noise going on around you. The studio-based shows were more comfortable, and the technicalities more reliable; nonetheless, five hours live on air, and sometime for much longer during the Olympics or other big events, make considerable demands on both mind and body.

I used to be able to get through the five hours, often without having to go to the toilet. I couldn't do it now. Food was taken on board as the programme went out. I was caught with a mouthful of sandwich on more than one occasion when an event finished abruptly or when the studio director cut back to me suddenly.

The winter programmes, when there was a full football fixture list, involved the presenter commentating on the results as they came in – originally on the teleprinter, later the videprinter. I thoroughly enjoyed this part of the show, exercising my knowledge of players and league positions and sequences of victories or defeats. I usually spent one day a week honing that knowledge: as a supporter of one of the smaller clubs myself, I knew how important these small facts and figures were to the fans around the country, from Aberdeen to Exeter.

Occasionally, with your mind racing, you would make the odd mistake, relying on the editor to correct you. Once I said, 'Southampton won 2–0, the same result as last year when they won 4–1.' During the videprinter sequence, we would go live to the grounds for reports from key matches. John Philips, the editor, would sometimes forget to tell me where we were going next and I would prompt him through the viewer. 'Now where shall we go to next?' I would say down the camera lens, and Philips would then tell me, 'Highbury, you prat', or he would simply tell me to keep talking till they had a reporter on the line. It was fast-moving stuff. Nowadays, Sky Television build a whole programme around scores and results information. It is skilfully presented by Jeff Stelling, in my view their best sports broadcaster by miles. I can see the buzz he gets out of the show. It used to be the same for me.

Martin Hopkins, who directed nearly every *Grandstand* show

I did, was an avid racing man. The custom was that he and the presenter would have a head to head bet on each race we were televising. He invariably won but it kept his interest at a peak.

For some of the years I was doing the show, the whole production team had to prepare quickly a five-minute sports bulletin for the South-East region. There were no reports or live action in this. The presenter simply read the copy put in front of him and hoped that the captions and still pictures fitted. Quite often they did not, and this became just about the hairiest programme that the sports department produced. Mostly, I managed to get out of it, and the broadcast was left to one of the newer faces; but those five minutes were always considerably more difficult than the five hours that had gone before.

While I found *Grandstand* challenging, presenting it always felt like it was something that came naturally to me. Around this time, I was asked to try something that really, really didn't come naturally. Not a lot of people know this, but for a time I tried my hand, or voice, at the art of football commentary with BBC Television. Now I was asked to do a test commentary. It was not an ambition of mine but Alec Weeks, the senior football director, and Mike Murphy, the *Match of the Day* editor, who eventually became my *Grandstand* boss, thought I would be a useful addition to the commentary team behind John Motson and Barry Davies.

My first attempt was a trial commentary at an international match at Wembley between England and Wales. I did my homework and found the job relatively simple. Football commentary is easy. It's good football commentary that's difficult. Weeks wrote to me afterwards. 'Your voice is clear. You have a wide range, your identification is sharp but your timing is appalling. We might get somewhere if we persevered on a few matches next season.' We must have persevered because I was booked to do my first match for real a few weeks later. The game was Bristol City against Wolves in the old First Division. Only about four minutes went out on *Match of the Day*, but the edit was awful – or rather it underlined my lack of technique as I was heard to repeat the same phrase over and over. The match editor had not really been very sympathetic to the new boy. I did a little better as I went along and began getting some big games. I remember being at Maine Road for Manchester City against Liverpool, and I also commentated on some other top matches. And I am still remembered by a few people in Wales for being the commentator when Swansea beat Preston North End at Deepdale to earn a place in the top division for the first time in their history. John Toshack was the manager. Nobby Stiles lost his job at Preston after that game.

By the time the European Championship finals came round in Italy in 1980, I was one of the commentators despatched to cover the event. Greece against Czechoslovakia stands out in my mind. I had seen neither team before the game. Some of the names were impossible, but I struggled my way through. On the way to the game, John Philips, my producer, who would eventually become the editor of *Grandstand*, had nearly killed us as he drove the wrong way up a motorway sliproad. He saw the oncoming traffic just in time. There was an advert at the time for an Italian car where one guy says 'But the steering wheel is on the wrong side'. His mate replies, 'The way he drives, it makes no difference.' It became a much repeated slogan during our stay in Italy.

Back home, I continued to do the odd game for *Match of the Day* and was called on again in a commentary capacity for the World Cup Finals held in Spain in 1982. I was the sort of 'Kim

Philby' of the team, the third man to Motson and Davies again.

A problem match for me there was Italy against Cameroon, who were then playing in their first ever finals. There was no television in Cameroon at the time, and so no chance of seeing a tape of their players. I was familiar with the goalkeeper and one outfield player, Roger Milla. The Italians, on the other hand, were nearly all big names. They were the easy part. But Cameroon had most of the play, held the Italians to a draw, and should have won. The Italian press destroyed the team and manager after the game, so much so that the Italian squad imposed a boycott on them. Italy of course went on to win the World Cup that year. Many red faces in the Italian press corps, but that was the end of my brief life as a football commentator.

Soon afterwards I was also approached by Aubrey Singer, who at the time was Managing Director of BBC Radio. Aubrey had a proposition for me. At the time, my television career was just about getting under way. I had done a few *Grandstand*s and was beginning to get the hang of it, but I still went back to radio for boxing and tennis commentaries. It was while I was covering the Wimbledon Championships for radio that Aubrey grabbed me. 'As you know,' he said, 'Bob Burrows has left us for ITV and I wonder if you would consider the possibility of becoming the boss of radio sport.' I was shocked and flattered. If the invitation had come a year or two before, when I felt terribly insecure on television, I think I would have jumped at it. I knew the radio set-up pretty well and had loved my time there; I also knew what a great department Burrows and Cliff Morgan had built. The trouble was that I was now thinking that I might carve out a bit of a future for myself on TV.

Did I really want to be on the administrative side of broad-casting? I thought about it very carefully and decided that I would gamble on making it on the box, though for a while afterwards, when things weren't going too well, I wondered if I had made the right decision. As it turned out, my good friend Patricia Ewing eventually took over the department and made a huge success of it. I know she thinks I made the right decision – not just for me, but for BBC Radio Sport.

I was destined for other things.

6

ALL TANKED UP

The 1976 Olympics in Montreal, Canada, were the Games at which the world discovered the fabulous talent of Sugar Ray Leonard. In fact it was the last Olympics in which the Americans dominated the boxing events. In addition to Leonard, they had a brilliant lightweight in Howard Davis, who was selected as best boxer of the entire Games, outshining even Leonard. Then there were the Spinks brothers at middle and light-heavyweight and the flyweight Leo Randolph. Five gold medals. They couldn't win the heavyweight gold though. That went to Cuba's Teofilio Stevenson, who had won in Munich and would collect his third gold in Moscow in 1980. In Britain's team were Pat Cowdell and Colin Jones, both of whom became outstanding professionals and contested world titles. Alongside them was Charlie Magri, a flyweight, who did win a world championship.

For these Games, BBC Radio had selected a certain Terry Wogan to be the presenter for the evening Olympic shows. Terry was based in London and turned out to be an inspired choice. An avid sports fan, though certainly no specialist, he brought just the right kind of irreverence and questioning approach to the broadcasts, plus of course his usual wit. 'Small-bore rifle shooting' was one sport out of which he got great mileage. I had many 'two-ways' down the line with him, both of us roaring with laughter.

One day I got an urgent call from BBC Television. Could I go into their studio and 'dub' some commentary on a few boxing contests – that is, record the commentary after the event – as Harry Carpenter had gone down with a throat infection. I was all set to do the job when Harry made a pretty swift recovery. Broadcasters do not easily give ground to anyone waiting in the wings.

My old mate Jonesy had a nasty experience in Montreal. Handsome devil that he was, he had no trouble attracting the ladies. One night he and a colleague, not me on this occasion, had gone back to the apartment of a very attractive girl and her friend for drinks. They were just enjoying their first one when there was a crash through the door and they were confronted by a rather large gentleman who turned out to be the husband of their hostess. The situation was manageable at that point, until he pulled out his hand-gun. This was when Jonesy, ever the erudite Cambridge man, proferred the wholly inadequate response, 'Now we don't want any unpleasantness.' They got out in double-quick time, and literally ran for their lives.

Off air, I was spending a little leisure time with Dr Liz Ferris, a diving medallist at the Rome Olympics, who was part of our commentary team. Liz introduced me to acupuncture, which certainly helped with some back pain I was having, and she also tried to teach me to do a 'tumble turn' in the swimming pool, with less success. I think that was what was giving me the back pain in the first place, but I still have fond memories of Lizzie's beaming smile and her head-back laughter as I nearly drowned on numerous occasions.

I got on with my radio work until it was time for the Games to come to an end. They had been pretty miserable in terms of British success. On the track, Brendan Foster's bronze medal at 10,000 metres was the only one won. But David Wilkie had won a swimming gold in the breaststroke, and we had done very well in the modern pentathlon, winning gold there too.

The pentathlon team was led by Jim Fox, a big handsome blond athlete who had all the girls swooning. The modern pentathlon comprises shooting, fencing, riding, swimming and running, and was originally introduced into the Games to replicate the tests that a military messenger might have to encounter during a battle. In the fencing section, Fox discovered that his Soviet opponent, Boris Onishenko, seemed to be recording hits electronically when Fox knew that no contact had been made. The British competitor reluctantly reported his misgivings to the authorities – reluctantly, because Onishenko had been a fellow competitor at many championships and Jim had counted him a friend. It was subsequently found that Onishenko had cunningly rewired his weapon in such a way as to allow himself to record hits when none had in fact occurred. He was thrown out of the Games in disgrace.

After the Games, Phil King and I decided to take a break in New York, taking a train, the 'Adirondack', down through southern Canada, through Vermont and New England. The journey was most comfortable and slow, but it was all the better for that, allowing us to enjoy the splendid scenery.

We had arranged to stay in the apartment of a New York-based BBC man who was going off on holiday elsewhere. It happened to be in the same apartment block, and on the same floor, as the film actress Angie Dickinson. She said 'Good morning' to me one day. I could hardly get over it. Kingy and I resolved to ask her out for a spot of dinner if we bumped into her again. Pipe dream. Phil and I enjoyed the bars of Second Avenue and one or two parties at the British Airways 'Speedbird' Club. I was offered a joint one night, but as a non-smoker couldn't handle the inhaling and my career as a drug-taker lasted all of two minutes. I was content enjoying a few beers.

Back home, I returned to the routine of presenting the radio sports programmes and endeavouring to see my son as often as possible. He was growing up fast.

I had given up trying to commute from Brighton to London each day and, while keeping my own flat on the coast, was sharing an apartment in London with a lovely lady called Patty Smith. I met her through her daughter, Jenny, who had told me her mother, who was divorced, was looking for a p.g., as she put it – a paying guest. Things got a little tricky for a time, because Patty was as glamorous as her daughter.

Later I shared a house with a great friend, Mike Greenlees, who went on to become a huge player in the world of advertising. We were two Jack the Lads for a time: nice house in Putney, which he owned, two sports cars parked outside, ready for action. We were rather like the Jack Lemmon–Walter Matthau pairing in *The Odd Couple*, advertising man and sports journalist, one tidy and organised (Mike), the other messy and disorganised (me).

As well as the sport, I was now asked to present a radio quiz programme called *Treble Chance Quiz*. The programme took two team captains around the country and they competed against each other with members of the public from the town we were visiting against an 'away' team. The team captains were usually Patrick Moore, the astronomer, and the late Ted Moult. The producer was a long-term BBC man, Michael Tuke-Hastings. Michael was fun but an absolute snob. Once, recording at Warwick Castle, he described our host, who seemed to me to be a perfectly charming and well-educated man, as 'strictly minor public school'. Another time, we were staying in a small hotel when the receptionist announced there was a telephone call for 'the Duke of Hastings' instead of Tuke-Hastings. Michael certainly acted like he should have had a title.

The next year he involved me in the overseas version of the show called *Forces Chance*, which as well as going out on Radio 4 was broadcast on the Forces network. This took me to Gibraltar, Malta, West Germany and the then divided city of Berlin. The show's next producer was Patricia Ewing, who went on to become the Head of Sport and Outside Broadcasts, and afterwards ran Radio 5. Pat was an ex-WRNS officer who introduced me to the delights of the old naval drink – a 'horse's neck': brandy with dry ginger. Ted Moult was involved in this show too, in which the celebrities took on teams from the armed services in general knowledge. Neil Durden-Smith, the husband of Judith Chalmers, plus the BBC's first female television newsreader, Nan Winton, were the other team members, although Sue Lawley soon took over from Nan. Some years later Ted, who seemed the happiest of men, took a gun and shot himself. No one understood why, least of all his large and loving family.

While in Germany we made a poignant visit to the museum at Belsen, where they say 'no bird ever sings'. We were treated royally by the Forces: the army breakfasts in the officers' mess, and getting our shoes cleaned by someone else, almost made joining up seem attractive. In West Germany we spent some time with a tank regiment and both Sue and I were given instruction on how to drive a tank. Later, when we went to Berlin, another tank regiment made us the same offer. I asked the corporal appointed to give me instruction if the tank in question was the same model as I had driven a few days before. It was. I told him to say nothing to the officer standing by, got into the driving position, started it up, shot around the compound a few times, over a few hills and humps, and delivered it back to the feet of the officer. He was white. 'Nippy aren't they?' I said. The corporal loved it.

7

GUN TROUBLE IN TEXAS

My ongoing love affair with boxing continued apace, and it was around this time that I covered Jim Watt's period as the World lightweight champion. Jim had been a useful boxer in a domestic sense until joining the Terry Lawless stable. Lawless helped him hone his skills to international level and had the connections to steer him to the world title.

Jim was a hugely attractive proposition for those of us in the media. He was very articulate and gave great interviews and of course has gone on to become an outstanding broadcaster on the sport. One of his title defences took place in the open air at Rangers' Ibrox stadium in Glasgow. His opponent was Howard Davis, the man who had been voted the outstanding boxer of the 1976 Olympic Games. Watt was too good for him though.

In 1981 I went to Houston, Texas to commentate on Pat Cowdell's challenge for the World featherweight title held by the Mexican Salvador Sanchez. It was a tough call for Cowdell. Sanchez was considered by many experts to be the best 'pound for pound' fighter in the world at the time. A few days before the fight, I took a taxi from the airport to my hotel and noticed that the glass was missing in one of the side windows in the back of the car. It had been replaced by a piece of cardboard.

'What happened to your window? I asked the driver.

'Oh, some crazy guy is taking pot shots at cars in the city,' the driver replied, seemingly unconcerned.

'Have they arrested him? I enquired.

'Nope, haven't found him yet.' I slunk down in the seat.

Later that evening it wasn't the sniper's gun I was worried about.

Suffering from jet lag, I had trouble getting to sleep but eventually nodded off with the light on. At around 3 a.m. I was awoken when the door to my room sprung open, held only by the security chain I had remembered to attach. Then, to my horror, a gun was poked through the gap and a voice said: 'Please come to the door and open it.' I thought, 'This is it. I'm in a violent city and am about to be robbed at best, and maybe shot as well.'

I managed to get a few words out. 'What the hell is going on?'

The voice replied. 'This is hotel security. According to our records this room should be unoccupied.' An accreditation badge was eased through the gap. The check-in receptionist had recorded that I was in another room. Her mistake could easily have resulted in a Lynam heart attack.

In the fight, Cowdell put up a valiant challenge before losing on points over fifteen rounds. Not long after, Sanchez was killed in a car accident.

I first came across Finbar Patrick ('Barry') McGuigan at the Commonwealth Games in Edmonton Canada in 1978. He was just seventeen years of age and boxing for Northern Ireland. This was an anomaly because Barry was actually from the Irish Republic and two years later he would compete in Moscow for the Irish Olympic team.

He was a sensation in Edmonton and made it all the way to the bantamweight final, in which he had to box a tough customs officer from Papua New Guinea called Tumat Sogolik. It was boy against mature man, but I called the fight narrowly for McGuigan. This was in the days before computer scoring came into amateur boxing. On television, Harry Carpenter felt that he hadn't quite done enough. As it turned out, McGuigan got the decision and his old club coach in Northern Ireland rang him to tell him that I had called it his way. It was just my honest opinion at the time, but Barry became a fan of mine, as of course I did of him.

The Edmonton Commonwealth Games had been my second trip to Canada. I enjoyed some marvellous hospitality, especially from a petite and vivacious girl who was working at the Games. I seemed to fall on my feet at these major tournaments.

Once again Wogan was orchestrating the broadcasts from his studio in London and persuaded me to sing the 'Londonderry Air' (aka 'Danny Boy') live on the programme after McGuigan's win. You would not have wanted to hear it.

On the flight home from Edmonton, a fellow commentator found himself seated between Mary Peters, the athletics gold medallist from the 1972 Olympics, and Anita Lonsborough, who had been Olympic champion in the swimming pool at the Rome Games in 1960. Both were travelling back in their pristine cream blazers provided by the BBC for the Games. Unfortunately my colleague had enjoyed a considerable amount of hospitality in the departure lounge, liberally topped up after boarding the aircraft, and proceeded to throw up. Two blazers and two gold medallists were despoiled in one ghastly moment. Embarrassed though he still is about it, he recently described it as 'a record that will never be broken'.

After these Games Barry McGuigan turned professional. I told my television audience on *Nationwide* to remember the name McGuigan. 'It's a difficult one,' I said 'but this boy will become a world champion.'

He duly fulfilled the prophecy on an unforgettable night at the Queen's Park Rangers football ground, Loftus Road, when, in front of a packed house, and after Barry's father had sung 'Danny Boy' (a considerably better rendition than mine) to the assembled throng, he outpointed a tough Panamanian, Eusebio Pedroza, to become the featherweight champion of the world.

I presented the live television broadcast that night with Alan Minter alongside me. Nineteen million viewers watched – the biggest TV audience ever for boxing in the UK. There were delirious scenes in the streets around West London after the fight. They were totally peaceful, but everyone was enjoying the victory for a super young boxer.

The following year I was back at ringside for the radio when there was an even more outstanding victory for a British fighter. This time the action took place in Atlantic City, on the eastern seaboard of the United States, where Lloyd Honeyghan was to challenge Don Curry for the World welterweight championship. The previous year, Henry Cooper and I had been ringside in Birmingham to commentate on a challenge by the excellent Welsh boxer Colin Jones against Curry. The American had won in four rounds and looked unbeatable. Henry remarked on the night that Curry was one of the best he had ever seen. Now, a year or so later, Honeyghan was up against this same man with

My maternal grandparents, Packo and Annie Malone.

'If the cap fits': me, aged a few months, with Packo.

Mum and Dad a-courting.

Mum aged eighteen, and just arrived in England.

Dad in tropical kit.

14279052. Pte Lynam T.
RAMC 3. BGH. 137
India Command.

To/ Desmond wishing
you a very happy
Xmas 1945. & New
Year. Be a good boy
& look after Mammie
& Nanna. I will send
you a small Xmas
Box later.
Lots of love from
Daddy ✗

BY AIR MAIL

Greetings from INDIA

FORCES MAIL
11 OCT 45

MR. D.___ LYNAM
___ FRANCIS. ST.
ENNIS.
CO CLARE.
EIRE.
IRELAND.

The letter from India, which I was too young to read.

Me in Mum's arms in Ennis.

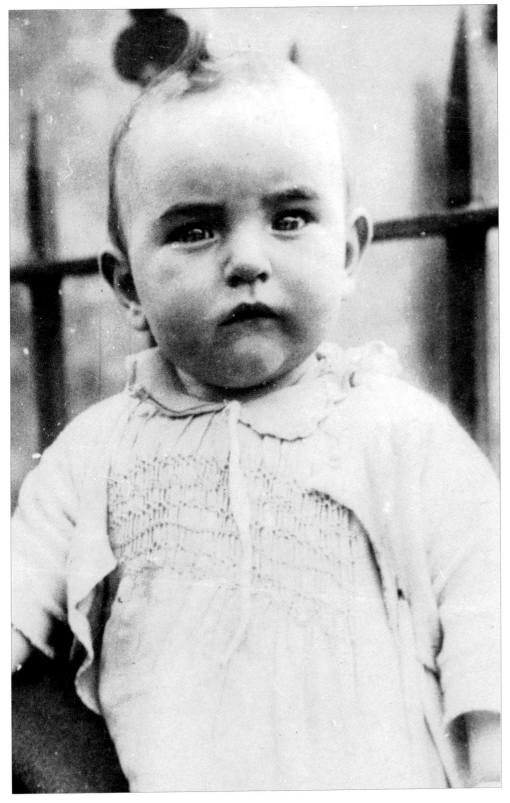

An early 'eyebrow' shot.

Not happy with the hair-do.

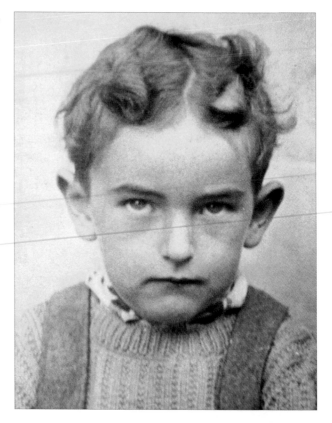

My first trip to
Father Christmas.

At St John the Baptist Primary – I'm back row right. Janice Prossor is centre row left, with the large bow in her hair.

Me with my younger cousin, Tony, on Brighton Beach.

Teenage years with Mum and Dad.

no home crowd willing him on. The British fighter went in to the ring a ten to one outsider, but he was so confident that he put a large lump of his purse money on himself to win.

My ringside partner on this occasion was the experienced boxing columnist of the *Sun* newspaper with whom I had enjoyed many trips around the world – Colin Hart. Neither of us could believe what was happening in the ring. Honeyghan was taking the fight to a great champion and beating him to the punch. By round six, Curry was overwhelmed and, extraordinarily, Honeyghan was the new champion of the world, plus the recipient of a nice lump of money from an Atlantic City bookmaker. It was one of the best-ever British boxing performances.

I had been to Atlantic City before. John Conteh had attempted to regain his World light-heavyweight crown there against the American Matt Franklin, who had become a Muslim and was now billed as Matthew Saad Muhammad. I had been asked to do the live television commentary on this fight, as Harry Carpenter was indisposed, and was working with a veteran television producer who at the time liked a drink. Our first morning meeting to plan the broadcast was at 9 a.m. in his hotel room. 'Right, what are you going to have?' he asked. 'I've got gin or whisky.' He was most put out when I declined. I was clearly not his kind of person at all.

In a pre-fight interview, Conteh decided he was going to remove one of the a's from 'Saad' and make his opponent 'Sad Mohammed'. It was a good line, but, as it turned out, Conteh was now just slightly past his best and was defeated over fifteen rounds.

There was no radio commentary on this fight because of the live television coverage, but my old sidekick Phil King was there to send back reports. One morning, he and I, with our press passes in hand, decided to gain entry to a press conference being given in our hotel by the singer Diana Ross. We were both huge fans and just wanted to have a look at her.

As her conference was going on, and the showbiz writers were asking her a lot of what we considered to be naff questions, Kingy said 'Go on. Tell her you're from England. Ask her a question.' I summoned up the courage and raised my hand. It was my turn. 'Miss Ross,' I said. 'I'm from the BBC in London. Do you have any plans to come and perform in England in the near future?'

'Not at this time. Next question,' she said. 'Thank you, Miss Ross,' I said, and sat down, red-faced.

'You prick,' said Kingy, absolving himself from his own idea but enjoying immensely my embarrassment at Miss Ross' brevity in replying.

Conteh's loss in Atlantic City was the second narrow defeat over fifteen rounds he had experienced in trying to regain the crown that he never lost in the ring. He had given up the title he had won by beating Jorge Ahumada in 1974 because of a contractual dispute. In 1978 he went to Belgrade, in what was then Yugoslavia, to challenge Mate Parlov, a former Olympic champion. This time I thought Conteh had done enough to win, but he was adjudged a points loser. Conteh thought he was on the receiving end of a dubious decision and there was a terrible row at the after-fight party, on a Danube riverboat hired to celebrate his victory, between him and Mickey Duff, his British promoter.

Alan Minter was one of the bravest fighters I ever saw. He beat Vito Antuofermo of America in Las Vegas to become the undisputed middleweight champion. It was no mean feat: Antuofermo had earlier defeated the fearsome Marvin Hagler.

Minter defended the title against Antuofermo in London; then came his second defence against that man Hagler.

I went to Jersey in the Channel Islands to do a television feature on Alan's preparation. In the interview, like all boxers, he was very bullish about his chances of victory. 'I'm not going to lose my hard-earned title to a black man.' he said. He didn't mean anything particular by it, but I could see that phrase causing mayhem, so I got Alan to do the interview again, advising him to find other words, which he duly did. However, on a live news programme, conducted by a less sympathetic interviewer, Alan fell into the trap of using the 'black man' phrase again. It brought a ton of criticism down on his head, and probably motivated his opponent greatly. I also met Hagler before the fight, when he came in to do a live interview on *Sportswide*. The producer given the task of looking after him was new to the complexities of the old Lime Grove studios used by the BBC at the time and he and Hagler managed to get themselves lost. There they were, wandering up and down corridors, peering into studios and offices, one of the most fearsome boxers of all time, and a novice producer. Hagler just made the broadcast in time.

The ring meeting of Minter and Hagler was brief but fearsome. It lasted less than three rounds, with Minter getting stopped with an awful cut. He was in serious trouble, but he had rocked Hagler with a tremendous punch before that and was even waving his opponent in to the fray.

When the fight was stopped, chaos broke out at the Wembley Arena, with some of the British fighter's unruly fans pelting the ring with bottles. Sitting at ringside, Henry Cooper and I were in serious danger of being hit. Henry was down and under the ring canopy like a rocket. Afterwards I teased him about how fast he had moved out of the line of fire when I had to keep talking.

'I never minded getting cut when I was getting paid for it,' he said, 'but I wasn't having it for nothing.'

While I had been in Jersey to preview the Minter fight I had bumped into Peter Batt, one of Fleet Street's legends. I knew him a little and had heard many amazing stories about him, most of them involving his fondness for a drink. One particular story sticks in my mind. The British press corps were in the Alps after a plane had crashed and they were busy seeking out any survivors. The word went out that a British man was recovering in a nearby hospital run by nuns. Upon hearing the news, the press boys hurried en masse to find him. After a long and torturous journey they got there to find 'Batty' tucked up in bed, having been found totally legless after yet another awe-inspiring drinking session. On another occasion, he had arrived home late and much the worse for wear to find that his wife had locked him out. Unperturbed, he decided to smash through the front door only to discover that he was two doors down. He had been sacked, or had resigned, from most of the tabloid newspapers, but he had a wonderful writing talent and always seemed to find himself back in work very quickly.

Now, like me, he was covering the Minter title defence. We discovered that there was a tennis court at the hotel where we were staying, and 'Batty' decided we should have a game. We borrowed the appropriate gear, grabbed some rackets and strolled down to the courts, where we found two rather cultured middle-aged ladies enjoying a game on the only court. 'Let's break them up,' said Peter, as if we were going to ask them for a quick-step, and we invaded the court. For the next hour the two ladies were introduced to a stream of pure Batt invective, words rarely heard on the tennis court unless John McEnroe is around. 'It must be effing deuce'; 'Terrible shot Des, you prick'. And much, much worse. To my utter astonishment the ladies remained and played alongside us as partners amidst fits of laughter; even more astonishingly, they invited us for 'another game tomorrow'. For these two very nice women, tennis must have seemed rather mundane thereafter.

It was 'gun trouble' of another kind a few years later in 1989, when Harry Carpenter and I travelled to Las Vegas to cover Frank Bruno's challenge to Mike Tyson for the heavyweight championship of the world. Tyson was in his prime, Bruno a big outsider. As well as covering the fight at Caesar's Palace, we had been asked to produce a preview show about the contest. The editor, John Philips, conceived a novel idea. Rather than just showing footage of previous fights and discussing the possible outcome, John's programme would be symbolic and imaginative. And so it was that Harry and I found ourselves out somewhere in the Nevada desert, at an old run-down western frontier town which was used for movie making. I say town – there was just a bit of dirt road and a few wooden shacks. The obligatory tumbleweed was in plentiful supply. There, Mr Carpenter, bespectacled as ever, and I would symbolise the Bruno-Tyson 'shoot-out' by having one of our own. We were issued with six-guns, holsters, and the rest of the paraphernalia of a couple of Wild West gun-slingers, and acted the roles out. We felt like a couple of right berks.

Later, the programme was both damned and praised. There was no middle road in terms of opinion. The critics either loved it or hated it.

When it came to the fight itself, I started the presentation and then handed over to Harry as the fighters approached the ring. Bruno, as challenger, was in first. Then I turned to see the champion striding forwards. He was wearing just one of those sleeveless towelling robes but as he was purposely making his way forward he tore it off and threw it to the ground. If the gesture didn't scare Big Frank, it certainly frightened me.

Bruno put up a bit of a show early on and caught Tyson with one big punch. It definitely had the affect of annoying the champ, who then proceeded to stop his man.

Frank's wife Laura did an emotional interview with me after the fight about her respect and love for her man. How sad that the marriage eventually came to an end.

There was a rematch in 1996 when the outcome was much the same except that Bruno seemed to enter the fight with his confidence already shattered. He looked as though he knew what was waiting for him.

Of course Frank achieved his life's ambition when he beat Oliver McCall at Wembley in 1995 to win a version of the heavyweight championship he had craved for so long.

As far as Tyson is concerned, I always found him mannerly and thoughtful when I interviewed him. I asked him once if he ever entered the ring 'scared'. I thought his answer would be full of bravado. On the contrary, he admitted that he was frightened before every fight. 'I know that the kind of people I have to fight have the power to extinguish my life if I get it wrong,' he said. What an answer.

When he first became champion, he came to Britain as a guest of the Anglo-American Sporting Club, whose Chairman Jarvis Astaire asked me to propose a toast to the new young star of heavyweight boxing. It was a 'black tie' affair and the organisers hired an apropriate suit for the champion but had a few problems finding a shirt for him. His collar size was something like twenty-and-a-half inches. I telephoned one of those upper class shirt-makers in Jermyn Street, London, and offered them the chance of some terrific publicity if they hurriedly made a shirt for Tyson. They turned up their noses at the prospect of being involved with a boxer. Now had he been a polo player...!

I put a great deal of work into my speech on the night and then to my amazement, Tyson, at only twenty-one years of age, got to his feet and responded in a charming and articulate fashion without a single note.

A couple of days before, he had been my guest on *Grandstand* and I had been warned that he could be surly and not very responsive. I knew, however, that he was a student of the history of boxing and I started him off on the great heavyweights down the years. He gathered it was a subject I knew a bit about too, and he ended up doing twenty minutes with me. I hate what has happened to him and what he seems to have become. At the age of twenty-one he was a fearsome young boxer in the ring. Out of it he was one really nice young guy.

While I was into boxing in a big way, for a time I also became the golf presenter for BBC Radio. In 1977 it was decided to take the golf show 'on the road' for the first time to cover the Open Championship at Turnberry from the course (for previous 'Opens', the presenter had stayed in Broadcasting House). Now I found myself in a position high over the eighteenth green at the famous course in Ayrshire watching Tom Watson play out of the bushes on the last hole to record one of his five victories by beating Jack Nicklaus into second place.

The following year I was at St Andrews to record a Nicklaus win. I also presented a couple of Ryder Cups. These were magical experiences.

At St Andrews, I met a BBC producer's secretary, a gorgeous girl who at eighteen years of age was much too young for me. Did that stop me pursuing her? I'm afraid it did not and she and I became an 'item'. I was still a good way from settling down into a solid relationship, though. Soon I was going to have to become a bit steadier in my private life. The trouble was, I was rarely short of a pretty girl on my arm. It sounds arrogant now, but I was spoilt for choice.

8

GERRY AND DEAN

As well as taking the radio golf shows 'on the road' for major events, Bob Burrows, who had become the ambitious and able Head of BBC Radio Sport, came up with the idea of presenting Wimbledon from the All England Club. Previously, a continuity announcer at Broadcasting House would simply link over for the occasional live commentary on a match. Now the whole broadcast came from Wimbledon, covering play from 2 o'clock in the afternoon until the last match had finished on the show courts. This enabled the broadcast to include not only commentary on the main games, but also reports from the outside courts and interviews with the stars and personalities there to watch the tennis.

In radio terms it became a major hit, a wonderful service for those who either couldn't get to a television set in the afternoons or those in transit. In fact, many people began to prefer to listen to the play rather than watch it. Peter Jones was the presenter holding the whole thing together in his immaculate style, but he saw little of the tennis as the programme was done in a tiny studio from where he could only see any action on a television monitor. Day after day during the Championships, major names from the world of showbusiness, sport or politics would be interviewed live by Jonesy between the matches.

I had been asked to have a crack at tennis commentary. Max Robertson was the doyen of radio tennis commentators at the time and prided himself on trying to describe every shot for the listener as it was played. This was a valiant and noble attempt at honest broadcasting but I had always felt that, although he showed a consummate skill in what he was trying to do, as a listener one had absolutely no chance of ever knowing where the tennis ball might be until one heard the score announced at the end of the point.

Our team of broadcasters included two great ex-champions, the legendary Fred Perry and the former World Number One of ladies' tennis, Christine Truman. Describing the play along with Max was John Motson, turning his hand to a sport other than his beloved football, and, amongst others, Gerald Williams, Norman Cuddeford, Tony Adamson and myself. Williams and I had discussed the art of tennis commentary on the radio and worked out a style in which we verbally followed the server. By describing what was happening to him or her, you could more or less tell the story of each point without gabbling too much. Previously, if you had a ladies' doubles between two players from, say, the Czech Republic against two from Japan, by the time you had mentioned all four names, the ball, had probably crossed the net four times. By concentrating on what was happening to the server – 'She serves, but is passed down the line', for example – the listener was given a better chance of understanding what was going on.

'Motty' was probably the most able of the 'new boys' at tennis commentary. He has always had a wonderful knack of relating what he sees to the listener in a kind of verbal shorthand, and if you only know him as a television commentator, a role he has fulfilled to the highest standards, for my money he is even more talented as a radio broadcaster.

He was once in a commentary position overlooking court two at Wimbledon when a producer spotted the famous film star, Jack Nicholson, among the crowd and invited him into John's commentary box to enjoy the play from there. Jack put on the spare pair of headphones and while 'Motty' was commentating, Jack heard an instruction from the editor of the programme which Motson had ignored. 'Johnny, they want you should give 'em the score,' said Nicholson in his best *One Flew Over the Cuckoo's Nest* drawl. To this day I often give 'Motty' the line.

Christine Truman was, and is, a sweetheart. She was beaten in the all-British Wimbledon ladies' final in 1961 by Angela Mortimer, but she wasn't fully fit at the time. While she was World Number One, her mother took her to one side after one important match at Wimbledon. 'Darling,' she said. 'You must stop playing the drop shot. It will give you a pinched face.' Can you imagine the Williams sisters getting such advice from their father? Christine played in different times. The most she ever won in those amateur days in monetary terms was a voucher for twenty-five pounds. Nowadays she would have become a multi-millionairess.

Occasionally she invites me to the All England Club for a 'hit'. I wouldn't dare take her on in a match because I probably wouldn't win a game. But I can bash the ball back and forth with Chris for some good rallies. Now and again she chastises me for a bad shot and I point out to her that, while she was number one in the world, I wasn't even number one in my own house.

Norman Cuddeford was a dapper chap who looked very much what he was in his 'day' job: an insurance broker in the City of London. Having been a part-time radio broadcaster for some time, he'd covered track and field at a couple of Olympic Games and had maintained both his professional standards and his position as an all-rounder on the wireless. He had once made a gaff on the *Today* programme when I had been presenting it. Norman had been monitoring a cricket score from a match being broadcast on another network. With his headphones on, and concentrating hard, he thought we were still rehearsing with him. When asked by Chris Rea, who was handling the sports desk that morning, to give the score he'd replied, 'No, I'm awfully sorry I can't.' Locked into his headphones, and unable to hear our producer. he said it a couple of times. I was hysterical and got up to leave the studio because I was making strange animal noises, as you do when you are not supposed to laugh; but I forgot that my headphones were attached to the desk and they promptly spun off my ears, hitting my co-presenter in the face. It was the complete 'Fred Karno' scenario.

Afterwards, Norman went to see Cliff Morgan, our boss at the time. 'Cliffy,' said Norman, 'I hope this morning won't affect me going to Montreal [i.e. to the impending Olympics].' 'Montreal?' said Cliff. 'You'll be lucky to go to the Albert 'all.'

In 1981, Bjorn Borg had won the Wimbledon singles title for five years in a row and was about to embark on the defence of his title once again. On the first morning of the Championships, I and my radio colleagues met to discuss our coverage for the day. One of our producers suddenly piped up: 'I've been talking to the pronunciation department,' he said, 'and apparently we've been getting it very wrong. Bjorn Borg should actually be pronounced Biern Bourra.' 'Do fuck off,' I said. 'By now he doesn't even call himself that. Where were you six years ago?'

Gerald Williams had been a respected sports journalist on the *Daily Mail* before becoming public relations officer for the Lawn Tennis Association. He was steeped in the game and there were few players of any age who didn't know and trust him. Gerry and I were destined to see quite a bit of each other in the next few years.

At the Wimbledon Championships of 2002, I was making my way through the crowds to get to my Centre Court seat for one of Tim Henman's emotional battles when I was stopped by two middle-aged ladies.

'It's Des,' cried one of them. 'Looking forward to seeing you and Gerry on the telly tonight,' said the other.

'We love that show,' added the first one.

I hadn't done that particular programme with Gerald Williams since 1989 and my last broadcast at Wimbledon for the BBC had been in 1999. A few minutes later the ladies probably realised their mistake, but they were suffering from what could be described as 'preferential television memory recall'. Frank Bough told me that once, fully ten years after his last *Grandstand* programme, on getting out of a London taxi, the cabbie left him with a 'Looking forward to seeing you on Saturday, Frank.'

Gerald Williams and I began our evening tennis highlights show in 1983. We are both great fans of the sport, but Gerald is a true aficionado who has devoted most of his broadcasting and journalistic life to it. We had been working together at Wimbledon for some years on the radio. Now I was being asked to present the evening television programme rounding up the day's main matches at the All England Club in a programme unimaginatively called *Match of the Day* – a filch from the football programme and somewhat confusing for the viewer. In due course the newspapers subtitled it 'The Des and Gerry show', but the BBC were against the 'cult of personality' in the sports department at the time, and so it remained *Match of the Day*.

I teamed up with Gerry and we decided that the show needed a bit of fun and some good opinions and that it should become a little less reverential to all things Wimbledon. We had great respect for the sport and the players; but when most tennis fans knew the result of matches by the time this programme was aired, we needed to wrap the tennis up with some decent journalism.

After our first effort, there was much humming and hawing in the television sports department. 'These two are demeaning Wimbledon,' was one cry. But the television audience loved it. We were getting a great response and, strangely enough, so were the establishment figures that ran the All England Club's marvellous Championship.

The chairman at the time was a gentleman called 'Buzzer' Hadingham. He looked to me as though he could have been a Second World War air ace and I always used to fantasise that his soubriquet 'Buzzer' had been bestowed on him because he'd lost a wing over the Channel, swum home, had a large gin, picked up a spare aircraft and shot down a couple of enemy planes before being back in time for a tea dance. Disappointingly, however, he was known as 'Buzzer' because a younger sibling had not been able to say the word 'brother' and Mr Hadingham had carried this juvenile nickname into later life. In actual fact 'Buzzer' had indeed been a war hero, winning the Military Cross and Bar during his army career.

Gerry and I decided 'Buzzer' Hadingham was a good candidate for a bit of teasing. We finished one programme with 'Buzzer's doing a great job.' Pause. 'Buzzer? Buzzer who?' Pause. 'You know, Buzzer Thingy.' Pause. 'Oh, that buzzer.' Williams and I were doing our Morecambe and Wise bit.

The BBC mandarins, thinking about their contract with the All England Club, were worried to death; but the next day 'Buzzer' rang up to say how much he had enjoyed the programme. We were home and dry. Around some serious tennis discussions – and, of course, the best of the highlights – Williams and I were having fun.

Once I borrowed a convertible car. At the end of the programme the angle of the shot made it look as though Gerry and I were both sitting in the car to leave for home. As I pulled away, it became clear that he was actually left behind on a bicycle, playing Laurel to my Hardy. Another time I left him up in a hoist, and once we began a programme with Pat Cash headbands on – we got so hysterical that we had trouble continuing.

On another occasion Gerry thought we were still rehearsing and at the end of his opening comment said to me 'Was that alright?' 'Of course it was,' I said and continued with the show as he realised at last that we were live.

The audience figures were climbing. We were caricatured on the *Spitting Image* show and got our puppets over to open one of ours. Patricia Ewing, who had taken over as Head of Sport and Outside Broadcasts for Radio, persuaded Gerry and I to become involved in a cabaret to mark the fortieth anniversary of *Sports Report*. Decked out in striped blazers and boaters, we sang a reworked version of 'Ah Yes, I Remember it Well', the Maurice Chevalier hit from *Gigi*, which I had rewritten to include the characters from her department. At the rehearsal, I found to my horror that Gerry was the only Welshman in captivity who was tone-deaf, but we managed to get away with it.

Our run came to an end when Gerry decided to take up a lucrative contract with BSB, which subsequently became part of BSkyB, and I began presenting the daytime coverage of Wimbledon. But they were good years.

John McEnroe was still playing during most of the time the 'Des and Gerry' show was running. We often had cause to criticise his behaviour, while all the time acknowledging his undoubted brilliance. After he stopped playing, and I began presenting the daytime shows at Wimbledon, I got to know him a little and realised what an extraordinarily charismatic and intelligent person he is. When he came in for interviews at the start of our broadcasts, he would leave it until I was about to ask him a question before he was seated and 'miked' up. Then he would be brilliant and incisive. I learned in due course not to worry whether he was going to turn up. He always did, but initially he gave us some scary moments.

Now of course he is the biggest asset to the BBC in its current Wimbledon coverage. More recently, Mac invited me to the launch of his autobiography, a compelling book. He referred to me in his speech when romanticising about one of his early tirades. 'Those were the days, when Des was on the right network,' he said. By then I had joined ITV.

In those years I quite often covered the tennis at the Queen's Club, the tournament sponsored by Stella Artois. One year, one of the sports producers, Chris Lewis, had heard that Dean Martin – of 'Rat Pack' fame – was visiting the tournament. Chris was adept at making contact with the stars and in due course got in touch with Dean's management to request an interview at the Club with the great man. I was the appointed interviewer and Chris and I duly presented ourselves at the Inn on the Park hotel in the West End to take Dean and his manager, Mort Viner, to the Queen's Club. The BBC had run to a stretch limo for the job of transportation.

I had been a tremendous fan of Dean Martin since my mother had taken me to see him and his partner Jerry Lewis in what, at the time, I thought were those hilarious films of the Fifties. I liked him as a singer too, and anyone who was a friend of Frank Sinatra would do for me.

So I was somewhat nervous waiting in reception. Mr Viner came down first to meet us and told us 'the star' would arrive shortly. A few minutes later, the lift gates opened and out stepped the legend. He looked immaculate, hair as thick and black as ever, high collared white shirt, black slacks, bright pink V-necked sweater. But as he got closer, Dean aged. He was, after all, well in his seventies at the time. He said very little, probably wondering what the hell he was bothering to do an interview for. In the limo I remember he spoke only once when Chris offered him a cigarette. 'Smoke, Dean?' asked Chris, to which the great man replied, 'Why, thank you, Chris,' in that unmistakable voice, the two of them bonding in their nicotine. To me those four words encapsulated 'Volare', 'Three Coins in the Fountain' and 'Little Ole Wine Drinker Me' all rolled into one. In short, I was totally in awe. And now I was thinking I had a problem. How on earth was I going to get an interview out of this man?

As we approached the Club, the manager was fretting about security. He didn't want his star getting mobbed. When we got out of the car and made our way through the club entrance, Mr Viner spent half the journey walking backwards to protect his man from the ensuing throng. But nobody approached him.

Mortifyingly for the manager of this superstar, two small boys did come and request autographs, but they wanted mine, not the signature of the elderly man in the pink pullover.

But when we arrived in the makeshift studio, Dean became alive. The lights went on, the microphone was switched on, and he was the big star again. He talked about his son Dino playing tennis with Jimmy Connors, about his friendship with Sinatra, and even went back to the old days with Jerry Lewis, leaving out the fact that in later life they were reputed to have hated each other.

When the interview finished, Dean once again became the monosyllabic elderly man in the pink pullover. We hardly spoke on the return journey. But I had met a hero.

9

OUR MAN IN MOSCOW

I had covered two Olympic Games for BBC Radio already, but by the time the 1980 Games in Moscow came round I was a fully fledged television man. My role was to be a roving reporter during the day and presenter of the evening highlights show.

The 1980 Olympics were fraught with problems. The Americans had boycotted them, as had several other countries, in response to the Soviet Union's involvement in Afghanistan. British Prime Minister Margaret Thatcher was also in favour of a boycott, but the British Olympic Association, underlining its independence from government, sent a team that included Steve Ovett, Seb Coe, Duncan Goodhew, Daley Thompson and sprinter Allan Wells, all of whom returned home with gold medals. Certain sports, however, such as equestrianism and hockey, took the government line and did not send representatives.

The BBC's coverage was somewhat diluted as they bowed to government pressure to stifle the celebratory aspect of the Games – by not showing national anthems being played, for example. It was not the BBC's finest hour.

I spent most of my mornings at the Olympic village, inter-viewing British team members or major foreign stars. Getting into the village each day was torture, the security being intense and heavy handed. My producer was a spiky little East-Ender called Bob Abrahams, who would have a row with the security guards each morning, and consequently took an hour longer than anyone else to gain entry. But he kept winning minor pyrrhic victories, which he said kept his pride intact.

The BBC organisation was slightly chaotic. With two crews out and about, both sets frequently ended up trying to do the same story in the same place, and we often wasted our time because the pre-planning was inept. As a result I formed the 'Wild Goose Chase Club', and later had ties made showing a lone white goose flying through the Olympic rings, which mem-bers of both crews wore proudly for some years.

We had not yet arrived at the mobile phone age, and our instructions came via a crackly radio communications system. One day a message came through telling me to make my way back quickly to our hotel, get a jacket and tie, and turn up at the studio, where I might have to present the afternoon's main programme because there had been a 'bit of a problem'.

The problem was that Frank Bough, the number one anchor-man for the BBC coverage, had had a blazing row with his pro-ducer, Jonathan Martin, and it looked as though Frank was not going to do the show. I rushed off in a state of nervous anxiety, and eventually arrived breathless at the broadcast centre to find that Frank had undergone a miraculous change of heart and was all set to broadcast. For the second Olympic Games run-ning, I had been denied my big moment.

During the Games, we were staying in a French-built hotel. Its design and accommodation were adequate, but it had certain drawbacks. For one thing, the radios in the room were listening devices for the hotel's security. These were the days when foreigners were considered highly suspicious by the KGB. Sometimes a few of us would get together and condemn the Soviet system for its inadequacies just for fun, knowing we were being eavesdropped.

It was also almost impossible to get served in the hotel dining room until we realised that bribery – or 'early tipping', as one colleague called it – was the currency of the day. When the food did come, it was ghastly and I spent a month living on bread and caviar, readily available at the broadcast centre, and bars of chocolate.

I got tickets one night for the Bolshoi Theatre. Moscow citizens, unless they were well connected, had little hope of ever getting tickets, but some were available for Olympic visitors. I took with me one of the Russian interpreters, a homely looking girl with a shiny Slav face. By the end of the first act of Mussorgsky's *Boris Godunov*, I had had enough and my translator friend and I adjourned to the bar, where babushkas in headscarves were dishing out glasses of Russian 'champagne', which was not at all bad.

My friend had seen the opera before and was equally bored by it, so we stayed in the bar for the rest of the performance – much to the amazement of the bar staff, who could not understand our disdain for an evening of musical privilege.

My friend, who spoke perfect English without ever having travelled far from Moscow, never mind outside Russia, was enlightening about her life and said her ambition was to live in the United States. I hope no one overheard her. But I never saw her after that night. I was told she had been 'transferred'.

After Seb Coe had lost the gold medal to Steve Ovett in the

800 metres we bumped into him in the village the following day. 'Hey, Coe, you've got to get your head up,' shouted one of our producers, Mike Murphy. I could not believe his gall in approaching one of our major sporting stars in such a way. Mike, though, was a self-confident young man to say the least. I thought Coe would be offended. He said nothing at the time, but years later, Seb told me that this rather clumsy rallying cry was just what he had needed.

He did get his head up and subsequently got revenge in the 1,500 metres, beating Ovett into third place. A very young Steve Cram was in that final too. His major moments were yet to come. As a reporter on site, I was gaining admittance into the preparation room before the race. The competitors were confined to a tiny space for half an hour before they were allowed on to the track. I'm sure that many races were won and lost during that claustrophobic half hour.

We were quite relieved when the Games came to an end. When we arrived back at Heathrow most of my pals were greeted by their loved ones, wives and families. There to greet me was – no one. I made my way to my lonely flat and unstocked fridge. I realised that this was the price I was paying for my playboy existence, and for failing to show commitment to anyone. The only thing I got close to that night was a bottle of whisky.

One other problem from my stay in Moscow was affecting me. It was a physical one. To my alarm, in my last few days away I had developed a rather nasty sore on the end of my penis. I knew this was not due to any sexually transmitted disease: I had been living like a monk for the past month, and I was meticulous in my personal hygiene. So what on earth was going on? I called up my friend Jill, who by this time was the senior nurse at a private health clinic in London. She couldn't stop laughing when I told her of my problem – she had seen the Lynam appendage at pretty close quarters in the past. She said I had better get myself round to the clinic and she would have a look.

So round I went and pulled out the old apparatus for her inspection. 'Ugh,' she said. 'That's nasty. Are you sure you've been a good boy?' I vouched for my recent celibacy and at that point she called in the senior physician, Mike Weston, who was also a very close friend of hers. Mike knew of my past relationship with Jill. The two of them poked at the offending pustule, and then Mike proclaimed, 'No problem. I'll give you some ointment, and you'll be available for socials within a few days.' It turned out that I had probably picked up a bug from unhygienic bedclothes in Moscow. Mike had never stopped laughing throughout my consultation; apparently Jill had told him 'Des is bringing his dick round for inspection.'

'Well, they're hardly going to come separately,' said Mike.

10

A CALL FROM ALI

In 1983 Muhammad Ali came to Britain to make some public appearances. The press were writing that he had not only lost his sparkle but seemed ill, that his years in the ring had taken their toll. He was forty-one years of age at the time. One morning, when I was presenting *Grandstand*, I got a call from one of his representatives. 'I am with Ali now,' he said, 'and he wants to come on your programme to prove to all his fans in England that there is nothing wrong with him and he's still the same old Ali.'

'Put him on the phone then,' I said. On came the familiar voice, words enunciated in a half whisper.

Arrangements were made to bring the great man into Television Centre. Later that afternoon, Ali arrived for the interview. As he entered the studio, something happened that I had never seen before or since. The entire crew, usually immune to the cult of celebrity, rose to their feet and gave him a round of applause. Although used to adulation, Ali seemed quite touched. But he was a pale shadow of the arrogant and combative interviewee that Michael Parkinson had to face years before. Ali had become benign. He struggled through the interview, often giving just one-word answers – unimaginable in his prime. He did go into a parody of his former self, did the old 'float like a butterfly' routine, and repeated one or two more familiar lines from the past; but it was all delivered in a sort of downbeat monotone. He explained that he wasn't ill; he just didn't have to go through the motions of selling fights anymore, so he now spoke in a quieter, more thoughtful way. He told me that he was devoting the rest of his life to his religion and to his eight children. The interview went on for ten minutes or so, but he was nothing like the man I had met in Zaire, Las Vegas and Malaysia in the past. It was all rather sad and afterwards I was convinced that Ali had slowed up dramatically and that he did indeed seem to have a health problem. I am sure that most viewers at the time would have drawn the same conclusion.

As far as I know, Ali did not return to a BBC television studio again until the *Sports Personality of the Year* programme sixteen years later, at which he was given a special lifetime achievement award. By this time, of course, his health had severely deteriorated. I had left the BBC a few months before that programme and I very much missed being there to meet him once again. On that occasion, the affection for him from all the other sporting stars present was clear. 'I may still make a comeback,' he joked, barely decipherable.

The year before, the BBC had come to me with the idea of having an 'Ali' night and I was asked to present the evening. The job would entail a trip to Ali's home town of Louisville, Kentucky, to Miami, and to his old training camp at Deer Park, Pennsylvania. I jumped at the opportunity, especially as I would be working with Stuart Cabb, one of the BBC's most imaginative and talented producers.

So it was that, one morning, I found myself in a queue of people in a launderette in a suburb of Miami. I was in the company of a short septuagenarian with mahogany skin and little hair. He was discussing with the proprietor of the establishment the contents of a blue bag that he had tipped out onto the counter. It became like a conversation from *The Odd Couple*, or perhaps *The Sunshine Boys*. Both men were raising their voices. There was a lot of 'What do I care?' and 'So who knows how many shirts there are?'

In Britain it would have seemed like a row. Here it was day-to-day banter. The septuagenarian had a twinkle in his eye. Always had. And that voice was the voice of the man who played a large part in changing the course of sporting history. He was Angelo Dundee.

In 1963, when Henry Cooper pulled out that famous left hook that flattened the then Cassius Clay, Dundee was the man who drew attention to a split in his fighter's glove, which gave Clay valuable time to clear his senses, recover and win, and maintain an unbeaten record, without which his journey to the heavyweight championship of the world would have been a more difficult one. How that split in the glove got there remains contentious. Again, when Clay wanted to quit in his fight with Sonny Liston for the title, it was the cajoling Dundee who made him get off his stool and continue.

Dundee had been in Ali's corner for all his professional fights but one. I was in Miami to hear about his life with the twentieth century's greatest sporting icon. The trip to the launderette had been part of the price. Dundee could always strike a deal.

Unlike Angelo, Ali's fight doctor, Ferdie Pacheco, had quit being part of the champion's team after his 1977 fight with Ernie Shavers, who had given Ali a torrid time and had had a

110

great chance to beat him. Pacheco had written to Ali after that fight explaining that he could no longer stand by and watch him take more punishment than was good for his health. Ali never replied, but Pacheco quit anyway and took no comfort from the fact that his point of view was sadly prophetic. Pacheco too was based in Miami. A successful artist, author, and broadcaster, as well as a medical doctor, he is an accomplished man with, shall we say, no detectable self-doubt. He articulated brilliantly the phenomenon that has been Muhammad Ali.

Then I went to Louisville to see Ali's birthplace and meet his brother, Rahman Ali, formerly Rudolph Valentino Clay, who had also embraced the Muslim faith. He too had been a heavyweight boxer, though without anything like his brother's talent. Rahman had seen our car pull up outside his timber-built bungalow and suddenly we were greeted by this bounding 54-year-old, looking like a black Captain Birdseye. Huge grey beard, open-toe sandals, topped off with a jaunty white sailing cap. Rahman introduced me to his third wife and his fifth wife. It was the same woman: they had remarried. We went to the bridge in Louisville from where the young Cassius, fresh back from the Rome Olympics in 1960, was alleged to have thrown his gold medal into the Ohio River after being refused service in a segregated restaurant. We also went to the gym where it all started after Cassius had gone to complain to a policeman that his bike had been stolen: the officer turned out to be boxing coach Joe Martin.

Then it was off to Pennsylvania and the old training camp that Ali used at Deer Park. By this time it was virtually derelict, but the log cabin where Ali and his team stayed was still there. It was an eerie place, purveying an air of sadness, of boxing ghosts, a nostalgia for lost times.

While in Miami, I had also volunteered to accompany Angelo Dundee on the coffee run to the nearest Starbucks for refreshments for him, his secretary of many years' standing and our crew. The secretary, possibly now of the same vintage as Angelo, had sternly reminded him before we left that under no circumstances could she take normal coffee; it had to be decaff. Her heart, you see.

I stood by in the shop, ready to carry some of the purchase back to the office while Angelo made the order, again with a lot of 'What do I know?' and 'What do I care?' thrown into the conversation. On the way out of the shop I happened to ask which of the coffees was the decaff. Angelo thought for a couple of moments, realised he had forgotten the special order, briefly contemplated going back, then looked me in the eye and said, 'Fuck it, I'll con her.'

Split gloves, coffee orders – all in a day's work for Angelo Dundee.

Many people remember Ali's presence at the Atlanta Olympics in 1996 when, with quivering arm, he lit the Olympic flame. Some thought it was sheer exploitation on the part of the organisers and that a sick man should not have been put through what clearly seemed like an ordeal. For my part, I thought it a valiant and brave act by a man who was able to cope with the downside of life as well as he had done with the spectacular highs he'd enjoyed as the world's greatest sportsman. Ali would not have been there had he not wanted to be. I was present in the stadium for the occasion, and it brought a tear to my eye. I was not alone.

11

FINDING A ROSE

My love life had been getting more and more complicated over the years. I was now in my late thirties and very much living the bachelor lifestyle, which meant too much bad food and probably too much booze. Luckily the drink never got a hold of me and I was careful not to let it interfere in any way with my work. I kept meeting gorgeous women but was finding it difficult to settle down with any one of them. There was my 'air stewardess' period, my 'model' period, and my 'BBC' period. The problem was, they intermingled.

There was a beautiful Asian model who did not drink any alcohol and would not go to bed with me before marriage. Romantically, that was short-lived, but we remained friends for some years afterwards.

There was the stunning blonde in her early twenties who made no bones about wanting to become Mrs Lynam. We had a great year or so together before I started messing her around. I still wasn't ready to settle down.

I had met an attractive Scots girl at the Open Championship

in 1978 and met another at a subsequent Open. They both lived in Glasgow and from time to time I would find myself out and about in that fair city with one or the other on my arm.

There was a third Scots girl, another real beauty, who was also on the scene for a while. What was it about these Caledonians?

One New Year's Eve I took her on a short holiday to a friend's house in Spain. On the way from the airport we were looking for a restaurant in which to celebrate the occasion. The ones that were open were fully booked and we were getting pretty desperate. At last I found a tiny bistro in the back streets of the town of Fuengirola. They had room for us. Relief. I deposited my girlfriend at a table and went off to park the car. Round and round the narrow streets I drove until eventually I found a space. Now I had a problem. Not only was I struggling to remember how to get back to the restaurant, I had forgotten to make a note of its name. In these mobile phone days the problem would have been easily solved.

For fully half an hour I found myself running up and down lanes and alleyways before, exhausted and breathless, I found it. My friend was entirely untroubled. She was enjoying a glass of wine, certainly not her first, as the owner and waiters hovered around her like moths to the flame. She was a cracker.

The villa of my dear friends, Mike and Sue Dring, became the 'compatibility' training ground for several of my girlfriends of the time. I took another leggy blonde there on another occasion. She seemed to have everything: looks, intelligence, a superb wit and she loved to play tennis. My kind of girl. Unfortunately, she also had a bit of a temper and would 'go off on one' from time to time. That relationship was doomed.

A year or so after she and I parted, I got a call from her. 'What are you doing this evening?' she asked. 'Oh, I'm going to an early evening drinks party at a friend's office,' I said. It was approaching Christmas time.

She told me that she was going to the birthday party of a girl-friend of hers and, as she hated going alone, would I go with her? In the end we agreed to go to both parties together.

After the early evening drinks, we headed for Chelsea in a cab and arrived at a flat where the revelry had obviously been underway for some time. In fact the party was to celebrate the birthdays of two ladies, both of them highly attractive. Even though I had not done a lot of high-profile television, I was cornered at the party by a chap who seemed to know all about my career on both radio and television and was clearly intrigued, if not by me, then certainly by the whole business of broadcasting.

I was finding it a little difficult to get away from him. I noticed that once or twice I kept getting a glare from this par-ticularly svelte blonde in a little black dress who was not only beautiful but oozed class. I found out later that she hadn't a clue who I was, that my 'fan' was her boyfriend, and that she thought it had been me boring the pants off him!

She intrigued me. I had to get her phone number. I had no clue at the time whether she was in a serious relationship or not, but at least I wanted to find out if I had a chance with her. She looked like a challenge to me. I wanted to know if she could smile as well as she could glare.

I managed to get her number and phoned her. I got a very frosty response, but under sufferance she agreed to meet me for a drink. Her name was Rose and that was the beginning of a relationship that, against the odds, has lasted to this day. Of course I have done my level worst to nearly ruin it on a couple of occasions.

The first occasion was early on. One of my Scots ladies was still on the scene and from time to time I was seeing her as well. She and Rose lived hundreds of miles apart but extraordinarily – wouldn't you know it? – they had a mutual friend, who was amazed to hear from both of them, separately, that they were going out with a chap called Des Lynam, the one who worked on television. Well there was only one of those, but there were two of them and I was in big trouble. Against the odds, Rose and I continued to see each other, though intermittently. It would be another couple of years before we moved in together.

From time to time I would also have lunch with another exotic creature. She turned out to be big trouble because 'she' turned out to have had a quite extraordinary past …

12

THAT WAS NO LADY

One quiet summer's morning, I accompanied a girl I knew to deliver something to a friend of hers. My role in this performance was merely that of transportation but I went with my friend to the door of an apartment in Kensington which was answered by a sultry looking female wrapped only in a bath towel revealing an intriguing décolletage, which immediately captured my attention.

'I'd better arrange a closer look at that,' I thought. I managed to prise the lady's telephone number out of my friend and duly called this subject of my excited interest.

A rather 'actressy' voice answered and was greatly underwhelmed by my suggestion of a meeting.

'But you know nothing about me. Why should you possibly want to meet me?' she asked. Some women have never understood that the initial attraction for men is nearly always physical. At that point I had no interest in examining her intelligence or possible common interests. In the end I persuaded her to come out to dinner one night.

We met on two or three occasions, and wherever we went she turned heads. She was six feet tall, taller than me when she wore heels, and there was something enigmatic about her. She would quite often seem to be elsewhere. 'God,' I thought. 'I'm boring this one to tears.' The usual chat lines were going down like lead balloons.

It was then I got the phone call one morning. The voice at the other end was female, but wouldn't give a name.

'Be careful with Caroline,' I was told. 'You obviously don't know, but she was born a boy and the press are on to her.'

I was unable to elicit any further information.

I had tried to get Caroline into bed after our second date, but she would have none of it. Now I wanted to find out the truth.

At our next meeting I was examining her like an antiques expert with a Louis XIV chair. She was tall, and her hands were quite big, although the beautifully manicured nails made them look ultra feminine. Her voice, which I had thought 'actressy', was certainly on the deep side, but there was no sign of an Adam's apple, and her breasts were magnificent. No. Someone was having a joke at my expense. I wanted to broach the subject, but how on earth do you ask a lady if she was born a male?

The answer was the booze.

We had had two bottles of wine, most of which I had drunk before I posed the question, almost certainly in a most ham-fisted way. Caroline was stunned. The evening was at an end.

I wrote a note to her afterwards apologising for the manner of my interrogation; but it became clear soon afterwards that my telephone informant had it absolutely right. The press were indeed on to Caroline, who had been a Bond girl and had taken part in a good number of advertising campaigns, including one for Smirnoff vodka. No one had any suspicions about this beauty until the press disclosures. Subsequently, Caroline produced a book in which she told her story. I was mentioned in it without being named, as a sympathetic friend, which indeed I became to her.

I continued to see her very occasionally for a few years without any romantic involvement. She was a troubled person. I remember once her saying that had she been born in Nazi Germany she would have ended up in a concentration camp. 'People like me would have been killed,' she said. She also expected to die young because of the shocks her body had to endure as a result of the operations and hormone treatments.

Whatever the complications of her life, I liked Caroline. I was perfectly secure in my own sexuality and had no trouble in telling friends that I knew her and saw her from time to time, usually for lunch. In the early Eighties, Caroline met an Italian who fell in love with her and wanted to marry her. Such a marriage would have been illegal and the relationship petered out. Later, she met another man whom she wanted to marry. He was Jewish and she went through a lengthy process of converting to Judaism in order that she could be acceptable to his faith and family. Rose and I were invited to the wedding, but we did not go. There was still that little problem. A marriage in the United Kingdom between a male and a transsexual was illegal. The ceremony did, however, take place and it was a big affair, with Caroline looking stunning in a white bridal gown. How she possibly imagined that it would all go off quietly without press attention, I cannot think; and of course once again the papers got hold of the story and it ended with the husband apparently denying that he ever knew of Caroline's past. This was an incredible claim, which she absolutely refuted. I think his family, and certainly the Rabbi who had converted her to Judaism, were pretty shocked though.

Caroline brought out another book. After the friendship and understanding I had offered her, she implied that there was rather more to the friendship than there actually was. Of course the *Sun* newspaper put it on the front page. All I had been was an occasional confidant and friend, but of course my name helped her sell the book. I remarked at the time that when I first asked her out I had followed my usual practice of not asking to see a lady's birth certificate.

I can only assume that Caroline was in desperate need of the money. She has had a tougher life than most people. Bravely, the year after her 'marriage' fell apart, she presented herself to the court of human rights in Brussels to have British law altered to allow her to change her sexual identity on her birth certificate from male to female, which would have given her the right to marry legally. Her plea was denied, despite some heavyweight dissenters amongst the presiding judges who thought she had every right to do so as in some other countries. Subsequently, as far as I know, Caroline did marry abroad, and I hope that, wherever she is, she is content at last. She may have been born into the male gender but in terms of her female looks, she was a definite 10.

13

BREAKFAST WITH BRISBANE

I had been to the Commonwealth Games of 1974 and 1978 for BBC Radio. Both trips, to New Zealand and Canada respectively, had been marvellous experiences. In 1982 the Commonwealth Games were to be held in Brisbane, Australia, and at one stage there was the prospect of my picking up my radio boxing commentary duties there. But I was summoned by the Head of Television Sport, who told me that he wanted me to be the main TV presenter for the Games.

'Great,' I said. 'But you will be fronting them from Television Centre,' he said. Not so great.

As it turned out, *Breakfast with Brisbane* was the first series of television programmes in which I really relaxed in front of the camera. I even felt I was doing the job rather well – up until then I had often been anxious before a broadcast; and although I had usually been able to hide my nerves, I had never felt entirely comfortable. It may have been something to do with the time of day, and the broadcasts seeming to be less formal, or at least I was making them so.

The shows began in the early morning by linking to our commentators at the events 'down under', where it was evening time. For me, it involved rising at about 3 a.m. to begin preparation and scripting before going on air at 6.30 or 7 a.m., depending on the day's major events.

For track and field events, my sidekick in the studio was Steve Ovett, gold medallist two years earlier at the Moscow Olympics, who was not competing in Brisbane due to injury. Daley Thompson was of course the outstanding decathlon star at the time, having also won an Olympic gold in Moscow and destined to do the same in Los Angeles in 1984; but on one of our shows, Steve described the decathlon as 'nine Mickey Mouse events and a slow 1,500 metres'. The Thompson fans were far from happy, but Steve was prepared to say what he thought. Nonetheless, Daley took that Commonwealth gold medal as well.

Steve and I hit it off together beautifully and produced some decent broadcasts. Coincidentally, we had gone to the same grammar school in Brighton, though at different times. When his athletics career ended a few years later, he spent a while working for ITV when they had a spell of covering track and field. I have always been surprised that he did not continue to pursue a career in the media. Steve was an absolute natural, but perhaps he was never asked or didn't push himself. He was always a free spirit.

Those early morning broadcasts got a great deal of attention at the time. They were the precursor to breakfast television, which began later in the year. The BBC were rubbing their hands with glee. We were doing huge audiences for the time of day, but breakfast television proper was unable to maintain them when they began broadcasting. People were much more fascinated by a little sporting competition with their breakfast than the doom and gloom of the daily news.

The editor for the shows was a chap called Mike Murphy, vastly intelligent, but with the syntax of a navvy. Mike was wonderful fun, of Irish stock like myself, but he had adopted the language and carriage of a cockney wide boy. However, he was never to be underestimated.

Once, when a new secretary joined the department, a young rather naive Sloane Ranger type, Mike shouted to her that he needed 'a black and fast' – 'Londonspeak' for a taxi. The bemused girl sprinted into the office with a black biro.

I had done one of my early *Grandstand* programmes with Mike as editor. At the Friday morning meeting, I said to him 'Now, how do you want me to start tomorrow's programme?'

'Well, here's my contribution,' he'd said. '"Good afternoon". 'Now I'm leaving the rest to you.'

The year before those Commonwealth Games, and after I had done a good few Saturday *Grandstand* programmes, I had been entrusted with a new series. It was decided to begin a *Sunday Grandstand* programme to run throughout the summer. This was a new departure. Prior to this, the BBC sports department had produced Sunday cricket only. Now with Grand Prix racing becoming more and more popular, as well as other big events transferring to Sundays, I was given this big new chance. The BBC even put on a press conference to announce the show. In the following day's publicity, *The Times* managed to spell my name wrong. So much for the big time.

Mike Murphy left the BBC in 1983, having edited both *Match of the Day* and *Grandstand* whilst still in his twenties and early thirties, to forge a career as an independent producer. Sadly he became a victim of cancer and died a few years ago.

His memorial service ended with the Guinness flowing at a great 'hooley', just as he had wished. We all left with a smile on our faces and with very fond memories of an outstanding and unique television man.

Around this time, the Open University asked me to be interviewed about the ability to 'take talkback', that is to listen to production instructions while you are saying something entirely different yourself. It's a bit like being on the phone when someone in the room is also talking to you.

The tradition in sports broadcasting, where events and information both come pretty quickly, is to have what is called 'open' talkback in which the broadcaster hears everything from the production gallery. If the programme assistant sneezes, you hear it. If the director and producer are screaming at each other, you hear that too. It has sometimes been the cause of the rather wide-eyed look on the Lynam face in your living-room.

Most other programmes use 'switch' talkback, in which the presenter is protected from the general badinage and only hears the director when a switch is thrown and the information is specifically for him or her, though some, especially if they are recorded, don't use talkback at all and leave any instructions to the floor manager.

The specific problems for a *Grandstand* presenter in my early days were that while you had to deal with the talkback you were also ad libbing or remembering lines – there was no autocue. In addition, if an item came off videotape, you had to give the director a keyword for him to run it and keep talking for exactly ten seconds in vision while the tape ran up to speed before it could be shown. Thankfully, television presenters now have the luxury of 'instant' videotape, and often autocue as well.

And so I was interviewed and examined by the Open University and they came to this conclusion. They didn't know how I managed to take the talkback – and neither did I.

14

NOTHING SUCCEEDS LIKE EXCESS

By 1984 I had emerged as the number one sports presenter for the BBC. Frank Bough had gone to breakfast television in 1982, and David Coleman's days as *Grandstand* presenter had come to a close. When the Los Angeles Olympics came round, I was going to be pretty high profile. The Commonwealth Games of two years earlier had been successful for me; but now much more attention would be paid to my skills, or lack of them, not only by my BBC bosses but also by the press.

For these Games, the time difference would mean that the main events would take place in the evening, British time, in peak-time viewing, and I was destined once again to stay in London for my presentational duties. However, I would travel to Los Angeles and spend a week or so previewing the Games and sending back reports before returning to London to occupy the presenter's chair for when the action got going.

My producer in Los Angeles was Bob Abrahams, my aggressive little sidekick from the Moscow Olympics, and he came up with a wheeze with which to open the very first Olympic programme.

He hired an extraordinary open-top car, an Excalibur, a modern replica of a Thirties American sports tourer. The plan was that I would make my opening remarks while driving this gleaming white beast to a camera mounted on a truck, which I would be trailing. We would drive just ahead of the latest Olympic torch-carrier, who would then be filmed as we slowed up and he passed us. I had written my opening, which was about a minute long. Now I had to drive this enormous vehicle, make sure I didn't crash into the truck ahead, and remember my words.

Off we went. Cue Des. 'In Los Angeles,' I began, 'nothing succeeds like excess.' I was about forty seconds into the spiel and going fluently. I could see the Olympic torch bearer in my mirror, when I suddenly heard, 'Sir, could you pull over to the sidewalk and get out of the vehicle please.' The cops had arrived on my outside and wanted me out of the way for the runner. We actually had a document from the LAPD allowing us to do the filming, but this had obviously not got through to the cops on the ground. We stopped, Bob came swaggering up, never one to use diplomacy when aggression will do, and very nearly got us arrested. In the end we did a re-take, speeding off to get in front of the torch-bearer again, who by now had long since passed us. Surprisingly, I got through the words again without a fluff. It was a smashing opening for the BBC's coverage of the Games, and was all down to Bob Abrahams' imagination. Of course the BBC have pulled out the film of me being stopped in my tracks by the police for the occasional showing on *Auntie's Bloomers* and suchlike.

So we had this fabulous car for the rest of the day. 'Right,' said Abrahams, 'I think we've earned a night out in this little baby.' Later that evening off we went downtown in the Excalibur, me driving, Bob with his arm out of the side and shades on. At one stage, we pulled up at some traffic lights, side by side with a Rolls Royce. The darkened electric window of the Roller slid down and a woman of some vintage, made up like Mae West, looked us slowly up and down. 'Say,' she said, 'you guys don't mess around.'

'We can do better than that,' I thought.

Then it was back home to London to begin coverage of the Games proper. Now I was working with John Philips, the best in the business at the time. He was a genius in television terms – flawed yes, but a genius none the less. We had already worked on *Grandstand* together where his humour and vision had produced some great programmes.

Once, on April 1st, I continued to broadcast to camera as a small scuffle amongst the crew behind me developed into a fully-fledged brawl. Some viewers caught on. Many others rang the BBC demanding that the perpetrators be sacked. It was of course an April Fool's joke, underlined when we replayed the whole thing in slow motion.

The combination of my writing and Philips' visual imagination gelled and we proceeded to get rave reviews for our Olympic coverage. But there was one big hiccup that nearly ruined the successful run we were enjoying.

John had been seeing a very beautiful girl called Jane. It was an on/off relationship, but it had been 'on' when he took her to a party arranged by one of our mutual colleagues and friends, John Rowlinson. Also present at the party was Seb Coe, Olympic champion and destined to retain his 1,500 metres title in Los Angeles. Seb took a shine to Jane. The feeling was mutual. In the middle of the Games, Philips suddenly found out that his girlfriend had flown to Los Angeles to meet up with Seb.

John cracked up. Now I had an editor on the verge of a breakdown: he couldn't eat, sleep or concentrate.

The story got through to the tabloid press and one Sunday morning as I drove up to the entrance to Television Centre, one of the porters approached me with the front page of the *Sunday Mirror*. 'I see that Coe's run off with your bird,' he said to me, with considerable lack of tact had it been true. The paper's banner headline had it there in black and white: 'Coe runs off with BBC man's girl'. Underneath it had a picture of me, with the caption 'worried'. The gateman had drawn the immediate conclusion that the *Sunday Mirror* had no doubt intended – there were more sales in Lynam's grief than in that of an unknown television backroom boy. When one read the text of course, John, who had surprisingly spoken to the press about his predicament, had given a quote that I was worried about him, which indeed I was.

John managed to pull himself together and got through the rest of the Games, but he spent many a very late night at my house going over his dilemma again and again. I had become presenter/psychiatrist. This experience should have helped me with one of my colleagues in 1984. Presenting some of the Olympic programmes alongside me was David Icke, a former professional goalkeeper who was now making his way as a broadcaster. He had been the butt of a few stories from the 1982 World Cup in Spain, where his fear of flying had caused a problem or two for the producers working with him. Mind you, that didn't stop him agreeing to be the presenter of the Farnborough Air Show not so long after – a bit like Julian Clary fronting the Rugby League Challenge Cup Final. During the Olympics, Icke took little part in the camaraderie of the broadcasting team and stayed somewhat aloof. One morning he was rehearsing his opening to a show. 'The big question today,' he said, 'is, can Carl Lewis win his fourth gold medal to emulate the great Jesse James?' It was a simple slip of the brain as he confused the famous bank robber with the pre-war track legend, Jesse Owens.

Now this sort of thing happens to any broadcaster, a simple error, which you either spot yourself or someone corrects for you – with luck before you share your idiocy with the public. But Mr Icke was so unpopular with his colleagues that they were of a mind to let him go on the air with the mistake. Luckily someone put professionalism before personal dislike and made the correction for him. He was uncharitable in his response, feigning that he knew all along and was 'having a joke'. We never became friendly, but I must admit that years later, when he was humiliated on the *Wogan* show after his 'Son of God' claims, I felt tremendously sorry for him. At that time he seemed to be unwell and the programme, I thought, took unfair advantage of him. Since then, he seems to have recovered his composure and as far as I know has cleverly carved out a role on the lecture tour circuit as he pontificates on world conspiracy theories for those prepared to listen, and has also written several books. Good luck to him.

Towards the end of the Games, as I thought might happen, the tabloid press had started to take some notice of me, for the first time. The *Sun* did a two-page profile and came up with the phrase 'Dishy Des', which has been dug up on numerous occasions since and for which I am truly ungrateful.

I received some 'herograms', as they are known in the business, from the BBC's top brass. Now I felt that I could not only do the job on television, but I could do it quite well.

I was getting delusions of adequacy.

*

It was at the next Games in 1988 that one of the biggest Olympic stories of all time emerged. As in 1984, I would present the Games from London but once again I would travel to the host city to film a preview progamme and so I found myself packing my bags for Seoul, South Korea.

The most exciting and eerie part of my trip to Korea was a visit to Panmunjom. To my astonishment, I realised that the North Korean border was only about forty miles north of Seoul, about as far as Luton from London. There, the respective soldiers of north and south glared at each other through binoculars and went through their respective rituals. I heard the repeated loudspeaker wailings from the communist side, regaling the south for their errant lifestyles. It sent a shiver up my spine as I recorded a small report on site.

But the real drama of the 1988 Olympics unfolded once I was back in London, presenting the coverage of the Games. British sprinter Linford Christie had seemingly failed a drugs test but was absolved later. He put it down to drinking 'ginseng tea'. I ribbed him about it at the next Sports Personality show. But then came the greatest shock of all: Ben Johnson, the world record holder at 100 metres who had just won the gold medal, failed a drugs test and was to be stripped of his title. I gave the news out live on one of our broadcasts, before we had the story confirmed. Someone had seen it written on the tapes by the French news agency, Agence France-Presse, and we went with the story, getting it out before our rivals or the news bulletins. 'If this is true,' I said on air, 'It is the biggest story of these or any other Olympic Games.' It was true alright, and dominated the Olympic news for the rest of the Games.

15

SPOTY

The *Sports Personality of the Year* show (SPOTY), formerly called the *Sports Review of the Year*, is the jewel in the crown of BBC Television's sports output. Even in recent times, when many of the major sporting occasions are seen not on the BBC but on other channels, it remains the most respected awards show in sport. In fact, other broadcasters have tried to emulate it over the years but have never been able to match it for the respect in which it is held, not just by viewers, but also by the sportsmen and women of achievement who make the programme what it is.

SPOTY started back in 1954 when Chris Chataway, one of the outstanding middle distance runners of the day, was voted Sports Personality of the Year, ahead of Roger Bannister, who had become the first man to break the four-minute mile barrier. Chataway had run in the race. Bannister had won it, but the viewers' vote went to Chris. The reason probably was that Chataway had run a brilliant 5,000 metres at the old White City just a few weeks before voting for the award began, beating the legendary Russian Vladimir Kuts and knocking five seconds off the world record in the process. Chataway's race was on live and had made a huge impact with the viewers. In contrast, the world mile record attempt had only been filmed by one camera on top of a van and had not been seen live on television. One of the most famous programmes on British television had begun its uninterrupted run.

Even when working for BBC Radio, I had never been invited to the show. I had watched it on television like everyone else and always thought it a rather nervy occasion. There was some lightness of touch and a few laughs; the racing drivers Jackie Stewart and Graham Hill had worked an amusing double act once or twice; but for the most part everyone seemed to be so stiff. It was rather like a school speech day.

When I made my switch to BBC Television, I began being invited to be part of the audience, which is mostly made up of Britain's sportsmen and women who have played some part in the sporting year, plus a good number of 'blazers' (sports administrators), and of course a host of BBC broadcasters, producers and management.

Sitting in the audience was actually quite nerve-wracking. Again, the formality of the occasion made everyone seem to tense up. I turned down my invitation a couple of times, finding it better and more entertaining to watch it in the comfort of my own home with a couple of beers. It was easier to miss the boring bits – and there were a few of those.

I appeared on the programme for the first time in 1982. 'Appeared' is perhaps not the right word: my voice was heard as I narrated one or two of the videotaped items. Then, out of the blue in 1983, the Head of Sport, Jonathan Martin, invited me to present the programme. This was a shock. Frank Bough, the regular number one frontman, had left for other pastures but there was still Harry Carpenter, who had been his co-presenter for many years, plus the likes of David Coleman and Jimmy Hill, as well as several others who might have considered themselves ahead of me in the pecking order to present the show. It had never occurred to me at that stage that I might have been selected, and I certainly had no intention of putting myself forward. It is extraordinary how difficult it is to get a break in broadcasting. But once you do, and if you show any ability, things tend to come to you by invitation. That certainly has been the case with me. I have never asked to do any show that has come my way in the last thirty-five years. Other people have kindly put me in the frame.

I must admit, the thought of presenting the programme sent a shiver of nervous anxiety down my spine, especially when I was told that I would be expected to take Frank's place and that Harry would remain the number two presenter. I would have been far happier slipping in behind him, but now I would be responsible for opening and closing the show.

I had already been working with a chap called Harold Anderson, my first editor on *Grandstand*. He was a Kiwi, a single-figure handicap golfer, and absolutely meticulous in his approach to programme-making. He and I were friendly but I gathered that he treated me with some suspicion, not being particularly enthusiastic about my so-called laid-back style. He was a believer in the 'sell it' type of presentation. That's what he had been used to. But he was now lumbered with me and we got together to prepare *Sports Review of the Year*, which would be broadcast on 11 December.

Unlike many awards shows, there was no team of scriptwriters to help the host: the custom in BBC Sport was that the presenter would be given a running order and then write his own script, something I was very happy to do and have always done.

I said to Anderson that the show always seemed 'edgy', and that I would like to lighten it somehow. As it turned out on the night, I was the one who was edgy. I now understood why. It was just such a momentous occasion. The sportsmen and women, most of them famous, were often in awe of each other's fame. And the 'blazers' often seemed bored when we were dealing with sports other than their own.

Steve Cram was voted Personality of the Year, having won the inaugural World Championship title over 1,500 metres in Helsinki that year. The familiar trophy was presented to him by Bobby Charlton, who is one of those famous names to miss out on collecting the award himself. I did my first interview on the programme with a young Frank Bruno and suggested he would soon be in the running for a world title. It took him another twelve years. Frank would play a prominent role in the show for many years to come, nearly always bringing the house down in the process with his wit and extraordinary use of the English language. We also had the car that had broken the world land speed record, reaching well over six hundred miles per hour. I remarked on the speedometer, which went from 0–800 miles per hour.

All in all, I managed for the most part to conceal my terror, got away with a few quips, and was astonished when we came off air to be hugged by Harold Anderson, in relief that I had actually got through the show without mucking it up.

He wasn't as relieved as me.

I would experience something like the same feeling once a year for the next fifteen years.

The *Sports Personality of the Year* show is rehearsed up to a point. You can go through the script and the videotaped items till you are blue in the face, but what makes the show stand or fall are the interviews with the stars and their contributions. There is no rehearsal for this. The sportsmen and women turn up on the night and usually the first inkling they have that they are going to be spoken to live on the show is when a sound engineer approaches them to strap on a microphone.

This affects people in different ways. Some suffer from 'first night' nerves. It is always a first night. Others rise to the occasion and become stars of the show. Frank Bruno, Jenny Pitman and others were always a delight to work with; some would be racked with angst.

In 1993 the Grand National had ended in chaos. Actually it had never started and the race had been declared void after the starting gate failed. John White had finished first in the 'race that never was', as Peter O'Sullevan had famously described it, on the Jenny Pitman-trained Esha Ness. On the day, White had done a brilliant interview with me, shocked seemingly that his 'win' would not stand.

For our SPOTY programme we had decided to transport the offending starting gate into the studio and I, suitably attired in bowler hat and trench coat, would 'start' the race all over again. White, whom I had recommended to the editor as a star interviewee, would delight the audience, I was sure. However, John, now able to see the whites of a few hundred famous eyes looking back at him, reverted to type: that of a shy Irish horseman, far different from the adrenaline-pumped loquacious chap I had interviewed at Aintree. 'Thanks for the John White idea,' the editor said afterwards.

I became associated over the years with the so-called stunts on the programme, not because many of them were my ideas, simply that I was the one who had to try to make them work, and with luck amuse the assembled throng and in turn the viewers. They were often bizarre, sometimes plainly ridiculous, and occasionally very funny. They did at least rouse the live audience from their slumbers. I usually introduced them with a line like, 'Now for the part of the programme our critics particularly enjoy', or 'Now the part of the programme that the editor thought up during a moment of self-doubt back in April'. It was a defence mechanism. The critics always hated these items. The viewers loved them.

One Olympic year, when our shooters had done particularly well at the Games, we decided to hold a duck shoot, rather as you might see in a fairground. The usual suspects, Bruno and others, would compete against each other. It didn't augur well for the show when the BBC safety officer managed (literally) to shoot himself in the foot during the afternoon rehearsals.

Another year, when the Europeans had won the Ryder Cup, we decided to have a golf game on the programme. We brought in a simulator that could measure the distance and direction of a golf shot. The electronics would assess the player's results. A few of us had a go in rehearsals and were unsurprised to find those results less than average.

On the night of the show we were rather more disturbed, when the likes of Ian Woosnam were unable to record anything other than a high slice, a shot he had probably never hit in his entire life. Bruno took part as usual with the fastest swing known to man. The inadequacies of the machine didn't affect him at all. He never actually managed to hit the ball.

There were often very nervous moments just before the show began. In 1986, when Steve Rider joined me as co-presenter replacing Harry Carpenter, the boxer Lloyd Honeyghan had been booked for the show and we had planned for him to be involved right at the start. Honeyghan had created one of boxing's biggest upsets that year, stopping the American Don Curry in Atlantic City to become the World welterweight champion. (I had been to the fight as the radio boxing commentator and had got to know Lloyd reasonably well.)

This was one of the rare occasions when I had actually spoken to the personality a day or two before the show to underline to them how important their contribution would be. All had seemed well at the time, but on the evening of the show we received a phone call from the driver who had been sent to pick him up that Honeyghan was refusing to get in the car. So I rang him. 'You must realise,' I said, 'that an appearance on this show can only do you good. It will further enhance your reputation. You know I'm going to look after you.'

'Well, I'll come if I've won,' replied Lloyd.

'In the history of the programme, nobody has ever been told before the show whether they've won or not, and that isn't going to start now,' I said. 'Now do yourself a favour and get down here.' It was true: down the years, the first time I knew the name of the winner was when it was announced. I had always told the production team to keep it from me so that I would never let the cat out of the bag during the show inadvertently or by nuance.

As it turned out Honeyghan was not at the show in time for his planned appearance, and so we had to do a hurried revamp of the opening. Halfway through the programme, out of the corner of my eye, I saw Lloyd arrive and slip into his seat. It was now too late to include him for an interview, although his achievement had been shown and referred to. At the after-show party, he pounced on me. 'I came like you asked,' he said, 'and you still didn't interview me. 'Too late, mate,' I replied.

Lloyd was in the top six personalities of the year, but Nigel Mansell won the coveted award.

That starting gate from Aintree had remained a jinx. I reminded the audience of 'the teeniest weeniest bit of a cock-up' at the National and then, just as I pulled down the starting handle to begin the review of the race, I caught my finger in the apparatus. I had to stifle a cry of pain, and bled my way through the rest of the show.

On one occasion I started reading a cue, only to realise that I didn't quite recognise the lines and that they should have been read by Steve Rider. The director had popped me up in vision by mistake. I got a fit of the giggles as I read on and then found to my horror that the cue ended with somebody's death.

There were many poignant moments in the programme over the years. In 1986 the jump jockey Jonjo O'Neil was a guest on the programme, his curly auburn hair gone from the treatment he was undergoing for cancer. Earlier in the year he had ridden Dawn Run to a famous victory in the Cheltenham Gold Cup, only for his serious illness to follow. He spoke bravely about his fight, encouraged by another hero of steeplechase racing, Bob Champion, who had had to deal with a similar illness and came through. Happily, so did Jonjo, who is of course now a successful trainer.

Some years later, Helen Rollason was present. She had also voiced some of the commentary in the programme. I gave her a special mention and there was instant applause from the audience for brave Helen, who was having her own fight against cancer at the time. Sadly, she died the following year but not before producing a most compelling autobiography – *Life's Too Short* – in which she told of her fight for life and her time at the BBC. She was an absolute delight.

The worst programme we ever did in my time was in 1990. Ironically, it was edited by John Philips, whom I have described elsewhere as the most talented editor I have worked with. But on this occasion John tried too hard and came up with the idea of dealing with the sporting year month by month instead of sport by sport, which had been the tradition. It was a valiant try but it didn't work. In some months barely anything happened; sports are spread over many months anyway, and so the programme suffered accordingly.

John had an idea for the start of the show that involved Steve Rider and myself rushing in from outside as though we were running late for our own programme, a highly unlikely event. We both looked like two wallies. Also, Philips was not a great fan of the interviews with the stars, which most other people thought formed an integral part of the show. John felt they were 'corny'; hence, in a year when England came so close to winning the World Cup, only to go out to West Germany in a dramatic penalty shoot-out, not a word was heard on the programme from the likes of Bobby Robson or Gary Lineker. I took it upon myself afterwards to drop a note to Lineker, apologising for not including him in the show. As it turned out, the award went to Paul Gascoigne. At least I managed to interview Gascoigne and, as Steve Rider pointed out in his excellent book about the programme, I 'expressed a prophetic concern that his off-field activities might damage his football, but Gascoigne was confident he would cope'.

Sometimes the programme seemed to coincide with the worst weather of the year. In 1991, Liz McColgan was one of the favourites to win the award. She had taken the 10,000 metres world title in Tokyo, a run described by Brendan Foster as the best performance by any British distance runner he had ever seen. On the day of our programme, after Liz had run her customary morning fifteen miles, she and her husband travelled to the airport in Scotland to fly down for the programme only to find themselves in a blizzard. They made it in the end by catching the train, but only just in time for her to pick up the trophy.

At the Olympic Games in Atlanta in 1996, Michael Johnson had his amazing 'double', winning both the 200 and 400 metres, the first man ever to do so, the former in an astonishing new world record time of 19.32 seconds. After his performance he was ushered into our studio by Daley Thompson to do a 'live' interview with me at the top of our show. He said he couldn't wait around, a matter of some ten or fifteen minutes, and so to accommodate him I would record the interview with him just before air time. Two minutes into the interview, he got up from the chair, took off his microphone and was walking from the studio. I thought his action quite rude, however fast a runner he was, and as he was leaving I remarked, loud enough for him to hear, that I never remembered Muhammad Ali behaving like that. He turned round and gave me a sullen glare.

So four months later, who was brought into my dressing room just before the start of *Sports Personality of the Year* to have a word with me about how I might conduct my interview with him? You've guessed it. As he walked in, he stopped for a second or two. 'We've met before, haven't we?' he asked. 'Briefly,' I replied, and we both left it at that.

I recently met Michael again at a sporting legends show I broadcast for BSkyB. He was charm personified and made a super contribution to the programme. But on the Sports Personality of the Year show in 1996 as it turned out, we paired him on the programme with the sprint champion Donovan Bailey and they produced a super interview as they sparred verbally about their respective merits as the world's fastest man. The heavyweight champion Evander Holyfield was also with us, and so was Frank Bruno, on the last of his many appearances on the show, having announced his retirement from the ring. He said he was now in the pantomime business full time.

My last programme as presenter was in 1998, my sixteenth show. Although I didn't know it then, my run was over.

Michael Owen received the award, after his brilliant goal against Argentina in that year's World Cup, and I had an uncomfortable few minutes in a Grand National simulator.

Sports Personality of the Year is part of the fabric of the British sporting life. The programme continues to do well, with a high critical appreciation and good audience figures; but it still doesn't quite manage to get away from its rather tense and formal style. Those 'stunts' of yesteryear existed to try and break the ice and I have long thought that the show would be even greater if the BBC hired the Royal Albert Hall and packed it to the rafters, not only with the sporting stars, but members of the public too. ITV do something similar with their annual television awards, a programme usually devoid of a moment's wit in its presentational style, but at least it benefits from the atmosphere.

Sports Personality of the Year needs to extend its boundaries, and the public's presence would give it a much-needed shot in the arm.

16

'A SIGNED AFFIDAVIT'

Although I have spent my television career largely in the world of sport, occasionally I got out of my pram and ventured into unknown territory.

I got a phone call one day from a chap called Alan Boyd, whose name I knew simply because I had seen his credit go up on screen at the end of entertainment shows like *Game For a Laugh*. Alan introduced himself and said he wanted to come and talk to me about a show he had for me. I told him that it was very kind of him to think of me but I was so busy with being the presenter of a large part of the BBC's sporting output that I was unlikely to have time for anything else. But he persuaded me to have a meeting with him and told me he had a tape to show me.

Alan came round to my house and put the tape in my VCR. I watched intently and within five minutes knew that he had a hit. He was showing me the American version of *How Do They Do That?*

The concept of the programme was that it explained things

143

that you had always wanted to know but never had explained to you before: pseudo-scientific with an attractive mixture of showbiz, beautifully packaged and presented by a male–female duo in front of a studio audience. The male partner was a man I had seen presenting sport on one of the American networks. He had grey hair and a moustache. 'What made you think of me, Alan?' I quipped.

'My company has the British rights,' he said. 'Would you be interested?'

I was.

Over the next few weeks, the sports department agreed I could do it and plans were made for the first series of twelve programmes. My American counterpart had a very pretty and clever sidekick. Now we had to pick a partner for me.

Alan put out his well-connected feelers, selected eight candidates, and arranged for them to record a much shortened version of the programme with me. They would all do it on the same day. Care was taken to avoid their seeing each other or knowing who their competitors were.

Amongst the trialists were Fiona Bruce, currently one of BBC's main news anchors and co-presenter of *Crimewatch*, and the throaty-voiced Mariella Frostrup; but the girl who caught everyone's eye, including mine, was a petite bundle of dynamite from Southampton, where she read the local news for the BBC: Jenny Hull. She sparkled and she got the job. We did three series of the programme together and I made a friend for life. Jenny was very telegenic and bright, but away from the cameras was one of the dizziest people I have ever met. Jenny buys a new car, prangs it on the way home. Jenny goes to airport, forgets passport. Jenny leaves home, shuts front door, drops keys down nearest drain hole, that sort of thing.

Almost every man who came into contact with her on the programme fancied her. It was no surprise when one of our guests fell in love with her and they got married soon after. His name was Nigel Marvin, who at the time had scarcely been on television but in recent years has completed several series on wild animals for ITV and Channel Five. On the day he met Jenny, he had come on the show to explain how you could programme swans or geese to fly to order so that you could film them in flight. The item had brought the house down because one of his geese had taken an unnatural attachment to my privates and wouldn't leave me alone. When I wrote to them, having been invited to the wedding, I told them that the goose and I were happily living together by the river. Sadly Nigel's marriage to Jenny was short lived.

How Do They Do That? was a big hit for the BBC for a while, claiming audience figures of up to thirteen million per programme and knocking the stuffing out of ITV's *The Bill*. We got our biggest audience one night when we showed an item about how audience figures are produced. A sample as small as 4,000 people record what they are watching, the results of which seemed to point to *Coronation Street* being the most popular programme in Britain on any given week. I have never met anyone who has been part of the sample; in fact I have never met anyone who has even known someone who has been part of the sample. Our intrepid reporters on the programme did however find and interview a couple of people who did this most rare of jobs. They obviously knew they were going to be on the programme, and they and all their friends pressed the right button. Our audience figure for a programme on audience research rocketed. Half a dozen or so people make a difference of around 2 million viewers. I feel strongly that the whole sample is questionable, and yet careers and reputations increasingly depend on the figures they produce. Network bosses and advertisers certainly seem to think that the system works, but it all depends on such a small number of people recording their viewing habits that I have my doubts. With the rewards for doing this being so small, how can they possibly entice a good cross-section of the population to do the job? I can't imagine anyone with a few bob being bothered. Perhaps that is why the less cerebral programmes appear to get the highest ratings.

One of my favourite segments on the programme was when Rory Bremner came on to explain how he does his impressions. Actually, he has a god-given talent, but he put me through the process of teaching me to do a 'John Major', which in the end wasn't too bad. Rory has been a good friend for years, and did me no harm at all with his impressions of me.

After three series, though, the attraction was beginning to wane as the programme ran out of ideas, just as the American series had done. I saw the writing on the wall and pulled out, leaving Jenny with a new partner, my old friend Eamonn Holmes. But the end of a good idea was not far away at that stage.

I also did the BBC's *Holiday* programme for a series in the late Eighties. Frank Bough had got himself into some difficulties and the BBC had decided to dispense with his services as the programme presenter. I was asked at pretty short notice to step into the breach. This was embarrassing for me. I liked Frank, whom I had always admired as an outstanding broadcaster. I had worked out that I could fit the presentational duties in with my existing schedule because, in those days, the programme was presented live from the studio, unlike now, when all the items are filmed on location. There would be some travelling involved, though, in particular a trip to Thailand, which sounded attractive.

I wrote to Frank explaining what I had been asked to do. He wrote back very charmingly, saying that he would rather someone he admired take over the role than anyone else.

The *Holiday* programme was fun, but the trip to Thailand gave me one of the most distasteful and frightening experiences of my life when, for the first time, but not the last, the tabloid press seemed out to get me.

Most people think that working on the *Holiday* programme and similar television shows is a dream job. There are certainly worse ones, but the travel schedules and the limited time given to each story make it less pleasurable than you might imagine. Also, the BBC, in its admirable desire to curry no favour and be impartial in its reporting, bought only economy tickets for air travel, even for fourteen-hour flights like the one to Bangkok in 1989. Arriving stiff, exhausted and jet-lagged, one had to move pretty quickly into broadcasting mode and I found myself, after just a couple of hours' sleep, doing pieces to camera from a long-tailed boat on the Chao Phraya River, and being thrown around the city centre in one of the famous three-wheeled 'tuk-tuk' taxis.

Bangkok was exhilarating and fascinating. One evening, in the company of two representatives of the Thailand tourist authority and members of our production team, we ventured into the nightclub part of the city to see the sights; and what sights we saw. There, whatever your sexual preference, it could be catered for. We had drinks at a few bars, one of which was a 'girly' bar, where the inmates made it clear that their services were very much available. I thought the girls pretty unattractive. They were mostly tiny with peasant faces, obviously trapped in a way of life from which they would have trouble escaping.

After a few days in the city we ventured north to Chang Mai to film the temples and other tourist sights. We had great fun in a massage parlour – nothing kinky, just the production crew, male and female, and I in the same room being massaged by several females, mostly using their feet. Very pleasurable.

We filmed on the island of Phuket in the Andaman Sea and then moved on to the Gulf of Siam and the small, and at that time still relatively unknown, holiday destination of Ko Samui, which could then only be reached by sea. There, it rained incessantly. The producer, Richard Lightbody, and I contrived a film story in which we sent an imaginary moving postcard home, one in which you tell lies about the wonderful time you are having. 'Weather wonderful,' I would say to camera (film of pouring rain); 'making lots of new friends' (film of deserted beach), etc.

We were staying in a remote but luxurious hotel, a couple of miles up a dirt road, that has subsequently developed into a popular holiday destination. The owner was an extrovert Thai who also owned hotels and property in Bangkok. He was very friendly, taking much delight in telling us about his time at university in the UK, where he could only get a third class degree in his studies because he had enjoyed the girls and the whisky too much. On my first day there I received a phone call from my agent in London. I was told that the *News of the World* had been on to verify my whereabouts because they had a story that one of the major networks in America was interested in signing me up to present one of their sports shows. I knew immediately that this was highly unlikely and I suspected that they had something else in mind.

The following day, having returned from filming on the island, the hotel receptionist told me that two gentlemen were waiting to see me. 'Who are they?' I asked. 'They are sitting

148

In the *Sports Report* Studio with my bosses, Cliff Morgan and Bob Burrows, in the foreground.

The 1974 Commonwealth Games BBC Radio team. I'm looking sinister on the back row. Dick Scales is in the centre of the back row. Peter Jones, Olympic swimming gold medalist Anita Lonsborough and Bob Burrows are centre front.

Me playing the fool in Hong Kong.

Peter Jones in Hong Kong.

World Travellers: Helm, Jones,
Scales and yours truly.

With my pugnacious side-kick, Bob Abrahams, to my left in Moscow, 1980.

At Panmunjom, Korea, in 1988 at the Seoul Olympics.

With 'Motty' and Vinnie Jones after Wimbledon's Cup Final win. We narrowly escaped a bath.

A publicity shot for the Grand National.

over there,' I was told, as the pretty Thai girl pointed to two rather scruffy individuals in the corner of the foyer. If you had gone to central casting for a couple of newspaper hacks, they would have come up with these two.

They both got up when they saw me and approached. One was carrying a camera. 'What can I do for you, gentlemen?' I asked.

The one not carrying the camera, dressed in a cream light-weight suit which looked the worse for his journey, and indeed his lunch, said that they were from the *News of the World* and informed me of a 'serious' allegation that, whilst in Bangkok, I had gone off to a room in a club and had sex with two girls.

I just laughed at them and told them that when I'd ventured into the nightclub area of Bangkok I'd been in the company of my crew and two members of the Thai tourist association at all times, and could prove it. I then asked them where they'd got their information from.

They said they had a written affidavit from a 'reliable source', and an affidavit from one of the girls.

They then made their cardinal error. The date they mentioned for my alleged transgression was the day before I had actually arrived in Thailand. I was somewhere over Asia in a Boeing 747. I pointed this out to them. 'Well, we may have got the date wrong,' said Mr 'Stained Suit'. 'So much for the signed affidavit,' I said.

The cameraman then took a few pictures of me. I did my best to smile. The tabloid press likes nothing more than that 'hunted' look of the accused. Extraordinarily, he told me he was a fan of mine, and particularly liked my boxing commentaries on the radio. They said they would be following the story up and I left them to refresh myself before joining my colleagues for dinner.

I was worried – not because I had anything of which to be ashamed, knowing that their accusations were groundless; but I doubted these two would want to return home without a story, having put their employers to the expense of sending them half-way round the world.

From now on I would be careful that there wasn't a girl in close proximity to me or my bedroom door in case a cunning photographer caught me in what might look like a compromising situation. In short, they made me somewhat paranoid.

When I joined the crew for the evening, they asked me what was going on, and so I told them. The hotel owner who was dining with us offered to 'arrange a little experience' for the two hacks who had been upsetting his valued guest. 'What have you got in mind?' I asked him. 'Oh, nothing too serious. Just a simple car accident,' he replied. I thanked him for his consideration but thought it better not to avail myself of his offer. I got the clear impression this sort of thing was not entirely unusual in this part of the world.

Later, one of the crew perhaps put his finger on the reason for the *News of the World*'s interest. They had just done an exposé on Frank Bough's personal problems. Perhaps someone on their editorial team thought it would be a scoop if they could uncover a bit of dirt on the man who had taken over from Frank. 'Des is going to Bangkok. You know what Bangkok is famous for ...' One could almost hear the editorial mind at work.

I heard nothing from the pair of scribes for a day or two, and actually began to worry that my host had decided to give them that 'little experience' without telling me. But I got on with my job, which included filming a meal at a typical Thai family house. We had been joined now by Christopher Matthew, who had been sent out to Thailand by the *Radio Times* to do a story about how a *Holiday* programme item is put together. Christopher got a cool welcome from me. I had had enough of journalists; but of course I soon realised that he was the Christopher Matthew who had written the highly enjoyable Simon Crisp Diaries, of which I was a fan. In fact I recognised his voice rather than his name because he had brilliantly narrated his stories on Radio 4 in his very distinctive manner. This highly civilised chap and I began to bond. Chris sat with us on the floor of this wooden house in the jungle where we were treated to all sorts of typical Thai dishes. My appetite was put on hold for a while after I saw a beetle as big as a mouse leap from one of the cooking pots, but after a couple of bottles of Thai beer I set about the food with relish. One dish was particularly hot, which I enjoyed, having always liked spicy food. Chris was not so keen on the fare, and asked me what he could take that was mild. The devil in me pointed to the curry that had made even me break out in sweat. He took a large mouthful. He took some time to recover, and has never forgiven me to this day.

Our Thai trip was coming to a close and soon we journeyed back to Bangkok for a last night at the fabulous Mandarin Oriental, one of the very best hotels in the world. After a splendid night at their River Restaurant, we gathered the following morning in the hotel foyer ready for departure to the airport. Suddenly I spied the *News of the World* cameraman taking pictures of me from a doorway. Then the journalist, whose suit had not visited a cleaner in the interim, approached me. 'Let me give you my card,' he said, 'in case you want to tell me any more about your night in Bangkok.' I turned on him: 'Why, in your right mind, would you think that I would ever telephone a little jerk like you?' I said.

151

I thought he was going to attack me and only the intervention of Christopher Matthew, who told him his behaviour was 'outrageous', stopped a potential brawl in this famous hotel, where Ernest Hemingway and Noël Coward had sat down to tea.

Of course the *News of the World* got me in the end, but it would be nearly ten years later and they needed no reporter. Foolishly, I had provided the source of their information myself.

Some years before my time with the *Holiday* programme I had presented *The Travel Show* for the BBC. This had a more editorial slant on the business of travel and tourism, and wasn't just a glorified holiday brochure. My co-presenter was Isla St Clair, who had become very famous while working on the *Generation Game*, that mainstay of BBC light entertainment for so many years. Isla did that programme with the late Larry Grayson, who was the host in between two periods of Bruce Forsyth's tenure of the show.

It always seemed clear that Larry, camp as you like and very funny, had little grasp of the rules or format of the *Generation Game* and Isla, in her bright and bubbly way, would steer him through it. She was a great favourite with the viewers, having been plucked from nowhere to do the show. She had been a folk singer and little known before being thrust into the full glare of the Saturday night viewing public. I went to the show once with her and Larry and it was clear that, without Isla, he would have struggled. But he was very funny.

When Isla's time on the *Generation Game* came to an end, the BBC began looking for another show for her, which is how she and I became paired together on *The Travel Show* – something of an adjustment for her after her time with Larry Grayson. Isla was great fun to work with and each week we would fly up to Manchester, from where the show went out live. Then we would convene at our hotel, where Isla, who never seemed to travel without her guitar, would always be ready to give myself and the team her rendition of an old Tibetan love ballad or a Peruvian mating song. The alternative was to get her drunk. Guess which alternative we usually chose?

Isla and I had a mild flirtation while we were working together. It ended with the series, but she was, and is, a lovely lady.

Actually, Isla introduced me to a friend of hers at the time, another singer, Barbara Dickson. I was a huge fan of Barbara long before I met her but now I had a privileged invitation to several of her concerts and we started going out together for a short while. My love life was so complicated at the time, though; I was also seeing the gorgeous Moira Stuart, who remains a good friend, and Barbara and I drifted apart.

I remember an incident that happened on the flight home from one of my last *Holiday* programmes for the BBC. I was flying back from the Canary Isles, having completed the programme, when a passenger on the plane tapped me on the shoulder. 'Mr Lynam, I presume?' he said. He looked and sounded a bit like Harry Enfield's 'Mr Don't' character.

'I have to tell you,' he continued, 'you are not one of the favourites of the wife and I but, as you are here, perhaps you would sign an autograph.'

My programme editor, Patricia 'Hot Lips' Houlihan, who was sitting next to me, mumbled, 'How rude,' which went straight over this individual's head.

'Thank you,' I said, 'that would give me great pleasure.' Where I got the next thought from I do not know: 'But when we are representing the BBC, and we bump into members of the public, we are now asked to verify that they have a current TV licence.'

'Of course I have a licence,' replied the man, 'but you don't expect me to carry it around with me, do you?'

'Of course not,' I said, 'but I'll need your name and address so that we can check it out.'

By now, Houlihan was wetting herself and it was all I could do to keep a straight face myself. 'Mr Don't' duly moved off down the gangway and then returned with his name and address neatly written on a piece of paper for me. I don't suppose I ever became one of his favourites – or the wife's for that matter.

Once or twice after my stint presenting the BBC's *Holiday* programme, I was asked back to be a contributor on the show. One trip was to the west of Ireland for a combined golf and fishing holiday. The golf appealed to me, but when I learned that the 'fishing' part would be shark fishing out at sea, my enthusiasm for the trip waned. Then it was explained to me that when the sharks were landed, they were tagged and thrown back and survived, and so I agreed to do the film.

The golf part was a joy. Christy O'Connor Jnr., one of Ireland's greatest players and a Ryder Cup hero, had opened a new course near Galway with a couple of partners, and I would play a few holes with him and talk about the venture and its facilities for holidaying golfers. It began with a stroke of luck. On the first hole we played, a par three, I hit a five wood stiff to within two feet of the hole. Christy put a six iron on the green, but a long way from the pin. I sank my tap-in for a birdie. Christy three-putted for a bogey. This was now on film. On the next hole, of course, I reverted to type and topped a drive about fifty yards, but Christy did a nice interview and that was the first part of the filming over.

Then it was off to the coast where the captain of the small vessel we had hired for the day advised us that the weather was going to be a bit rough and it would be better to leave our fishing trip to the following day. Unfortunately, BBC resources and timing meant that the filming had to be done there and then, or not at all, and we took to the Irish Sea with one very nervous reporter.

It got worse. A few miles out, the engines were cut and the boat started to roll from side to side in pretty big waves. I suddenly spotted the cameraman leaning over the side in a fashion that indicated all was not well. Next to go was the sound man. At around this time, the fishermen on board were mixing up the live bait they used for the sharks. The very smell of this was enough for me. I was as sick as I had even been in my life and I wanted to die there and then. But there was still filming to be done. So midst throwing up, the film crew and I attempted to report on the fishing trip. One shark was pulled out that had been tagged once before off the Bay of Biscay – here was a shark that was getting used to travelling by boat for a while now and again. It was tagged again and set free once more. I would have been willing to dive in with it and give up the ghost. But eventually the engines were started and we were making for the little west coast harbour again. My sickness disappeared as quickly as it had arrived, but unfortunately the man with the green face would be seen on the *Holiday* programme, trying to look as though he was having a good time.

Another non-sport programme I got involved in during the Eighties was *It's My Pleasure*. This was a sort of *Desert Island Discs*, but instead of picking their favourite records, guests were invited to select eight clips of their favourite television shows. It had always seemed an obvious follow-on from the famous radio programme, until you realised that most of the clips that people might choose were very expensive to show because of the broadcasting rights involved. Guests usually ended up with a couple of their own selections and then a few that we had convinced them to include for budgetary reasons.

The show was recorded at the Greenwich Theatre in London in the afternoons before a live audience. I would usually record two shows at a time and always had a few jokes with the audience beforehand. These would sometimes go well, and sometimes not. One day I was dying on my feet before the recording began. My tried and tested one-liners were going down like a pork chop in a Jewish butcher's. Even when I introduced the guests, familiar and famous names, to the assembled throng, it got little response. We got on with recording the shows – again little or no reaction from the audience.

When we had finished I collared the producer, Phil Chilvers, and asked him why the audience had been so dismal. He made enquiries. 'You haven't lost your touch, Des,' he said. 'Apparently, you've been working to three coach loads of Norwegian tourists.'

I never found out what they'd been doing there – and nor probably did they.

Among the guests on the show was the lovely Irene Handl, the celebrated comedy actress who had appeared in countless films and television shows. Before the recording I found her slumped in her dressing room, looking pretty ill. I told her that her health was rather more important than the show and that we could arrange a car to take her home.

'No, don't worry my dear,' she said. "Doctor Theatre will look after me. I'll be fine.'

She seemed to recover pretty quickly and did a sparkling interview, but I learned to my distress that, just a few days later, Irene sadly passed away.

'Doctor Theatre', as she put it, had provided only a temporary respite, and we had lost one of our great comedy actresses.

That was my only incursion into the world of the 'chat' show on television; but when Terry Wogan was doing his thrice-weekly spell on BBC 1, his producer, Peter Estall, took me to lunch to try and persuade me to become one of Terry's stand-in presenters. I did not take up that particular challenge at the time.

There was another show that I didn't do which I might have done.

I was approached once by a producer from the department that broadcast factual programmes.

'Des,' he said, 'we've come up with an idea which we think will be a big success, and which we feel may be right up your street. It will be a programme about crime and the solving of crimes. We will invite the public to help the police. It won't go out every week but we reckon on doing it, say, once a month and the running time will be approximately an hour.'

There was an ITV crime-solving show hosted by Shaw Taylor at the time called *Police Five*, which did last for just five minutes. 'A sort of *Police Five* stretched to an hour?' I said. 'It'll never work.'

The programme, of course, was *Crimewatch* – still as successful as ever.

Of course I have 'guested' on many programmes over the years. I once went on the *Wogan* show, with disastrous results.

While I was waiting in the wings to join Terry, an assistant producer had explained to me that the previous show, a few nights before, had ended with a gag about piña coladas. She asked if I would take out a tray of them for Terry. I had no objection to this but, as she handed me the tray, the drinks toppled all over my shirt, tie and jacket. I was about two minutes from being introduced. They wiped me down as best they could, but my nerve was shot and Terry, who I knew reasonably well, must have wondered if 'I had the drink taken', as he might have put it, I was so twitchy. I had the drink taken all right, but unfortunately the application had been purely external.

17

A TOUCH OF THE DIMBLEBYS

In the Queen's Silver Jubilee year of 1977, BBC Television was planning to mount a huge outside broadcast to celebrate the occasion. It was a big event also for BBC Radio. This was my last year in radio before I moved over to television, and I was asked to present the broadcast.

This involved a day-long programme, with some of the famous radio broadcasters of the day, such as Brian Johnston, Wynford Vaughan-Thomas and Alyn Williams. I felt pretty humbled by this kind of company, but I managed not to embarrass myself or the broadcast.

Twelve years went by before I was once again asked to be involved in an outside broadcast other than sport. This time it was for television.

Following the tragic events at Hillsborough stadium in Sheffield in April 1989 when over ninety fans were crushed to death during the FA Cup semi-final between Nottingham Forest and Liverpool, a memorial service for the victims had been arranged to be held at Liverpool's Protestant Cathedral. The producer of the TV coverage was Tim Marshall, who was very experienced in these sorts of sombre occasions, and Helen Holmes was to be my adviser-cum-researcher. Helen had worked not only with David Dimbleby but also went back to the era of his famous father, Richard. Realising she had a novice on her hands, Helen became quite a disciplinarian, and was pretty fearsome to work with. She took no prisoners, our Helen. In fact she frightened me to death.

On the day of the broadcast, I began to wonder why on earth I had let myself in for this kind of commentary. It was not really my kind of thing at all. Definitely no jokes.

During the service, a lone choir boy had sung 'You'll Never Walk Alone', the Liverpool Football Club anthem: there was not a dry eye in that great cathedral, or, I suspect, among the viewers at home. I had to speak at the end of the boy's magical performance, and my voice crackled with emotion. I felt at the end that I had not contributed enough in the way of commentary. Frankly, I had been concerned not to commit myself too much in areas in which I was really an innocent.

In fact, once or twice, Tim had suggested the odd comment over my headphones; but I'd ignored them. I suspected he was less than pleased with me.

However, one thing happened that surprised me. My uncle, Dr John Clark, to whom I was close but who had never once complimented me on any broadcast I had ever made, wrote me a lovely letter in which he said he had been proud of me and that I had kept up the tradition of Richard Dimbleby, whom he had admired so much. This was praise indeed.

Tim Marshall also wrote to me: 'When I listened to the tape on Saturday night, I was even more aware how measured and sensitive your commentary was. My wife commented that it was a joy to hear a commentator using words sparingly, but on the occasions they were used, they were made to count. It was also significant that supporters came up to you afterwards and thanked you for coming to Liverpool.'

But more surprising than Tim's letter was the note from my slave driver, Helen. She wrote: 'I've just had a chance to look at the Liverpool tape and I hasten to send my congratulations. Such programmes are among the most difficult of any events to do and you got exactly the right note first time … It was great working with you. Here's to the next time.' Helen's meticulous research, together with her no-nonsense approach, had helped me through it. She was one of the 'old school' and David Dimbleby, with whom she worked on many state occasions, told me once that she had never stopped frightening him either.

If they all thought I had done a reasonable job, that was good enough for me. I never looked back at the tape of the programme myself. I suspect I would have been rather less impressed than they were.

18

MR AND MRS MERTON

One day in the early Nineties I got a phone call from a radio producer called Richard Edis. He had an idea for me. Throughout my career I've been lucky enough to have been regularly approached by people out of the blue who wanted me to broadcast for them. So I went to meet Richard in the roof restaurant of the St George's Hotel, next to Broadcasting House in Langham Place – a regular haunt for radio personnel.

With Richard were a couple of young guys looking for their first success – Simon Bullivant and Bill Matthews. They had come up with an iconoclastic sports quiz that Richard thought would make a nice radio show and he wanted me to be the host/quizmaster. What they did not have was a title for the show. Over lunch we fiddled with a few ideas and then for some reason I thought of 'They Think It's All Over', which I suggested would be quirky enough to fit the show. Of course, this was the phrase made famous by the late Kenneth Wolstenholme when commentating on England's victory in the Final of the 1966 World Cup, so it was already in the public's consciousness.

In due course Richard hired Rory Bremner, already famous for his brilliant impersonations, and comedian/writer Rory McGrath to be the team captains; the remaining panellists would be different sporting guests for each edition.

We had a radio hit on our hands and did three series of the show. It was gaining some interest from television and eventually, under the control of the independent production company TalkBack, we were asked to do a pilot programme. The TV version was somewhat harsher than the radio show, which had been witty and cerebral and had somehow benefited from the imagination that radio engenders. On TV, the ideas did not quite stand up in the same way, and it all seemed a bit too contrived. Rory Bremner and I watched the pilot show together, and we both hated it. Neither of us wanted to do it. I was also concerned that it would be difficult to appear on television one minute doing the legitimate sport and the next moment taking the mickey out of it. So I turned down the offer of being the TV host.

BBC Television, who were convinced the show would be as huge a hit as it had been on the radio, tried to coax me into the role. But I resisted, and the whole thing was put on ice for well over a year before it saw the light of day with a young comedian called Nick Hancock at the helm. Gary Lineker and David Gower were on the panel, along with Rory McGrath, who had no inhibitions about the transfer to television. With respect to Gary and David, both of whom I admire for their sports broadcasting, I thought they never looked comfortable on the show. Instead of being clever it seemed to survive on laddish interplay between the panellists as they went out of their way to insult each other. It was not the show it had been on radio. However, it has had a great run and has brought success to the two boys who came up with the concept in the first place. I am delighted for them. Don't worry about royalties for the title idea, lads.

Extraordinarily, as I write this in the winter of 2004, I have just returned from a meeting with the BBC, who in an attempt to make the programme less laddish, have asked me if I might take over the hosting role from Nick Hancock, who had apparently been thinking of quitting. Once again, though, I felt that it was not quite for me and turned it down, despite the lucrative fee.

Then, irony of ironies, I bumped into Nick Hancock at a football match between Brighton and Stoke City – we are respective fans of each club.

'Hello, Des. I'm still doing your job,' he joked. Nick knew I had started the show on radio, and he chuckled. I said nothing about my meeting with the BBC.

As a postscript, one person who was singularly unhappy with the title of the show was Kenneth Wolstenholme, who thought it demeaned him. In fact it prolonged his fame for having come up with a phrase that had been so appropriate at English football's finest ever moment.

Another show I guested on was the *Mrs Merton Show*, that wonderfully inventive vehicle devised and presented by Caroline Aherne. Her character described me as 'the menopausal woman's Tom Cruise', and of course she asked me if my bowels were regular.

I had seen the show a few times before I went on it and had witnessed Debbie McGee being asked what first attracted her to 'millionaire' Paul Daniels, a brilliantly clever and wicked line that people still remember. I also saw the boxer Chris Eubank on the show and wasn't sure if he had worked out that 'Mrs Merton' wasn't a real person.

I had also seen one or two guests attempting to compete with the host and lose out badly in terms of wit. I made a decision that, whatever 'Mrs Merton' levelled at me, the best way to deal with it would be to keep smiling and roll with the punches. As it turned out, I got a very easy ride with her and enjoyed the experience enormously.

Some years later, I went on the Mr Merton show – Paul Merton's *Room 101*. This show was also great fun to do and I endeavoured to abolish, among other things, politicians (for obvious reasons), teeth (which I described as being a design fault), and golf. 'But you play golf,' said Paul. 'Yes, but if it didn't exist, I wouldn't have to,' I replied.

Merton had come up with a wheeze after I had told him over lunch that I could bounce a golf ball on the end of a wedge for a good while before it fell to the ground. I had agreed to do it on the show and asked for a piece of matting from which to flick the ball up onto the club face. The piece of matting found for me was too solid, almost like an upturned broom, and in rehearsal I could not manage to get the ball onto the club. I realised I would have to begin the trick by dropping the ball onto the club face, which made it much more difficult to get the rhythm going. In rehearsal, the most 'uppies' I managed was about ten. When we came to record the show, I did twenty-four in one take and brought the house down. Golf was thus discarded into *Room 101* as my reward. I also put France into the room, on the basis that David Ginola was too good-looking and they kept winning the major football tournaments, even though they were really only interested in cycling. A few weeks later, Anne Robinson got herself all over the papers for trying to discard Wales. Anne though, was rather crueller in her disposition.

I ended my performance on the show with a rap. I had described rap music as being a contradiction in terms, so the programme writers produced one for me to do. I had got the girls in my office to take me through the kind of hand gestures that rappers use when performing, and I think I gave a good parody of the genre which the studio audience enjoyed. Strangely, I thoroughly enjoyed performing it. Silly old ham.

Chris Evans is not everyone's cup of tea, but when he was presenting his live entertainment shows I thought he was outstanding. He seemed to have no fear and was thoroughly disarming towards his guests, all of whom he would take the mickey out of, whilst at the same time paying homage to them – a difficult art which only Jonathan Ross currently can match. Evans' disappearance from our screens is, in my view, a loss to British television.

I went on *TFI Friday* a few times, and also *Friday Night with Jonathan Ross*, but I have never 'done' *Parkinson*. I have been invited, but while Evans and Ross use the guests as a vehicle for humour, Parkinson is a more considered interviewer and, frankly, I have never wanted to talk about myself too much on that kind of interview show. I know that writing this book might seem to contradict that philosophy, and that by doing it I may well have 'Parkied' myself.

Incidentally, when *The Premiership* ended and ITV hired Michael Parkinson to take over the late Saturday evening slot, they benefited from a huge financial deal. They no longer had to pay for the rights to show the football; they simply had to pay Parky instead of me, plus fees for the guests. I reckon hiring Parkinson from the BBC, instead of costing ITV money, has saved them over sixty million pounds a year.

19

SEE NAPLES AND DRY

Having covered the 1982 World Cup finals in Spain as a commentator, I would spend the next five World Cups as the front man: four of them for the BBC and the 2002 finals for ITV.

The two major terrestrial broadcasters were co-rights holders for these major football occasions, with the BBC usually easy winners in terms of audience figures when the two went 'head to head' on a game. This was mostly avoided except for the occasional England match or the actual Final itself. The critics were usually more positive about the BBC's coverage, but of course they had the benefit of broadcasting uninterrupted by commercials.

Back in 1970, ITV actually had the better of the ratings. They had been the first to come up with the idea of a panel of experts to discuss the action, and the combination of Jimmy Hill and the likes of Malcolm Allison and Derek Dougan had proved irresistible to the viewers, especially as they were contentious and amusing.

In those days, of course, you had to get up off your backside to change the channel, and broadcasters had a better chance of retaining the loyalty of viewers if they attracted them in the first place. By comparison, the BBC coverage was pretty orthodox. I was working on the finals for the radio from London and suffered with the rest of the nation when England lost to West Germany, having been two goals up in the quarter-final.

By 1986, my first World Cup on television as presenter, the panel was a constant part of major football broadcasts for both channels. At the BBC we made a big play about signing George Best as one of our experts. As the first broadcast got closer, no one had actually had a meeting with George for some time and we were getting concerned about his first appearance. Our concern was not misplaced. George was going through one of his 'difficult' periods and never in fact turned up for any broadcast.

Those who did turn up for that series included Andy Gray, a long way from the finished broadcaster he has become on Sky Television, and the late Emlyn Hughes, the former Liverpool and England captain. Alan Mullery and Lawrie McMenemy made some appearances too.

The programmes were presented from London with the commentary teams at the matches in Mexico. This of course was the 'Hand of God' World Cup when England were cheated by Diego Maradona, plus a referee and linesman who, extraordinarily, missed the foul. At least Gary Lineker won the 'Golden Boot' as top scorer with six goals.

The summer of 1986 was a busy one for me. As well as covering the World Cup and Wimbledon, I was fronting the Commonwealth Games in Edinburgh. It rained for virtually the entire duration of the competition. The distance athlete, Liz Lynch (later Liz McColgan), was one of the stars of the Games, winning a gold medal on the track for her native Scotland. 'See you, Lizzie Lynch' was a phrase I used about her, which she reminded me of at a recent *Sports Personality of the Year* show.

At the Wimbledon Championships I had briefly met Anita Dobson, who had become famous for her role as Angie, the pub landlady in *EastEnders*. She had been having some photographs taken with the late Sir Peter Ustinov, a big tennis fan, in one of the hospitality marquees. The photographer was racking his brains how to get some sort of 'slant' on the photos. 'Why don't you get Ustinov behind the bar to pull a pint for "Angie",' I offered. It was hardly brain surgery; but that is what they did, and the photos made the following day's papers.

I didn't even speak to Miss Dobson on that occasion but I noted how nice she seemed to be – more attractive when not having to play the role of aggressive Angie.

Shortly afterwards, the BBC decided they would mount a programme previewing Frank Bruno's world title challenge to the American Tim Witherspoon, which was to take place at Wembley Stadium in the open air. I was to present the show live from Wembley, and as well as the usual pre-fight footage we would have some guests on the show. Someone had spotted in the newspapers that Anita Dobson was a big Bruno fan, and she was invited to appear. She turned out to be a very bright guest, a super personality with a good knowledge of boxing. After the show we agreed that it might be nice to meet up for a drink some time, the kind of suggestion that is often made after people have worked together.

In Edinburgh a few weeks later, I came down for breakfast one morning, ready for another marathon programme ahead of me. As I approached the table where a group of my colleagues were sitting, it suddenly went very quiet. 'Have I forgotten my deodorant this morning?' I said. 'Something seems to be up.'

169

'We'd better show him,' said Penny Wood, our programme assistant. 'Show me what?' I asked. Someone then produced the front page of a tabloid newspaper. There were separate pictures of me and Anita Dobson, with the headline 'The new man in Angie's life'. It was not the best start to my day. I explained to my colleagues that the statement might be just a little premature, bearing in mind we had not even had a drink together; and then, of course, I immediately thought of home. The other papers would be bound to follow up the story. There could be reporters on the doorstep at that very moment. I rushed for the phone to explain to Rose what had happened, before she found out from some other source. Then I arranged to block the story from gaining further 'legs'.

Subsequently I realised that Anita might have mentioned in conversation on the *EastEnders* set that she had met me, even that we had got on well together, which was true. Someone had put two and two together and got a front page out of it. There is not much that is said on some 'soap' productions that doesn't find its way into the tabloid press. There are those earning a regular income out of such 'revelations'. I never met Anita Dobson again until I was on holiday very recently. She was staying in the same hotel with her husband Brian May, guitarist with the rock group Queen. We smiled and said 'Hello', and that was that. Eighteen years of our lives had disappeared in the interim. We still hadn't had that drink. But I expect someone, somewhere, will reckon that 'That Des Lynam used to go out with that Angie, you know.'

Aside from football and my regular stints on the summer Olympic Games, it also became my task to front the Winter Olympics. On several occasions, the pattern that had been set for the summer Games was used: I would travel to the venues

170

to do a preview and then be back in London to present the action when it began.

In 1988 I travelled to Calgary in Canada, from where I sent back several reports. I had never been so cold in my life. One day the temperature touched minus forty and my moustache was frozen solid, not to mention the hairs in my nostrils.

These were the Games of 'Eddie the Eagle', Britain's representative in the ski-jumping. He became hugely famous for a time, not because of his prowess at the sport but because of his comparative ineptitude. While others jumped off the ramp, Eddie more or less dropped off. Having said that, I went to the top of the ski-jump, and as far as I am concerned he got full marks for having had the guts to do it at all.

I could never take the Winter Games as seriously as their summer counterparts and used to have some fun with the events.

Apart from skating, in which Torvill and Dean were our great hopes after winning gold at the previous Olympics, Britain had little chance of bringing home any medals; the boys in the pub certainly weren't likely to be discussing who was favourite for the biathlon. This is where Nordic skiers stop every now and again to shoot at a target with a rifle. 'You can't get a ticket for this north of the Arctic Circle,' I said.

And of course there was the luge doubles. 'Here's the plan,' I said. 'Two guys get into tight rubber suits, then one gets between the other's legs, then they get on their backs and they slide down the hill on a tea-tray. And we're showing it before the watershed.'

By 1990 I was well entrenched as a football presenter, along with my other duties with BBC Sport, and was greatly looking forward to the World Cup in Italy. By now we had a super production team plus a panel of experts including Jimmy Hill and Terry Venables, which meant the programmes would always be interesting, and sometimes controversial.

The signature tunes for major BBC sporting series have often been memorable, and once again we were racking our brains to come up with something that the viewers would catch on to for this World Cup.

I was at home one day and mentioned this to Rose. She immediately suggested using the magnificent Italian tenor, Luciano Pavarotti. We played a few tracks and I went humming into the BBC next morning and put my idea, or rather Rose's idea, forward. With one or two it fell on deaf ears. Their view was that you couldn't use a vocal: it had never been done. But Brian Barwick, the editor for the series, thought the idea was a great one and between us we came up with 'Nessun Dorma', on the basis it was simply a great aria with a fantastic climax. We put some football pictures to it and it worked superbly well. Only later did we realise that 'Nessun Dorma' meant 'none shall sleep' – most appropriate while a World Cup is going on.

It became an instant hit and turned Pavarotti from an opera star to a megastar in the United Kingdom. I reckon he owes us a few quid.

Once again I was fronting the shows from London but we had the idea that from time to time I would hop on a plane and introduce the programmes from the actual stadia. This would not be from a temporary studio, such as we used much later at ITV for Champions League presentations, but in a standing position somewhere in the ground. The problem with that was that it was virtually impossible to hear any talkback instructions. It would have been possible, had I worn headphones that blocked out ambient noise; but my BBC bosses, none of whom had actually experienced standing in front of a camera in a crowded stadium, insisted that headphones were visually unacceptable and that only an earpiece would be used. ITV had gone down this road with all their broadcasts from Italy, and it had certainly not improved their coverage. Communications between production and presenter, and indeed between presenter and pundits, had often seemed fraught. With modern television techniques, you can always make the presenter look as though he has the stadium backdrop behind him anyway. If it was right to present most of the programmes from London, why was it appropriate to change the style of the broadcast, indeed jeopardise it, especially as in my case I would be talking to the experts back in London? There was I, 'on the spot', putting questions to those who were not. However, if that was what they wanted to do, I was not about to argue about a few days in Rome and Naples.

It was a trip that I will remember with a shudder for the rest of my life. In the middle of the best of times, I was to experience the very worst of times.

The Republic of Ireland team, under the guidance of Jack Charlton, had qualified for the 1990 finals for the first time in their history and they were making it a fabulous experience for their players and fans. They had got as far as the last eight, a tremendous achievement, and were up against the hosts Italy at the Olympic Stadium in Rome. As an Irishman, I was delighted by their exploits and on the way to the stadium for the match I'd got caught up in the frenzy of enjoyment: the whole of Ireland, whether or not they had tickets, seemed to be present.

Inside the stadium I was perched high up at the back of one of the stands. I managed to present the show, despite hearing little of the instructions in my ear, reasonably smoothly. Ireland were knocked out of the finals at last, by a single goal from the Italian centre forward Schillaci; but you would not have known they'd lost. The Irish fans celebrated long into the night, delighted by their team's progress to the later stages of the competition.

I tried to get to bed at a reasonable time. In the morning I had to journey by road down to Naples, where it would be England's turn to face a quarter-final. Their opponents, the best team to come out of Africa at the time: Cameroon.

The following morning, in the company of Bobby Charlton, we were driven to Naples for England's big match. This was one of the occasions when both the BBC and ITV would be covering the game. It was important to stamp the BBC's authority on the broadcast to make sure that, as usual, we would take the lion's share of the audience.

Once again I found my position was standing high up at the back of the ground, from where I would start the broadcast.

Shortly before air-time, some officials decided we were not in the right position and shuffled us to another site. Camera and sound cables were unplugged and we gathered ourselves together to go live once again. I completed a rehearsal of the opening. Smooth as you like. I had a confidence gained by experience that whatever happened in a broadcast I would be able to cope with it. My colleagues were confident in me too and so, I felt, were the viewers. 'Relaxed and smooth' were the adjectives often used about me by television reviewers and critics. In fact I was always a little more nervous than they thought, but I knew I hid my nervousness well and would often try to inject some humour into the broadcast. After all, this was just sport. The nation may be hanging on the result, but it was just a game. And for me this was just television.

I heard the countdown in my ear. 'Thirty seconds to you,

Des.' Ten, nine … two, one, cue. Having just heard the opening to the show off tape, which included some commentary on Cameroon that I hadn't quite heard in rehearsals, I decided at the last minute to change my opening words slightly. I would try to be clever. Anyone can do a prosaic opening. I'll try to smarten it up a bit. But my brain got stuck between what I had been going to say and what I now intended to say. As I stumbled, the producer in London tried to help me, giving me my original words in my ear. It did not help. I froze. I stared at the camera for what seemed like a lifetime. My career was going up in smoke in front of me. I was horrified. My brain would simply not engage. Now I was panicking. Now I wanted to be anywhere else. I desperately hoped that this was a nightmare, that I would wake up to find that all was well, and that it wasn't really happening to me – a dream not unknown to broadcasters. But it was horrifyingly real. It couldn't be. I was Des, unflappable, in control, smooth.

The horror only lasted a few seconds for the viewer and I got through the rest of the programme. I tried to make a joke about it, which probably fooled no one – certainly not me. I came up with a phrase, 'See Naples and dry'. But why had my brain not worked for me when I needed it?

The match happened around me. I couldn't have cared less about the outcome. At the end I met with John Shrewsbury, the director on site, who apologised to me for not 'covering me up' with another camera shot, but he had been as shocked as I was. I apologised to the people at the other end of the line in London. I was actually shaking with disbelief that this could have happened to me.

No post-match chats and drinks for me. I fled to the underground car park, where I knew our car would be waiting to take us back to Rome. I wanted to talk to Rose and have her comfort me. I knew she would be worrying for me, but this was before the mobile phone age and I couldn't. I leant on the outside of the vehicle, in despair. This was the end of my career. How could I face the nation after this? I had embarrassed myself in front of fourteen million people.

The journey back to Rome was virtually silent. Bobby Charlton didn't mention my lapse. I couldn't bring myself to. He briefly spoke about England's narrow win. They were now in the semi-final of the World Cup, and in sight of victory. But none of this mattered to me. Bobby slept for some of the journey. Outside, the rain was teeming down. The black skies and stormy weather perfectly fitted my mood.

Back at the hotel in Rome, I telephoned home. Rose was in shock. She tried to comfort me but she also knew that I'd had a disaster. I didn't sleep a wink. I convinced myself that my career was over. I'd had a great twenty-two years, and now I would do something else. I could not face a television camera ever again. I would not put myself through it.

The following morning, the pain of my embarrassment had not gone away; if anything, it had increased. I kept trying to tell myself that, in the grand scheme of things, embarrassment was all it was. Nobody had died, though I felt as though I had.

I had been very proud to have got to the position I had done with the BBC. I knew that I had mostly done a good job. I'd tried to change the style of presentation of sport, and bring a little more humour into the broadcasts; at the same time I hadn't been afraid to criticise our own output, or some of the decision-makers. I'd never curried favour with the bosses, and had always said what I thought. Now I felt my strength of position had been undermined by my own fallibility.

The phone rang in my room. Here comes the press, I thought. The voice on the other end was familiar. It was Phil King, who had been working on the England–Cameroon match for our rivals, ITV.

Of course he knew all about my debacle – ITV would have been keeping an eye on our broadcast, as we would on theirs. It would undoubtedly have been the talk of their post-match get-together on into the night, and discussion had probably resumed round the breakfast table. There will have been one or two who were not entirely unhappy about me falling on my face. I had always strongly backed the BBC case against ITV on these big occasions and some would have felt it was high time I took a fall. I don't blame them. Phil, my old friend from radio days, for whom I provided refuge when his first marriage had broken up, was not among them. He told me he was on his way to see me.

'You need to get away from people for a few hours,' he said. He did not go into the whys and wherefores of the previous evening. Phil knew instinctively how much I was hurting. He knew how professional I was. How my pride had taken a tumble.

'Get your kit on,' he said. 'I've got a car and driver outside.'

I was consumed with my own misery, but he wouldn't hear of my protestations. I avoided a few faces I knew in the hotel foyer on the way out and sank back into the comfort of the ITV Mercedes. Ironically, no one from the BBC had thought to come to my rescue. They were probably too embarrassed.

'Now,' he said, 'first a little coffee and brandy is called for,' and off we went to a small café he knew. There I went through my horrors once again. I still could not understand how it had happened or adequately explain it.

Then it was time for a little contemplation and some physical exercise, a combination that has been succour to sinners and saints down the years. We went to St Peter's, the mighty bastion of Roman Catholicism, the largest church in the world. There, as Phil stood by, I lit a candle and asked for forgiveness, not for my failure, but for my selfishness. There were so many less fortunate than me. I was ashamed to be wallowing in so much self pity.

Then we took the 537 steps up through the dome of that great cathedral designed by Michelangelo. It was physically demanding. I was serving my penance in the company of my atheist friend, one of the most Christian men I have known.

The following day I flew back to London and home. The World Cup was now reaching fever pitch in terms of public interest. England were in the semi-finals. Their adversaries, the old enemy: West Germany. Paul Gascoigne was making headlines. Lineker was scoring goals.

I steeled myself for the next broadcast. In fairness, there was never any question, from the BBC's point of view, of my not continuing. Some bosses might have panicked, thinking that I'd lost it and that I might perhaps do something similar again. Brian Barwick and Jonathan Martin took the view that I hadn't become a bad broadcaster overnight, just an unlucky one. I was grateful to them. I presented England against West Germany from the studio in London. It was of course one of the most memorable sporting occasions ever. Gascoigne shed his tears. The penalties were missed and England were out. I finished the broadcast by saying, 'If you're going to have a few drinks tonight to drown your sorrows, do it safely, not aggressively. Be proud of England's performance in playing so well.'

A few days later we presented the disappointing Final between the Germans and Argentina – very much an anti-climax.

Gazza came home to sackloads of fan mail and mega-fame. Bobby Robson came home to curse his luck, look to the future and tell stories about Gascoigne playing tennis the night before the most important match of his life until the manager had caught him. And I went home to the realisation that I wasn't as good as I thought I was. I hope, as a result, that I became a better and more humble person. Perhaps it was something I needed and had been lying in wait for me. Never again in the next fourteen years of my career as a sports broadcaster would I take for granted that it was all a piece of cake.

After a summer break I was back in harness with *Grandstand* and other major programmes; but it wasn't until the next World Cup, four years later, that I felt I had exorcised the demon that had entered my brain on that summer's night in 1990, when I had seen Naples and dried.

Oh, and the press. They were extraordinarily forgiving. Most papers never mentioned my lapse. Russell Davies in *The Times* wrote that I had had a momentary lack of my usual fluency but had soon recovered my normal style. I have many times cursed the British press; but this was an occasion when I blessed their understanding.

Soon after the end of the World Cup, in October 1990, I suddenly found myself being asked to make a presentation to members of the House of Lords. The idea was to make sure that certain sporting events remained available to all viewers – the so-called listed events such as the Cup Final, the Olympic Games and Wimbledon. A new broadcasting bill would have allowed any of these events to be sold off to the highest bidder. If that was a satellite or cable channel, then the mass of the British people would be deprived of seeing them.

179

Paul Fox, the Managing Director of BBC Television, had asked me to make the presentation. 'They're more likely to keep awake if they see a "face" rather than a "suit",' he said. I did a bit of homework and discovered that the Derby, Grand National, Wimbledon, and the Test Matches had all been pioneered by members of the House of Lords: 'So many members of this House,' I told them, 'were instrumental in those events and many others becoming part of the fabric of British life, we now depend on you (their successors) to ensure that the British public as a whole can be assured of continuing to enjoy them on the television screens.'

I made my speech and sat down, thinking I had not for one moment captured anybody's attention. 'It would have been nice if they'd listened,' I told Paul Fox. It was then explained to me that it was normal procedure for the Lords to mumble their arguments amongst themselves as they hear yours. No insult had been intended.

I am happy to say we still have the listed events in this country available to all. In 1998, under the Labour Government, they have actually been extended.

Sky Television has done a wonderful job in making so much sport available to those who wish to pay for it; but, to my mind, it would be unthinkable for major events like the World Cup or the Olympics being only available on subscription television or, worse still, 'pay per view'.

20

THE KING OF DENMARK

The 1992 Barcelona Olympics were a real pleasure to cover. The Spanish – more particularly the Catalans – put on a tremendous Games. The opening ceremony, with its flamenco theme, was for my money the best ever.

Having presented the two previous Olympics from London, it was a delight to actually be in the host city for the duration of the action this time. Once again, Martin Hopkins was the BBC's main player in setting up the BBC coverage. Martin would go on to run the BBC's coverage of the Athens Games of 2004 before finally retiring after many years of valiant service for the Corporation.

He had found us a nice, small family-run hotel in Sitges, a beautiful little seaside town just down the coast from Barcelona. A few months before the Games began, the town's mayor wrote to him to say that they were going to present him with 'A Friend of Sitges' award for the business that he would be bringing to them. It was then I told him that there were many people who were friends of Sitges because it was Spain's gay capital. Despite his several visits to the town, this had passed the very straight 'Hoppo' by.

Unable to collect his award in person, he decided he would send them a cassette of a thank-you speech, which I persuaded him to record in Spanish. Martin didn't speak a word of the language but I spoke a little, and so I wrote the speech for him and rehearsed him through it.

In it, I included, for my own amusement, the phrase *Quiero encontrar muchos amigos nuevos* – 'I want to meet many new friends'.

As well as organising the coverage, the industrious Hopkins also directed most of the major programmes at the Games. One afternoon I was sitting in the studio watching the action alongside the excellent David Moorcroft, the former athlete, my regular partner for major track and field broadcasts, when 'Hoppo' suddenly said in my earpiece: 'Look lively. We're going to cut out of the action in a couple of minutes for you to interview the King of Denmark. He's on his way into the studio.' 'The King of Denmark?' I said to Moorcroft. 'Know anything about him?' The question fell on deaf ears.

A few moments later, this tall, tanned, good-looking man came in, accompanied by our programme assistant, Penny Wood, and a couple of other people. Moorcroft and I rose to our feet and greeted our special guest. Just before I was to interview him live, I happened to ask him how he felt his country was doing at the Games. 'Well,' he said, without much trace of accent, 'we have done OK in sailing, and it was a great lift when our girl athlete won the sprint hurdles yesterday.' I racked my brains for a moment. A Dane in the sprint hurdles? It was won by Patoulidoo Paraskevi of Greece after the favourite Gail Devers of the United States fell. It suddenly dawned: this King of Denmark was the former King Constantine of Greece. 'Hoppo' and I and our team screamed with laughter long into the night about how close I got to the 'King of Denmark' interview, which would certainly have become a collector's item.

'Who did you think he was?' I asked. 'Fucking Hamlet?'

My next big assignment was to be the 1994 World Cup finals, a tournament that turned out to be one of the few not to involve England – a big disappointment for all. Graham Taylor's team had failed to qualify, thus reducing the value of the event dramatically for television viewers at home. Once again, though, Jack Charlton's Irish Republic side had qualified, and of course we at the BBC were pinning our hopes on their having a good run.

The plan for me was that I would fly out to Dallas in Texas with our commentators. Then I would move down to Florida, where the Irish team were based, and film some preview items with Jack and the team. Then it would be back to London to present the matches from there before returning to the States to broadcast the Final from Los Angeles.

I spent a couple of days in Dallas and thoroughly enjoyed the experience of visiting the Kennedy Museum and listening to recordings of the President's memorable speeches. I understood why he had been able to affect so many people and why his assassination had been such a tragedy for America, and the world. His voice was haunting.

I stood with other colleagues on the grassy knoll from where conspiracy theorists thought shots had been fired in addition to those from the rifle of Lee Harvey Oswald. All of us were moved by the experience. The usual banter amongst broadcasters on tour was put on hold.

In contrast to the BBC, ITV had decided to present all their shows from the United States, but this time, instead of the presenter moving from stadium to stadium, possible in a relatively small country like Italy, they'd decided that the broadcasts would be done from a studio in Dallas. This made absolutely no sense to us at the BBC. If the studio had no outlook, what possible advantage would it give the viewer? They might as well have had a studio in London like us.

It would have been different if it had been, say, the Olympic Games, where most of the competitors were in the one place, and athletes could be brought to the studio for interviews and guest appearances; but with the World Cup, the players were spread all over the United States.

ITV had found a new presenter for this World Cup – Matt Lorenzo. I knew him a little as he had worked at the BBC as an assistant producer. He had been looking for a break into performing and it had come with ITV, rather than the BBC, who always seemed suspicious of 'behind the scenes' people looking to get in front of camera.

I had actually worked with Matt's father, Peter, who, after a lifetime as a sports journalist in Fleet Street, had joined the BBC Radio sports department while I was still there. Like Peter, Matt had a ready wit and I was pretty sure, as were ITV, that they had found a broadcaster with potential.

He and I met up in Dallas and had a few drinks together. 'You know, the press always compare presenters and commentators and pundits on these occasions and they will have you against me,' I said. 'Just bear in mind, it's not you against me, it's us against them.' We had a laugh about it and wished each other well.

Unfortunately for Matt, ITV in their pre-World Cup press conference had dubbed him 'the new Des Lynam'. This was embarrassing for me and did him no favours either.

Matt did not have a great World Cup. He didn't ever stare at the camera speechless, as I had done four years earlier; but he came over a little gauche and under-prepared. He wasn't aided by one or two of his studio pundits who seemed to offer him little help.

Matt got a panning in the press, and so did ITV for their 'bunker' studio in Dallas, as it became known. It was the beginning of the end of Matt's career with ITV. Subsequently he moved to Sky Television, where he has yet to become one of their stars. For my money he could have been pretty big in the business, but he had a shaky start and he's been lumbered with it.

Some years after his ITV World Cup, Matt gave an interview to a football magazine and was reported as having told them that in the conversation he and I had in Dallas, I'd said that it would be 'between you and me, and I will win'. Anyone who has ever known me in the business will tell you that I would never say such a thing. I've been competitive – I always want to do my job well; but to shove it down someone else's throat is simply not me. Matt wrote to me, saying he had been misquoted; but the damage had been done. I came out of it looking like a big head.

The Irish team's camp in Florida was the worst possible base for them, with sky-high temperatures and humidity. They were killing themselves in training alone. Jack Charlton did a super interview after pouring us both a couple of Guinnesses from the barrel the stout makers had provided for him in his hotel room. As usual, Big Jack was compelling to listen to, but as ever he found it difficult to remember the names of his players. I was reminded of a press conference he held before a match at the previous World Cup, when his team had been written on the back of a piece of card, or some such, and he had struggled to

185

read the names. I had been watching the occasion in the company of his brother Bobby, who wept with laughter as Jack ploughed on with the 'big lad' and 'the ice-cream man'. He occasionally used to refer to Liam Brady as 'Ian', which understandably infuriated one of Ireland's greatest ever players, unhappy with being confused with the Moors murderer.

After the interview I flew back to London in the company of Brian Barwick. During the flight, he managed to tip a bottle of Krug champagne we had been given by the air stewardess, plus a half bottle of Gevrey Chambertin, over both of us. We got off the plane at Heathrow not only smelling like alcoholics but with red stains down the legs of our nice fawn summer slacks.

Ireland proceeded to delight their fans again, especially with an historic win over Italy earlier in the tournament: a single, beautifully-taken goal by Ray Houghton gave them sweet revenge for the defeat of four years before.

For me it was then back to the States in the company of Barwick, Jimmy Hill and Alan Hansen to broadcast the Final between Brazil and Italy. Having made a few bob for Luciano Pavarotti at the previous World Cup, I was now delighted to be given a ticket to the 'Three Tenors' concert in LA on the eve of the Final. Terry Venables and his wife came as well.

In the audience, and within a few feet of me, sat a host of mega-stars. Giles Smith wrote in one of the broadsheets later: 'All Hollywood was there: Dustin Hoffman, Charlton Heston, Walter Matthau, Gene Kelly, Arnold Schwarzenegger, Tom Cruise, Nicole Kidman, Frank Sinatra and Desmond Lynam.'

No irony deficiency from Giles.

The Final was a bore – goalless after extra time, with Brazil running out winners on penalties. The extraordinary thing was that despite the USA being a relatively minor soccer country, the stadia were absolutely packed for every match. The World Cup USA was a big success, contrary to many forecasts.

A year or so before the World Cup, I had done a 'question and answer' for a women's magazine. Not the sort of thing I have usually bothered with, but a journalist rang my office one day and she seemed nice and so I went through the 'What's your star sign' and 'favourite colour' routine with her. One question she also asked was, 'Who was your first ever girlfriend?' 'Her name was Janice Prossor.' I replied. 'She went to my primary school and when I was about eleven years of age I was desperately in love with her. She was beautiful then and I suppose, all these years on, she still is.'

I was pretty sure this was unlikely to embarrass anyone. I knew that my junior school classmate had emigrated to the United States many years before. But a few weeks later I got a letter several pages long from San Francisco, from the said Janice. An aunt in England had sent her the magazine. In the letter she told me about her life and how it would be nice to meet up some time and talk about our respective experiences. I wrote back and told her that in the summer of 1994 I would be in California.

A couple of days before returning from the World Cup Final, I took a short flight to San Francisco. Waiting for me at the airport was the young girl I had known in my boyhood. She was unmistakable. She told me I was too, despite the silly moustache.

We spent a blissful day together seeing the sights and reminiscing. She was into her second marriage and had two grown-up sons. We both wondered 'what might have been', and then we said goodbye. As I waved to her at the barrier at the airport, I realised that, like the song says, I had left a little of my heart in

San Francisco, and I thought about the passing years and how quickly our lives ebb away.

At the end of our World Cup broadcasts, Malcolm Kemp, the executive producer, wrote to me: 'Thanks for a smooth and professional performance ... in difficult conditions.' I had been involved in some major television events since Naples, such as the Olympics in Barcelona; but now at last I felt I had shaken off the four-year-old albatross that had been hanging round my neck.

21

SEXY FOOTBALL

The year 1996 was a massive one for BBC Sport, with the European Football Championships being held in England, the biggest football occasion at home for thirty years, plus the Olympics in Atlanta. I was to be the presenter of both, plus the little matter of the Wimbledon Championships. This was a tough schedule, but I was happy to have the faith of my bosses that I could cope with it all.

Football had 'come home' and there was great expectation that Terry Venables' team could actually win a major competition for the first time since the glorious World Cup victory of 1966. The Dutchman Ruud Gullit, one of the greatest footballers of recent years, was now making his name as a coach with Chelsea and we decided to bring him on to our team as an additional pundit. On the first day, we all boarded our BBC coach at Television Centre in London to drive to the first match we were to broadcast.

As Ruud got out of his chauffeur-driven Mercedes to get on the bus, he was busy on his mobile phone and wasn't paying too much attention to the vehicle. But as he put his foot on the step, he paused for a moment, gave the bus the 'once over', and exclaimed, 'What is this shit?' Ruud had been used to the type of coach used by the likes of AC Milan. Our mode of transport was much more the BBC 'cost-cutting' variety of bus. He was not impressed. I immediately thought he might not blend in with the squad. But I could not have been more wrong. Ruud was a delight and on air he and Alan Hansen combined to make our broadcasts zing. He coined the phrase 'sexy football'. The females on our team knew exactly where the 'sexy' was coming from.

The tournament was a big success, and after a shaky start against Switzerland, England hammered Holland, sneaked past Scotland and Spain, and were within sight of the trophy. However, once again, it was the Germans who barred the way to ultimate victory at the semi-final stage. Paul Gascoigne, who had scored his memorable goal against the Scots, so very nearly won the match for England; but it went to penalties, with the seemingly inevitable outcome. At least Gareth Southgate got a pizza advert out of his miss.

Venables had lost a European Cup Final with Barcelona on spot kicks. Now he had done the same in the semi-final of a major international competition. It was dreadfully disappointing. 'There we are,' I said. 'No use crying for what might have been. Not for more than a couple of years anyway.' As broadcasters, at least we had done a good job, and the BBC picked up several broadcasting awards for the shows. Patrick Collins in *The Mail On Sunday* thought we were like Tyson against Bruno in our domination over ITV's output.

The channel rivalry was certainly in evidence at one point in the Championships when Paul Gascoigne had agreed to do one post-match interview for television; the idea being that both BBC and ITV would take it. But of course there was the little matter of pride as to whose reporter would be used.

The BBC producer and his ITV equivalent met. 'What would you like us to ask on your behalf?' asked the Beeb's man. 'I don't know what you're talking about,' said the ITV representative. 'We haven't decided who's doing the interview yet.'

'Yes, we have. We tossed for it and you lost,' was the reply.

'Well,' said Mr ITV. 'You didn't toss with me, my friend, and I am the official ITV tosser.'

For some time after there were members of both companies wearing t-shirts bearing the logo 'Official ITV Tosser'.

The ITV man in question was Gary Newbon, who I got to know well when I joined ITV, and who was always bright and breezy and tremendously supportive. He conducted interviews on our Champions League games and had done a fair bit of national broadcasting over the years, but was mostly confined to the midlands region, where he was Head of Sport.

At one of Ron Atkinson's charity golf days I introduced Gary as 'a legend in broadcasting (pause) in a regional sort of way'.

He loved it.

My performances apparently caught the eye of the comedian and playwright Arthur Smith. Arthur had produced a hugely successful West End play called *An Evening with Gary Lineker*. It had little to do with Gary, but the action took place while the World Cup finals had been going on. Using a similar theme, Arthur now decided to produce a television play entitled *My Summer with Des*, about a fantasy romance happening while Euro 96 had been taking place.

In the play, clips of one or two of the things I had said would be used and I would also have to record a few other inserts. The play was actually about a potential love affair and the actors taking the principal roles were Neil Morrissey and Rachel Weisz, who later went on to be a Hollywood star.

I actually had to film one scene with her, in which we were passing the Neil Morrissey character with the two of us ensconced in the back seat of a car. There were about ten re-takes, for lighting, camera angles, etc. I would have been happy to have gone on all night. Rachel was a delight and later, in a magazine interview, said some very complimentary things about me. Golly gosh, blushing time again.

The play was broadcast on BBC1 prime time before the World Cup of 1998. I watched it from behind the couch. Clips of my original comments from Euro 96 worked well, but the bits I had to act were pretty awful. Stupid old ham trying too hard. Nonetheless, Arthur Smith had given me a wonderful experience.

In 1996 I was also once again at the Olympics, this time in Atlanta, Georgia. Some of the programmes were presented from a studio at the broadcasting centre; at other times I would be at the athletics track to open the show. One night, my co-presenter was the gorgeous Sharron Davies, the Olympic swimming med-allist. Our position was next to the VIP area, and on this occasion the US President himself, Bill Clinton, was present. He was just a few yards away from us. We'd finished our rehearsal of the opening of the show and had half an hour or so before we went on air. I noticed that every time I looked towards Clinton he was staring past me to Sharron, who that night was wearing a very tight mini-dress. She looked stunning. 'When I tell you,' I said to her, 'just give Clinton a little look and smile.' She did, and his face lit up.

Here was a man who definitely liked the ladies, and made no bones about it. If he could have escaped his retinue, Sharron would have been on a promise.

22

HAVE I GOT A SINGER FOR YOU!

One summer I went to Portugal for a photo-shoot for a magazine. At the end of a long day I adjourned to the nightclub attached to the hotel on the sunny Algarve.

That night I saw and heard a singer who made the hairs stand up on the back of my neck. Her voice was haunting. She was quite beautiful too and came from the old Portuguese colony of Mozambique. After her performance I invited her to join our table for a drink and to find out a little more about her. There was no ulterior motive behind my invitation: she was with her husband, who was also her manager. When he found out I worked for the BBC – in fact he recognised me, having spent some years in London – he gave me his business card. 'We would love to do some work in London. I think my wife would be a big hit there,' he said. I had to agree. Her voice was Bassey-like, but in my judgement had more depth, and she was stunning to look at.

I told them that when I returned to the BBC, all I could do was pass on their contact numbers with my recommendation to the appropriate person. I obviously underlined that I had no power or influence in the world of entertainment, which they understood.

I had met Jim Moir on a few occasions, at BBC receptions and the like, but our paths had not crossed in a broadcasting sense. Jim was something of a legend in the world of television entertainment. He oversaw every hit show on the BBC for many years. A good number of household names owe their popularity and fame to the good judgement and loyalty of Big Jim. He also happens to be funnier than most of them.

On returning to the BBC after my Portuguese trip, I telephoned Jim's office and asked his secretary if he could spare me a couple of minutes.

I duly arrived at his door, and in I went. A beaming Jim got up from his desk and shook my hand.

'You look well,' he said. 'Obviously you've been away.' Then he asked: 'Do you know what my predecessor Bill Cotton told me when I took this job?'

'No,' I said.

'He told me that every now and again you'll get some prick knocking on your door who's been abroad and found a singer for you.'

'You bastard,' I said, got straight up, and left the office after throwing the singer's card on his desk. I could hear his screeches of laughter behind me. His response to my visit had been entirely intuitive. I had said nothing to his secretary about my reason for wanting to see him.

I phoned him straight away and we had a great laugh about it. He explained that the current state of light entertainment was undergoing change. 'When did you last see a singer on the BBC?' he asked.

Not long after, Jim left television, somewhat disenchanted

with the way things were going, and became BBC Radio's publicity guru. He did the job well, but it was a great waste of his skills. Jim had showbiz running through his veins. Soon, however, he would be back dealing with talent. Jim became Controller of Radio 2 and made that network hugely successful. Now it was Jim's turn to put a call into me.

We lunched at one of those gentlemen's clubs in St James's – I think it might have been the Reform – where, over steak and kidney pie and several bottles of excellent wine, Jim put a proposition to me. He told me it would make me 'rich beyond my wildest dreams'. I knew what radio paid. This was a splendid exaggeration, but it was 'Jimspeak' for there being a nice few quid in his proposition.

He wanted me to take over the John Dunn Show, which ran every weekday evening on Radio 2. John, who had been on the network for many years and whom I knew quite well (indeed, I'd sat in for him for a couple of weeks some years before) was retiring. But before going, he'd slammed the regime of John Birt and the BBC management in general. It was most unlike him. Something had obviously upset him. He had been one of the stalwart voices of BBC Radio for years and he was a peerless interviewer. Sadly, John died in 2004. Apart from sitting in for him a couple of times over the years I had also been his guest on the show and he was so comfortable to be with, and prompted you so well, you ended up giving a much better interview than might otherwise have been the case.

'I'll take you back to your first love: radio,' said Jim. 'You'll be a sensation.'

I said to Jim: 'Every now and again, some prick will ask me to work five days a week on radio in addition to presenting most of the major sports events on television.'

'*Touché*!' he said.

I told him that it was a fabulous offer and that I was very flattered, but that I simply could not do it justice.

We staggered out of the club and fell into a taxi.

Later, after discussing the matter with Jane Morgan, we came up with an idea that did see me back on Radio 2.

We offered Jim the possibility of my doing Friday evenings only. I had time for it and we could make the programme the start of the weekend. Jim loved it. I loved it. Jim hired Johnnie Walker, a veteran radio man, to take over Dunn's slot from Mondays to Thursdays, whilst I did the Friday show. Soon I found my mugshot on hoardings all over London, and indeed on double-decker buses, as the BBC announced 'Des Lynam, now on radio too'.

'It has come to pass,' said Jane. 'A face like the back of a bus.'

My programme would be a mix of music and star interviews plus the usual radio blend of travel information, news and sport.

I was asked to do a pilot show, just to get used to the format and the workings of the studio. The singer Lulu very kindly came in to be the star guest on a show that she knew would never hit the airwaves. She was a delight.

The prospect of my going back to radio created quite a bit of newspaper reaction, most of it very favourable; but after the first show was broadcast, one critic wrote, 'TV's Mr Smooth hits the rough.' Roland White, in the *Radio Times*, wrote, 'There are disadvantages of being a great bloke. The first is that we're all waiting for you to prove otherwise ... this is a long-winded way of working myself up to a terrible confession. I didn't enjoy Des's new radio show. Des was simply too smooth.' This criticism seemed to be made on the back of one show. White did like my interviews with Elaine Paige and Lee Evans but thought I needed a sidekick, someone to bounce off, in the way that Wogan uses his producer – a formula Jonathan Ross has excelled in. He was right. I felt exposed talking to myself and was much more comfortable with the guests or teasing the traffic reporter, Sally Boazman. But for the remainder of my time with this radio show it was decided I had to fly solo. I got a bit better at it, though.

We had great success in delivering big stars to the programme, none bigger than the singer Cher, who had just come off a plane at Heathrow and seemed very jet-lagged. To be frank, she didn't warm to me, and I didn't take to her. Our chat must have been like listening to paint dry.

Among the best guests were Neil Diamond, Joan Collins, Caroline Aherne, Cilla Black, Barbara Windsor, the Spice Girls and Paul O'Grady. Paul had genuinely travelled to Broadcasting House by tube and we made out that he had come with his Lily Savage gear on. Before our interview, Paul had reminded me of a recent meeting when he was hosting the TV show *Blankety Blank* in his Lily Savage character. I remembered what fun it had been watching Lily, who didn't seem to have a clue about the rules, and couldn't care less, make a series of brilliantly performed 'cock-ups'. It was absolutely hysterical. Paul's mistakes would have made a great late-night show on their own. I enjoyed it more perhaps in light of my only other appearance on *Blankety Blank*. Years before, in the early Eighties, when Les Dawson was the presenter, I came on as one of the celebrity contestants, and it was obvious that my television appearances on *Grandstand* and the Commonwealth Games hadn't made much of an impression on Les. He kept getting my name wrong.

'It must be difficult for you,' I said. 'After all, there are two syllables in each word.' The producers cut my remark out of the finished programme. My son Patrick, who was only about ten years old at the time, had come to the recording, and he got it absolutely right afterwards. 'That was embarrassing, Dad,' he'd said.

I also remember that I was once induced to film a sketch for Paul's *Lily Savage Show*, in which I and a few other television performers, including Michael Ball, played alongside the star, who was 'Shanghai Lil'. I was the barman in the nightclub and for the first time on television was seen singing, mercifully briefly.

We also convinced Joan Collins to come on my radio show and were all absolutely mesmerised by her lips, painted and glossed, with a life of their own, it seemed. Dale Winton also came on the show and was so much wittier and funnier than his television persona. He was also quite wicked when the microphone was turned off – a dangerous strategy: never say anything you don't wish to be heard in front of a microphone. Engineers make mistakes sometimes.

A particular favourite of mine came on the programme: the American–Jewish comedian Jackie Mason, whose show I had recently seen. A few nights after the interview, I found myself in the same restaurant as him. He completely blanked me. I might have come from Mars. He still makes me laugh, though.

During the series I had a scoop. I had bumped into Paul McCartney just once in my life as we came out of adjoining dressing rooms at Television Centre when I was presenting *Grandstand*. To my amazement, he had seemed as delighted to meet me as I was to bump into him and he told me he was a big fan. 'Hang on a minute,' I said, 'this conversation is the wrong way round.' As we were talking, Brian Barwick, my programme editor, was walking by. There is no bigger Beatles fan than this son of Liverpool, and to this day he holds it against me that I continued my conversation with one of his greatest heroes and did not introduce him. 'I passed by about eight times with my tongue hanging out,' said Brian, 'and you bloody ignored me.' Anyway, a few months before my radio series began, Paul had lost his beloved wife, Linda, to cancer, and in the interim had given no interviews. I wrote a personal note to him to say that if at some time he wanted to talk about the awful experience he had gone through, I would be honoured to conduct the interview with him. I pointed out that I hoped he could trust me not to include anything in our talk he did not want broadcast. A few weeks went by and I had almost forgotten about it when I got a response. Paul would do the interview with me.

And so I found myself at the famous Abbey Road Studios in North London to be greeted by this icon of popular music, and we sat down to record. It was the most moving interview I have ever conducted. Paul spoke lovingly of his wife, and especially of her final day when she told him she could not get out of bed. 'I know, you want a bit of a lie-in, love,' he'd said. She passed away later that day. In the middle of the interview, Paul broke down. I broke down with him. The listeners merely heard a slight pause, which told its own story. I didn't want the great man to be embarrassed in any way. He talked a great deal about the good times with Linda. 'We fancied each other something rotten,' he said. 'That's all it was. Our kids used to laugh at us. We'd be standing in the middle of the kitchen, kissing and stuff, and they'd say, "Look at the state of you two".'

We played the interview over two programmes. I felt it was strong enough and long enough to make a separate programme by itself. I was told that Radio 2 was not really a 'speech' network, but they were too protective of the interview to pass it on to Radio 4.

Paul, of course, has found happiness again with Heather Mills, who seems to get something of a bad press. 'Speak as you find', my mother used to say, and when I have met Heather I have always found her delightful and entirely unpretentious. She came on the *How Do They Do That?* programme not long after she had recovered from losing her leg in that famous accident with a police motor cycle. She had lifted the studio audience, and I am sure the viewers as well, with her courage and humour. I described her on the night as an 'absolute tonic'. There were some envious broadcasters on Radio 2 who thought that I had been 'given' the McCartney interview. They would have been unaware that it stemmed from my having the initiative, or perhaps cheek, to write to Paul on a personal level.

Afterwards Paul was criticised because, despite his stance on animal welfare, he admitted that Linda may have taken some drugs that had been tested on animals in an attempt to prolong her life. I was sorry that I had exposed him to that criticism and wrote to him accordingly.

I stayed with the radio show for getting on for a year but when I moved to ITV it seemed inappropriate to continue with BBC Radio as there was so much ill-feeling against me from other quarters of the Corporation at the time. Jim Moir thought it would be OK to continue, but I did not feel comfortable with it and left. I wrote to Jim, apologising for having to make my decision. He wrote a charming note back, thanking me for making such a positive contribution to Radio 2. 'The Radio 2 audience loved you as I did,' he said. I was greatly touched by his kindness and understanding. 'Once a *mensch*, always a *mensch*,' he used to say. I presumed that was a compliment.

23

NATIONAL DISASTERS

As with several other sports, such as tennis and golf, BBC Radio had decided to present major racing occasions 'on site' – that is, the presenter would actually be at the occasion rather than following the previously accepted practice of linking to the commentators at the event from the safety of Broadcasting House.

There was no bigger racing occasion than the Grand National at Aintree; and so I began presenting the show from the course. Judith Chalmers, famous for her travel programmes, but an excellent all-rounder, was part of our team. Her responsibility was to take care of the 'personality' interviews. The main race commentator was Peter Bromley, a man with a stentorian voice, authority, and great experience. Had Peter O'Sullevan not dominated racing on television, Peter Bromley would certainly have done so, and become equally famous. As it was, he was a delight to work with as far as I was concerned, but he was certainly a man who didn't suffer fools gladly. He used to have some fearsome run-ins with our old radio boss Angus

McKay, but only by correspondence – they had long since stopped talking to each other.

An example of their mutual loathing is apparent in two memos that passed between them. Bromley had been asked by McKay to do a one-and-a-half minute piece from the Cheltenham Festival meeting looking forward to the Gold Cup. However, the race on the Wednesday, the Champion Hurdle, provided what he thought was a first-class news story. The race was won by a one-eyed horse called Winning Fair ridden by the first amateur to win it since 1938. Bromley therefore began his report with a twenty-second mention of this before dealing with the Gold Cup. The next day he was admonished for departing from his brief.

Memo from Peter Bromley to Angus McKay:
I acknowledge that I departed from my brief and spoke for 20 seconds on the Champion Hurdle and apologise if it spoilt the impact of the piece about the Gold Cup. However I would like to point out that:

1. I was convinced there was a news story in the Champion Hurdle.
2. I suggested the 20 seconds on the Champion Hurdle to the producer before the programme who accepted it.
3. I did not over-run.
4. I did tip the winner of the Gold Cup.

Memo from Angus McKay to Peter Bromley:
1. We weren't.
2. He didn't.
3. You're not expected to.
4. You are expected to.

And these were grown men.

In 1980, Bob Champion joined our team to give us the benefit of his experience as a top jump jockey. Bob was at the time enduring treatment for testicular cancer. On the morning of the race, when he turned up, I and my colleagues were shocked by his appearance. The muscular, spare rider of before had given way to seven stones of skin and bones. His hair had disappeared and he had that yellow pallor of the seriously ill. Not one of us would have given him a hope of survival. However, he remained cheerful during the day and certainly added to our broadcast with his knowledge and inside information.

Fast forward now to the next year. Bob has not only recovered, but is back in the saddle; not only that, but on a horse he had ridden to third in the Gold Cup two years before. Bob was actually winning the race. In the interim, the horse, Aldaniti, had broken down, injured, and, it was thought, would never race again. And so this unlikely combination of horse and rider, both of whom had been written off, produced one of the greatest National stories ever. The occasion was made into a most moving film with John Hurt playing the part of Champion, and the emotive music from the film has been used in every television broadcast of the National since.

Rather as I had been doing with my boxing commentaries, I was being seconded back to radio from television to cover the Grand National. But soon, because I'd taken over the main presentational role on *Grandstand*, I would have to relinquish my radio work at Aintree. Now I would be presenting the occasion for television.

Almost every year, the great race produced a special story. Two years after Bob Champion's victory came the first-ever woman to train a National winner: Jenny Pitman with her gelding, Corbiere. It was the beginning of a seventeen-year-long series of Grand National interviews between me and Mrs P.

For the 1986 National, we had come up with a wheeze to publicise our coverage of the race: Des would have his own runner, and of course, if it won it would mean that he would have to interview himself. Naturally there was little hope of that happening. I leased a 13-year-old called Another Duke, who had seen better days, to run in my green-and-white colours. It was a rank outsider but was going well until it was brought down by a falling horse. On board was Paul Nicholls, now a hugely successful trainer.

The Clerk of the Course at Aintree at the time was John Hughes, a character who certainly enjoyed a drink, but which never seemed to impair his excellence at his job. I knew him quite well, but he told me that he and David Coleman had always gone out to dinner on the eve of the National, in order to make sure they were 'singing from the same hymn sheet' for the following day's major television broadcast. I had no real desire to do this, because I was already feeling the pressure of having to cope with one of the most difficult outside broadcasts that BBC Television produces. I needed an early night and no booze.

Hughes, however, saw my less-than-enthusiastic response to his invitation as something akin to bad manners. In weakness, I succumbed and so, despite turning down three out of every four drinks offered to me, I arrived at Aintree the following morning for my first television Grand National with a throbbing pain over one eye that underlined my stupidity of the night before. Hughes greeted me, looking as fresh as a daisy. 'You look a bit pale,' he said, which did nothing for my confidence.

As it turned out, I got through the five-hour show without mishap. Last Suspect, owned by the Duchess of Westminster, who had also owned the famous Arkle, won the race at 50–1 with the Welsh jockey, Hywel Davies, on board. Corbiere was in the frame again, third this time. As I walked to the BBC caravan, having come off the air, the headache, which had all but disappeared for the length of the broadcast, came back with a vengeance. I just about managed to avoid throwing up. For the ensuing fourteen years I was rather more careful with my eve-of-National preparation.

When I first started doing the show for television, I would spend the previous two days at the racecourse trying to glean what information I could for the big day itself. What usually happened was that one would be pulled from pillar to post by the punters, who would demand photos or autographs, or just a chat. After a couple of years, I realised that staying safely in my Liverpool hotel, watching the Thursday and Friday racing on television and going through my preparation quietly, was the best course of action.

Of all the sports I presented, I probably had to work hardest on the Grand National broadcast, or, rather, preparing for it. While the likes of Richard Pitman, who has done magnificent work on the show over the years, were steeped in National Hunt racing, I came to it in a professional sense just once a year and I had to mug up seriously. The journey up to Liverpool from London each year would rush by as the hours were filled with Rose springing questions to me about the history of the race, previous winners, owners, trainers and the unexpected runners. I did not profess to become an instant expert, but you had to know enough.

Once I saw a young female presenter on another channel suggest that Desert Orchid, the famous grey horse, 'would be worth a fortune at stud', not having understood what a gelding was. Or perhaps wasn't. I once asked Jenny Pitman why gelding a horse didn't reduce its athleticism. 'Wouldn't work in humans,' I said. 'No, you'd lose a bit of your sparkle, Des,' she replied. The idea of having a non-expert presenting the occasion was that it was precisely that: an occasion, a day for the British sporting public, not just for racing aficionados. Sue Barker has now taken over the role of main presenter. Like me, she is not a racing specialist, but she does her homework. While I understand most sports commentary, which has no great mystique about it, I have undying admiration for those exponents of the art of 'calling the horses'. Imagine forty runners travelling at high speed over thirty fences, in often awful weather conditions. Most of the horses look much the same, except for the occasional grey. The commentator's only means of recognition is the colours worn by the rider, which are often not dissimilar to those of other runners. Now you have to transfer the immediate recognition of colours to the name of the horse and rider. Oh, and you had better not get the wrong one first past the post. If you ever go racing, and you are looking for the horse you have backed, you know just how difficult it is to find in a reasonably large field of runners.

The BBC has been blessed with the very best in the business when it comes to racing commentary. Bromley, O'Sullevan and now Jim McGrath on television, have been outstanding exponents of this extremely difficult technique. One night before a National, the BBC asked me to do an interview with Peter O'Sullevan and for him to show the amount of work he put into his commentaries. Peter produced the incredibly complicated chart he prepared, using coloured crayons on it. There was every conceivable piece of information about the following day's runners and riders. On the actual day, though, he would have little time to refer to it. He hoped that by writing it all out he would cement most of it in his brain. I was amazed to witness Peter enjoying an excellent bottle of claret the night before. 'Aids the sleeping process, old boy,' he said. O'Sullevan, of course, also had another gift: that wonderful instrument, his very special voice. He maintained the highest of standards before calling it a day in his eightieth year.

Before one of the Nationals, I flew to Ireland to interview J. P. McManus, who had a runner that year. JP used to be described as a bookmaker and gambler, but in recent years he has become mega-wealthy, investing on the currency markets with his pals Dermot Desmond, major shareholder in Celtic Football Club, and the billionaire Joe Lewis. And of course he owned a large amount of Manchester United stock, before selling out to the American Malcolm Glazer.

Having landed at Shannon Airport in the west of Ireland, we were escorted to JP's waiting helicopter, to take us on the short journey to his home in Tipperary. Conducting an interview with McManus is not the easiest of broadcasting tasks. He is self-effacing and modest, and gives little away. His house was magnificent. 'If ever I thought I would own it, I'd have made a better job of the foundations,' said JP, who had driven the bulldozer for the builders as a young man, some years before he found his route to wealth. Over lunch we were offered the most superb wines, while our host, a teetotaller, drank his usual pint of milk. 'That stuff will clog up your arteries and kill you,' I told him. 'And the booze will ruin your liver and kill you,' he responded. 'Yes, but I'll be too pissed to care,' I replied. Soon we were back in the helicopter to Shannon. We were a little late for our scheduled flight, but JP radioed ahead to hold the plane for a few minutes. The power of one of Ireland's major players and a most charming man.

When Martell Cognac took over sponsorship of the National, they once or twice took those of us involved in the broadcast down to their estate in France for a bit of a 'jolly'. There, some of us would have a round of golf and be given a tour of the brandy-making distillery. We were told about the 'angel's share' – that part of the distillation process that is lost in vapour and gives the area its distinctive aroma – and were each presented with a special cognac made in the year of our respective births. On one occasion we were also shown how the barrels were made. The families of coopers involved had a history as long as the Martell family itself and had been involved in the business for generations. Peter O'Sullevan and I watched in awe as these sturdy men with rippling muscles bent the timber and then wrapped the red-hot steel around the shaped oak to create the finished product. It was artistic and strength-sapping at the same time.

On the return journey from Cognac, Peter and I were invited into the cockpit of the Martell Lear Jet, where we received a few minutes' 'flying information' from the pilot. As we regained our seats, Peter, in that wonderful voice, nudged me. 'You know,' he said, 'with a bit of decent instruction, I reckon I could fly one of these things.' There was a thoughtful pause, and then: 'But I'll tell you this, I could never make one of those fucking barrels.'

Martell had become the sponsors of the Grand National in 1992, taking over the role from their parent company, Seagram Distillers, who had achieved the ultimate publicity coup the previous year when the race was won by a horse called Seagram. The National, under these two banners, enjoyed its most stable period for years. For a long time, the very existence of the race had been in doubt. The involvement of Seagram was really down to a great lover of the National, Ivan Straker, who had been the Chairman of Seagram in the UK. With the race continually in a financial plight, he had made a special appeal to Edgar Bronfman, President of Seagram International, and his organisation came riding in to the rescue of one of Britain's greatest sporting institutions.

But in the second year of their sponsorship, Martell were to experience a total cock-up.

The race became void following two false starts. It was a black day for Aintree, racing, and, indeed, British sport. Jenny Pitman was deprived of her second Grand National winner when her horse, Esha Ness, got round the course in first place, all to no avail. Many of the entries had failed to start, or got caught up in the starting tape. The subsequent enquiry apportioned some blame to the officials involved, but they were not helped by an antiquated piece of machinery used for the starting gate.

For me, as presenter of the programme, this was a big story. I was in my element as I questioned everyone concerned: the jockeys who had got round, those who hadn't started, angry trainers, and, of course, the bookmakers, who told the nation's punters what would happen to their money. I also spoke to a dismayed Patrick Martell, the urbane head of the French brandy makers, who must have been wondering what he had let his company in for. People were queuing up to give their view of what had happened, and why. These are the times in a live broadcast when one hopes one can put names to faces, or, if you obviously cannot, that the editor or producer will give you a prompt. All was going well until a young man to whom I had been speaking that morning over breakfast was next in line to be interviewed. His name just would not come to me and obviously my colleagues in the scanner van were having their own doubts as to whom I was now interrogating. Then, all of a sudden, it dawned on me. I was talking to Marcus Armytage, who as an amateur had ridden Mr Frisk to National victory a few years before, in a record time for the race. In my sudden relief I over-compensated with his name and when I looked back at the tape afterwards, I found myself using 'Marcus' almost between words.

The race starter himself, Captain Keith Brown, had been spirited away out of reach of the media. But I caught up with him a year later, a few days before the 1994 National. He explained rather poignantly that the unfortunate events of the void race had virtually ruined his life.

People afterwards kept congratulating me on how I coped with the situation on the day. Actually, it was a journalistic dream, a real story to get your teeth into; but, of course, a total embarrassment for the organisers. Incredibly, our viewing figures went up. British television watchers are obviously more mes-merised by a cock-up than by anything going smoothly. The following year, the National was back to normal, with Richard Dunwoody winning the race for a second time. His mount, Miinnehoma, was owned by the comedian Freddie Starr, who was not actually at the race but we got hold of him on the tele-phone. As it turned out, my interview with him was bizarre because, while viewers could hear my end of the conversation, they could not hear what Freddie was saying. I can only tell you, it was just as well. Then, in 1995, Jenny Pitman got her second National winner after all, when Royal Athlete romped home.

The post-race interviews were sometimes terrific. After his win on Rough Quest in 1996, Mick Fitzgerald described the experi-ence as 'better than sex'. The lady in his life was not best pleased.

Daisy performs at Wimbledon on a rainy 'Take Your Dog to Work' day.

With my pal, Gerald Williams, who's slightly younger than the car.

Proposing a toast to World Heavyweight Champion Mike Tyson with Jarvis Astaire between us.

The Grand National Squad in Cognac with those ...ing barrels. Sir Peter O'Sullevan is third from the right. Martin Hopkins and Julian Wilson to my right, and Dave Gordon is extreme left.

With Grand National
sparring partner,
Jenny Pitman.

With dear Jill, Jeremy
Guscott, Annabel Croft
and Gordon Ramsay in
an 'Eat More Fruit'
campaign.

Meeting John Major
at No. 10, not a
grey man at all.

With Rose – we've had a great life together.

Presented to her Majesty with Sir Peter O'Sullevan.

A *Holiday* programme
pose in Venice.

Sir Paul gave me a great
interview.

Damon Hill wins Sports Personality of the Year, and graces the programme like his father before him.

Cher and Meatloaf on the radio show: he was fun, she was jetlagged.

With Alan Hansen and Mark Lawrenson on MOTD – both brilliant to work and laugh with.

With Hill, Hansen and
Ginola at the 1998
World Cup.

Celebrating 40 years of
Grandstand with the
presenters.

The 1997 National was going to be an even higher profile occasion than normal. It was the 150th running of the race and the Princess Royal would be present to unveil a bust commissioned in honour of Sir Peter O'Sullevan, my friend and colleague, who would be commentating for the last time – 'Bowing out before I outstay my welcome,' was Peter's way of expressing his decision to retire. He created a laugh when the bust was unveiled: he reckoned that it was facing away from the course 'so as not to frighten the horses'. In addition, nine of the previous winners would be present to parade before the start of the race. All in all, there was a wonderful day in prospect.

I did an interview with Ginger McCain, trainer of the great Red Rum. Ginger, incredibly, would win the race again in 2004 with Amberleigh House, some thirty-one years after his first win with 'Rummy'. Mick Fitzgerald was back, and the glamorous Gee Armytage, who had ridden in the race, was on the programme. The National is a big television favourite in the Far East and the producer, Martin Hopkins, arranged for a group of twelve Singapore nightclub hostesses to come on and be interviewed. They were extremely good-looking girls, but not one of them spoke English. Hopkins had assured me that some of them could, but the boys in the production scanner had a great laugh when I ended up with a little egg chow mein on my face.

Mike Atherton, the England cricket captain, came on, and then Jenny Pitman for one of our annual verbal jousts. This time, live on air, Jenny suggested it was about time I made the lady in my life, Rose, 'a respectable woman'. Jenny herself was about to marry her long-time partner, David Stait. I was not entirely delighted with that particular invasion of privacy. 'Thank you for sharing that with the nation, Jenny,' I said. A friend later told me that my eyes went suddenly cold as I said it, but we ended with a smile and a joke as usual.

I heard later that the Princess Royal was sitting in the production truck and had hugely enjoyed the sight of me squirming. 'She was roaring with laughter,' said Hopkins afterwards. Then on came the Hollywood legend, Gregory Peck. His performance as the small-town lawyer in *To Kill a Mockingbird* was one of my favourite film performances of all time. He was as charming as I expected him to be. I was in good form. The programme was going well.

Then disaster. At 2.49 and 2.52 precisely, Aintree received warnings that bombs had been placed at the course. Earlier in the week, three bombs had been placed on the M6 and the motorway had been closed. The warnings, because of the nature of their delivery, had to be taken seriously. The Grand National, and the thousands of people there to enjoy a great day's sport, were in serious jeopardy.

The key personnel at Aintree quickly conferred with the Merseyside Police to decide what should be done. Soon an announcement was made that the course had to be cleared. The safety of the thousands of people present, and of course the horses, had to take precedence over the event itself. The Aintree Press Officer, Nigel Payne, was rushed to me at my presentation position to explain exactly what was going on. Together we watched the early consequences of the announcements on a television monitor. Extraordinarily, people were evacuating Aintree not only in good order, but in good humour too.

I kept broadcasting from my position near the winners' enclosure until the police decided we had to move. Now I had lost control of the broadcast and was close to being removed from Aintree altogether. My floor manager, Chris White, and I found ourselves in a pretty exclusive group, which included the Princess Royal and Gregory Peck, who were being ushered out of the course by senior officers of the Merseyside force. When I realised what was happening, I said to Chris, 'We can't follow them. They're taking us out. They think we want to go. I've got a broadcast to finish.' Chris and I broke free from our entourage and now found ourselves battling against the crowd to get back to wherever I could pick up the broadcast again. The punters were asking me what was going on, giving me plenty of good-natured banter in the process. 'Only just turned up, Des?', 'You're going the wrong way', 'Shouldn't you be on the telly?' I was having to cope with this maelstrom and, worst of all, with my ignorance of what was going on and where I should be. My talkback system had long since become detached. Eventually we found our way to the horse-box car park, where I was hurriedly wired up again and resumed the broadcast. There was no shortage of people to interview. The fact that I could do this at all was down to the foresight of a BBC cameraman, Howard Woosey, who had rolled up a length of cable and carried it off with him to our new position. I spoke to jockeys, trainers and officials, all highly indignant and frustrated by this potentially dangerous interruption to what should have been a great day's sport. Jenny Pitman spoke movingly and emotionally: 'How could they do this? They're supposed to love horses,' referring to the acceptance that the bomb warnings had come from the IRA. Then came the extraordinary exchange with Charles Barnett, the Clerk of the Course. He did his best to explain what was going to happen. There would obviously be no further racing on the day. He finished by saying, 'Everyone must leave and that means you, too, Desmond.' The police had decided that the whole place had to be cleared.

Nobody was even allowed back to their cars. I know of several cases where people had left their dogs in their vehicles, giving them much cause for concern.

The BBC's broadcast from Aintree was about to be suspended. but first there was an exemplary commentary from Jim McGrath, now the main Grand National commentator but that year still the Number 2 to Peter O'Sullevan. Jim was perched in his position high over Bechers Brook, and from there described all that was happening. Jim kept going fluently and movingly for about fifteen minutes, describing the dramatic scenes that were unfolding in front of him. It was a marvellous feat of broadcasting. Once again the audience figure rose as the drama of all that was happening became compulsive viewing for millions.

Gary Lineker, who was in the BBC office at Television Centre, had presented *Football Focus* as usual at lunchtime and was staying on for *Match of the Day* in the evening. But when we closed down early at Aintree, he suddenly found himself thrust into the *Grandstand* presenter's chair in the studio. For the first time in his fairly limited broadcasting life, Gary found himself without a script and with no preparation, having to pick up the broadcast. He was having to ad lib about a very delicate situation and then had to cope with the videprinter as the final football scores came hurtling in. He found that more difficult than he ever thought it could be. Gary described his experience later as one of the scariest things he's ever had to do, 'like taking penalties for England, but it lasted a lot longer'. Then, bizarrely, he found himself interviewing me down the telephone about the latest news from Aintree.

I was then finished for the day. There was nothing further for me to do, but I hung around in the Aintree car park for a few hours. There was a strange atmosphere. People were enjoying a joke and having a laugh. British people in times of crisis always rally round – the Dunkirk spirit. Drinks were dispensed. No one knew at that point whether or not there would be a Grand National that year, and so we had a gentle party.

The BBC's veteran Aintree producer, Martin Hopkins, summed up all of our feelings that evening. 'We were all pissed off at being mucked around by a bunch of lunatics.' But he, the editor, Dave Gordon, and the race director, Malcolm Kemp, for whom this was his first Grand National (what a baptism of fire), had assured Aintree that if they decided to reschedule the race, the BBC would accommodate it any time, any day.

I felt sorry for the sponsor's Chairman, Patrick Martell, who, before his company's involvement, scarcely knew what National Hunt racing was. Now, within the space of four years, he had witnessed 'the race that never was', as Peter O'Sullevan described the void race of 1993, and now another debacle. He was probably thinking he should have put a few francs into the Tour de France instead, but, stoically, he and his company stayed with the National for quite a few more years.

By the end of the day, Aintree was empty save for a full car park. No one was allowed to take their cars out until the next day – apart from me: I had asked the police inspector in charge if he could make an exception in my case, as I had to return a borrowed Jaguar car the next day. He agreed to the request, which upset one or two people, and Rose had to negotiate this high-performance vehicle back to London as I stayed on to find out what was going to happen. She managed to get home unscathed. Eventually it was decided that Aintree would try to run the race on Monday. This would need a fantastic piece of reorganisation.

My Sunday was pretty relaxed. I got myself a ticket for Liverpool's home match against Coventry. In a big upset, the visitors won, ruining the championship chances for the Merseysiders. Some of the jockeys went as well, still wearing their riding breeches and colours, covered by macs or overcoats, because they hadn't been able to retrieve their normal day clothes.

The race on the Monday turned out to be a big success. Aintree let the public in for free and the television audience was bigger than ever. About twelve million watched, many of them anticipating possible further trouble, no doubt. I interviewed Peter O'Sullevan, who was finally about to do his last commentary, and he got a great reception from the crowd.

I must admit I was considerably more nervous than usual during the broadcast. There were several hints that further bomb warnings had been made and everyone connected with the programme was a bit edgy. We went on the air at 4 p.m. and the Grand National of 1997 took place at last, won by a horse called Lord Gyllene, who had led all the way from the first fence to win by some twenty-five lengths, ridden by the appropriately named Tony Dobbin.

My abiding memory of the Saturday is how well the people reacted. There was dreadful inconvenience for thousands, not to mention the possibility of extreme danger. Everyone, including many of the Liverpool people who opened their doors to strangers, behaved commendably. The best thing of all was this great part of Britain's sporting heritage survived and did not bow to the behaviour of a group of extremists. The message from Aintree had been clear: no giving in.

24

IF I COULD KEEP MY HEAD

Some time before the World Cup finals to be held in France in 1998, I wrote to the Managing Director of BBC Television, Will Wyatt, copying the letter to the Controller of BBC 1, Peter Salmon. 'Dear Will,' I wrote.

> Sooner or later I suspect that you will become involved in the planning for next year's World Cup finals.
>
> Preliminary negotiations are already underway with ITV under the so-called 'gentlemen's agreement'.
>
> I would like to impress upon you the strength of feeling in the sports department that while we play the role of gentlemen, ITV get away with murder. To put themselves in an equal sharing position (of matches to be broadcast live) goes completely against past experience of audience research, reaction, not to say broadcasting awards.
>
> We think that with England and Scotland's presence, the finals taking place in our time zone will be the biggest sporting event ever. Forget the Olympics.
>
> We desperately want the BBC to make a decision that

we will cover all of England's matches live whatever the opposition decide to do.

Any sharing agreement can take place after that. The audience will back us and we will do our utmost to earn that confidence as we did in Euro 96.

This is the opportunity for the BBC to regain its mark as the sports channel during 1998. God knows we need to.

Niall Sloane, the editor of football, had backed my stance. So had all the people working on the BBC's football output. In fact they were at least as bullish as I was, and I wrote the letter on their behalf.

The viewing public had voted many times with their remote controls. They preferred the big occasions on the BBC. But the powers that be decided that, although they had every right to broadcast all the World Cup matches live, as had ITV, it was better for the viewer to share the games and then be able to offer alternatives to football when a match was 'on the other side'. This would have made sense to me if the BBC had only one channel. They had two.

Also, they were concerned that there were the Wimbledon Championships and other summer sports to consider. The football had to be worked in and around these events. The BBC did not want to be accused of sporting overkill. They also knew that ITV always ran to the press if the BBC threatened not to share, claiming that the BBC did not have the viewers' interests at heart.

And so my plea was turned down and on the night of 30 June 1998 I sat in the dark of the BBC studio on top of the French Automobile Club offices on the Place de la Concorde, next to the famous Hotel Crillon in central Paris, as England played

Argentina in St Étienne. Beckham got sent off, Michael Owen scored his wonder goal, and England lost. It was all live on ITV, not the BBC. Later, ITV quite rightly crowed about their audience figure, some 27 million people, one of the biggest UK sports audiences ever.

The BBC mandarins realised they had missed an opportunity to mark the famous occasion with the BBC brand and from then on became much more bullish in their negotiations with ITV over major football. Unfortunately, by the time they did, it was working not for me, but against me.

Overall, the World Cup in France was a big success for the BBC, despite missing out on the biggest match for British viewers. Once again, the broadcasting philosophies of the two terrestrial organisations had differed.

While Bob Wilson found himself flying, driving or catching trains all over France to present his next match for ITV from one or other stadium, we at the BBC were in our comfortable, indeed perfect, position in those studios in central Paris. We had pitched for them against the German broadcasters and luckily managed to gain the position with views over the city. It gave the broadcasts a very French flavour. Before one match I did a brief travelogue for the viewers in which I picked out several landmarks before we got on with the football.

The disadvantage was that we watched all the games on the television, just as one would at home, and missed some of the crowd atmosphere; but of course the viewer missed nothing. Our remoteness did not detract in any way from the opinions we voiced on the action. The broadcasts were actually better for our peaceful surroundings. We just missed the personal experience of being at the games, but we were spared the chaotic travelling, which I learned later had worn poor old Bob to a frazzle. Once again the ITV broadcasts occasionally looked uncomfortable. Ours tended to be much more controlled and we had a great deal of fun doing them. Besides, we were not there for our own experience of the event, but to do our job in the best way to the advantage of the viewers.

I had the benefit of working with a cracking group of experts. Firstly there was Jimmy Hill, proudly wearing his St George's Cross bow tie when England played. Alan Hansen was at his imperious best; Martin O'Neill and Ally McCoist brought a certain amount of quirkiness and humour to our shows, not to mention their considerable expertise. And then there was David Ginola, charming, handsome, and entirely pissed off at not being part of the French team. (David actually fell asleep during one of their matches.)

One day before a game, there was a surprise visitor to the studio. We suddenly and unexpectedly found ourselves in the presence of the singing star, Robbie Williams. He had been watching the shows on television, worked out where we were, and decided to pay us a visit. We put him on the show, and live in front of camera he peeled off his jacket, to reveal a T-shirt on which was emblazoned 'Des is God'. He gave me no warning of it. The production team told me later I actually blushed on camera, something they had never seen before. I told him if there were any gods around it certainly wasn't me.

The discussions on the game worked well. I felt in good form. The editor was the battle-hardened Niall Sloane, with whom I had shared an excellent Euro 96, and the director was Paul McNamara, one of the best in the business who, a few years later, was to follow me to ITV.

Jimmy was experiencing his last big event for the BBC. He had shaken hands a couple of years before on a two-year

222

agreement that would take him up to and including this World Cup but his contract would not be extended beyond. Jimmy would be seventy years of age during the tournament, but he was less than pleased that the end of his BBC career was in sight. He felt he had plenty left to offer.

From time to time, his opinions made some of his fellow pundits fall about. The Romanian team had all dyed their hair blond before a match. Jimmy thought this a good ploy, 'anything that helps you pick out a team-mate quickly is good,' he said.

'Doesn't do a lot for the Swedes,' I retorted a bit too tartly, as the others smirked.

Before our last programme it was suggested to me that, on behalf of everyone, I should wish Jimmy good luck in his retirement. Knowing him well, I realised that I had better mention the plan to him. 'Don't do that,' he said. 'I'm not retiring. The BBC have chosen not to renew my contract, that's all. I still want to work.'

And so Jimmy's last hurrah was uncelebrated on our last show together, and as a result I later received letters from viewers criticising me for not giving him a decent farewell.

Final broadcasts on big occasions nearly always end with a visual round-up of the major memories of the event. This is usually accompanied, not by a narration, but by music. I happened to mention to the producers that, with all the ups and downs experienced by the England team, especially Owen's great goal, and Beckham's (in my opinion) grossly unfair sending-off, I was reminded of Kipling's poem 'If'. Perhaps we should end our last programme with those words put to pictures, I suggested.

It was thought to be a decent idea, a bit different from the norm, and one of the producers dug out a recording of the poem and put it to pictures of some of the football highlights from the previous month. It worked beautifully, but it was thought the words were delivered too theatrically, which might not appeal to our football fans. 'Why don't you read it, Des?' said one my colleagues. 'You sound a bit more common.'

France won the World Cup for the first time, beating Brazil in the Final.

We had screened a copy of the Brazilian team sheet, which had been submitted before kick-off as is routine, and were astonished to find that Ronaldo, their great striker, had been left out. Then, to our amazement, he was hurriedly reintroduced to the starting eleven: the suspicions were that the Brazilians' sponsors had demanded his inclusion. I did a two-way with John Motson at the stadium and we made the most of the story before the match got under way. Two old hacks like dogs with a bone, we were.

That night Paris was the place to be. The streets were thronged. Everyone in celebration mode, kissing and hugging everyone else. Along with one or two of my colleagues we battled our way down to the Seine where the BBC were 'pushing the boat out' with a party on board a boat. Director General John Birt turned up, exhausted from having walked most of the way from the stadium. One of our broadcasters had convinced the DG's chauffeur the car was for him and the boss had been left to find his own way back. One thing that John Birt did very well at the BBC was to hold some very entertaining gatherings of eclectic talents.

Packing the deck of the boat, we all revelled in the success of the previous few weeks: superb programmes, well received by the public and critics alike. Albert Sewell, long-term servant of the BBC as the football statistician whom I had dubbed 'Albere' for the series, reckoned that the last night he remembered to match it was on VE Day when he was a teenager.

I forgot my other problems for the night and proceeded to invest in a world-class hangover.

25

FRONT PAGE FOOL

During the 1998 World Cup, my BBC bosses were amazed to pick up the *Sun* newspaper to find my picture on the front page promoting that paper's coverage of the event. It was something that I should have cleared beforehand, and they could not understand why I had got involved with a newspaper promotion at all. The supposition was that I had been paid handsomely. Actually, I received not a penny; but I had, temporarily as it turned out, bought myself some piece of mind.

A couple of days before, early one morning, I had been walking back to my hotel when a reporter from that newspaper approached me, introduced himself, and told me that he and his newspaper knew I had just come from seeing a certain lady in her hotel.

It was true. My immediate reaction was to punch this individual right in the face, but I knew instinctively that these types do not travel alone – there would be a cameraman lurking somewhere out of sight. So I merely mumbled about my private business being nothing to do with him, left him standing there, and hurried across the River Seine, past the Louvre, and back towards my hotel.

It was a beautiful early summer's morning. Paris was at its most beguiling, but the storm clouds were gathering for me. I had had the feeling that something like this was going to happen. The woman in question had pestered me to death to allow her to come and visit me during the World Cup. I had run out of excuses, and so she had made her way to Paris. Not for the first time, I had succumbed to her attractions – something I cannot explain to this day. She was no beauty, rather one of those women in middle age who try a bit too hard with the make-up and clothes. In actual fact I was embarrassed by her appearance, but a part of my anatomy had taken over from my brain and I was out of control. She seemed very experienced in how to snare a member of the opposite sex.

The newspaper probably had pictures to prove my dalliance. What on earth was I going to do? I wasn't concerned for myself, but for the hurt I was going to cause the woman I had shared my life with for some fifteen years. I thought long and hard. I took another walk and found myself at Notre Dame, that ancient and beautiful cathedral in the centre of the city. There were quite a few British visitors who recognised me and said hello. Unusually for me, they got a grim response.

I hurried back to my hotel room and picked up the telephone. I dialled the number for the *Sun* newspaper in London and asked to be put through to the editor. As it turned out, I spoke to the deputy editor, Rebekah Wade. I complained to her about the intrusion into my private life by the paper's reporter, emphasised that I wasn't actually married, and that although a story about an affair would be interesting to the public, it was not in the public interest to know about it, as laid down in the guidelines of the Press Complaints Commission. I was not a politician asking for people's votes; I had just made a private mistake, and whatever relationship I may have had was certainly at an end.

Rebekah asked for some time to look into the matter and an hour or so later telephoned me back. She said that her paper would not be publishing the story, but that I probably owed them a favour. My part of the bargain was that front page appearance, which had confused and upset some of my colleagues.

The woman in question? Well, I had made a mistake. I had gone behind Rose's back and had the occasional meeting with this person. I spent the few times I had with her trying to extricate myself from the web I was caught up in, only to find myself getting more deeply entangled. She did not actually say so, but I always had the feeling she would run to the press when the relationship ended. And so I tried to break away gently, simply by not being readily available. All the time, the guilt for my behaviour was crippling me. Here I was presenting the World Cup, getting tremendous reviews, broadcasting as well as I had ever done, with this over-painted albatross around my neck. I told her about my encounter with the *Sun* reporter and that she should immediately return home. It would be impossible to see her again. Strangely, she did not object. It was as though her task had been fulfilled. I felt I had fallen into a trap. The *Sun* may not be printing a story, but somebody would. Eventually.

After the World Cup was over, some contacts of mine in the newspaper business had heard murmurings concerning a story about me being hawked to the press. I knew it was only a matter of time before I would have my private life dissected over the nation's breakfast tables.

I decided that I had to come clean with Rose, and so I told

228

her about the affair. Firstly she laughed. She could not believe it when I told her who the person was. Rose said that she could almost understand if I had found myself falling for a young beautiful actress or model; 'but that ravaged old tart,' she said. And then she cried, long and hard, and I cried with her and begged her forgiveness and understanding. My spies told me that the following Sunday, the *News of the World* would be printing the story. I decided to flee to Spain. We were going on that Sunday anyway with our usual group of friends, so I brought the flights forward. I told Rose that even if she didn't fancy my company very much, she too needed to be out of the firing line for a while. With our rented villa not quite ready to receive us, we checked into a small hotel on the Costa del Sol that we had stayed in together fifteen years before and where we had enjoyed a blissful time. Now the hotel had lost some of its magic and looked to be in a rather shabby state – a metaphor for my life, I reflected.

As it turned out, there was no story in the paper that Sunday. In fact there was no story for several weeks. We got on with our holiday. All credit to Rose; although she was cool with me, she never showed her troubles to our friends, who still could not understand why we had changed our flights and went out a day or two earlier when we always used to travel together. They found out why some weeks later.

In due course, one of those brokers in other people's misery sold the story, not to one paper, but to two. The fee involved I learned was something like £100,000, too much for one of our famous Sunday tabloids to pay, so two of them clubbed together. I hope the payee paid her tax on the sum.

You will have heard of that much used phrase in the theatre, 'the show must go on'. Well, I have done shows on the television with headaches, feeling sick, and suffering from colds and flu; but now I was going to do a programme shaking with fear and embarrassment.

One Saturday, in September of 1998, I was told that the *News of the World* and *The Mail on Sunday* were about to expose me the following day as a 'love cheat'. I telephoned my editor at the BBC, Niall Sloane, and explained my predicament to him. He was enormously sympathetic. I wondered whether or not to turn up for the programme. I didn't want to put the show at risk by not being able to perform to my usual standard. 'Those bastards would love you to miss the show,' he said. 'Don't give them the satisfaction of being able to print that you went missing.'

I had hoped he would take that stance. I wanted to show I would not be cowed by them, even if I had erred in my supposedly private life.

The day went by more or less as usual. Alan Hansen and Trevor Brooking, the production staff, and I settled down to watch the afternoon's games. Then I wrote the script for the show, trying to keep my mind off the sword of Damocles about to cut off my balls.

The norm for *Match of the Day* evenings is that around 9.30 p.m. the early editions of the Sunday papers arrive. The pundits check that the sports pages are not running with anything they have not been aware of or might have missed. Then we would turn to the front pages of the tabloids and, with the rest of the nation, read about the discomfort of the latest celebrity to be caught 'in flagrante'. But now it was me caught with my trousers well and truly around my ankles.

Niall and I had thought of Alan and Trevor and the team getting hold of the early edition, only to find that I was all over them. It would have been embarrassing for them to have to

230

cope with. Niall therefore decided that, on that evening, there would be a 'delivery problem' and the papers wouldn't arrive. I remember Alan complaining bitterly at the incompetence of the BBC at not being able to check the papers.

I had asked my agent, Jane Morgan, to rush down to Victoria Station, one of the best places in London to get the early editions, to take a look at the damage being done to me. She phoned me at about 8.30.

'How bad is it?' I asked.

'Bad,' she replied.

'Page one then, I guess.'

'Yes, and pages two, three, four, and five, and the promise of more to come next week.'

I had been done over good and proper.

Now I had to do the programme. Tricky.

After I'd made it through the broadcast, Niall Sloane brought me the early editions of the Sunday papers he had cunningly concealed from our football experts. They made horrific reading. It was one thing to have been a fool in private. Now I was publicly humiliated. Of course, the details of my relationship with the woman were exaggerated and embellished. 'It says six times a night. I don't even yawn six times a night,' I said to Niall, dredging up a smidgeon of humour from my tortured mind. There was even a picture of me leaving the woman's rented flat on my first ever visit there some months before. How extraordinary that a photographer would just happen to be handy to record the event. It seemed to me that it had been the beginning of what one could be forgiven for thinking might have been an elaborate newspaper sting.

I drove home in a daze and told Rose to get her things together. We would try and avoid the press follow-ups by escaping to our house in Sussex. There, we went through what had been written. I told her what was true and what to my mind had been invented.

One of the papers, which had not paid for the story but had taken it from those who had, a common practice in the tabloid business, had the cheek to write their front page as though I had given them an exclusive interview. I had not spoken to the press at all. The two papers that had paid for the story never approached me with their accusations. They simply printed it all from what they had been told by their informant.

Rose and I had a tortured night, neither of us sleeping a wink. Although Rose had known about my unfaithfulness for some weeks, now that it was all laid out in black and white made it even more unbearable for her.

Bryony Hill, Jimmy's wife, a dear and faithful friend, came to her rescue. Rose drove off to the Hill household for some comfort.

I stayed alone, contemplating the probable break-up of a relationship I had put in deep jeopardy.

A couple of hours went by before I heard the sound of tyres on the gravel drive. To my surprise it wasn't the press, but Jimmy Hill. He had come to get me. 'Not a morning to be alone,' he said. I found out later that, just as we sped away, round the corner came a press squad looking for me. It was a narrow and timely escape.

He took me off to his house in the country, where I met up with Rose again. Her tear-stained face told the story. Bryony welcomed me. Neither she nor Jimmy was making any judgements about me. They both put a metaphorical arm around us and took care of us. Once again we were in receipt of true friendship. I hardly deserved it.

I had another programme to do on the Tuesday night, a live UEFA cup tie. Once again Niall Sloane insisted I do the show, and I had no hesitation in agreeing to fulfil my obligation.

In the meantime, on returning to London, my home was besieged by the press. At one time, there were probably as many as a dozen reporters and at least as many cameramen outside my door. Most of them were ringing the doorbell at all times of the day or night. We felt under siege. When Rose had to go out to the shops, I told her to look her best and force a smile. 'Don't see yourself in tomorrow's papers as the downtrodden victim of all this,' I said. 'That's the picture they want.' She bravely put her war paint on and sailed off in her car, beaming and waving like she hadn't a care in the world. It was a performance that brought a tear to my eye. How could I have hurt this lovely woman so much?

I took our West Highland White Terrier, Daisy, for a walk. Of course we got photographed. 'One female who won't say a bad word about Des Lynam,' said one of the captions the day after. There was a picture of Rose looking absolutely beautiful.

I made no comment to anyone, only saying that I would not discuss what should have been my private life. However, I'd referred the matter to my lawyers, who advised that it would be better to issue some kind of statement to the press in order to help bring the matter to a close. In the end, I was simply quoted as saying that I had made an error of judgement in my private life and was sorry about it, or something equally bland.

On a chat show recorded in Dublin a few weeks later, I said what I really thought. I told the presenter, Ally McCoist, that 'any woman who kisses and tells for money is just a hooker who defers payment'. The comment brought the house down. I received prolonged applause. I had joked to Ally that the papers knew I was out on the town with somebody during the World Cup in France: 'I thought, damn, Jimmy Hill has spilt the beans on us.'

As it turned out, the woman who had sold her story became the subject of press speculation the week after her exposure of me. *The Mail on Sunday* had investigated her and alleged that she had been married three, if not four, times, was several years older than she claimed and had falsified her educational background.

I was contacted by the daughters of an elderly man who had fallen for this woman's charms, had married her late in life, and had left her all his money after a late change in his will.

All this just underlines what an extraordinary lack of judgement I displayed in getting involved with this kind of person in the first place. She flattered me. I fell for it. Stupid fool.

On the Tuesday programme I had to do while the press activity was raging around me, Martin O'Neill, the highly successful football manager, was a guest. His Leicester team had played on the Sunday. 'As you can imagine, I needed my Sunday spiced up, so I watched your match with Wimbledon,' I said to him.

Martin knew where I was coming from and gave me a wry smile. The *Independent on Sunday* the following week wrote about my remark and self-deprecation. 'Never underestimate Des Lynam,' said their reviewer. Nice of him at the time, but it did little to alleviate the pain I was in and, more importantly, the suffering experienced by Rose. Could we survive?

As it turned out, there were no further revelations the following Sunday. Little had been left to people's imagination by the first articles; but of course every columnist on every paper had their opinion about my behaviour, the woman's behaviour, how I had dealt with it, and whether or not it would be damaging to me.

Some, mostly the females, were pretty critical in their views. Many saw it as a bit of a joke. Will Carling, not to mention Bill Clinton, were having their own troubles at the time, and there were several articles that lumped our respective infidelities together, like it had been some kind of orgy. I bumped into Will shortly after and he thanked me for taking the heat off him for at least one Sunday.

The cartoonists got involved. There was a particularly clever one in the *Daily Express* in which a harassed BBC executive had six phones on the go and was yelling into one of them 'Technically we can't impeach the presenter of *Match of the Day*'.

At home, the days were difficult. Then Rose and I made a resolution. We would either part, which seemed a terrible waste of a loving relationship that had outlasted many of our friends' marriages, or we would endeavour to put the matter behind us and continue to live together.

I had told her that, while she would never be able to forget the horrors of being paraded as a victim in the national press, if she was going to let it come between us on a day-to-day basis, if the relationship was now to become a recriminatory one, then it would be better to end it and go our separate ways. Rose decided that we would start afresh. We have never regretted that decision.

We received numerous letters and calls from many friends, and one or two famous names, wishing us well. It was truly heartening.

Not long after the debacle, we decided to take a few days' break in Rome, just to enjoy that historic city and its restaurants, and for Rose to do some shopping. While we were there, sitting at an outside table having some lunch, I spotted a man placing his jacket over an elderly lady's handbag. He was clearly attempting to steal from it. Without thinking of the consequences, I got up and grabbed him and he pulled a knife on me. Thankfully, he didn't use it but scrambled away. I fully expected him to be waiting round the corner with his pals, and we stayed on in the restaurant for rather longer than we needed. I received thanks from the lady in question after it was explained to her what I had done, and nothing further happened.

But of course, as Oscar Wilde wrote, no good turn goes unpunished, and once again the tabloid press, this time the *Sunday People*, had me on the front pages. They had missed my 'thief-collaring' but just happened to have a photographer around at other moments during our break.

I was front page again. Above a picture of me and Rose looking thoughtful, was the banner headline 'Forgive Me'. Underneath it said 'Cheat Lynam Takes his Missus to Vatican to Repent his Sins'. It was a picture exclusive by one Jason Fraser, top honcho in the grubby little business of spying on people in public places.

We had been followed everywhere. There were pictures of me 'gazing mournfully into space simply lost in thought'. Actually I was sitting in the sun, bored rigid, as Rose was trying on dresses in a clothes shop. They got some tin-pot psychologist to say there were tell-tale signs of a 'broken man'. Of course, the photos were carefully chosen to back up the story. They could have had plenty of us in fits of laughter, but of course those were not quite what they were looking for.

'Onlookers' were quoted – i.e. the hack who was following us – 'that we were miserable'. We most certainly were not. We had a super time together, forgetting our recent woes completely.

According to the paper, I went to the Vatican for forgiveness and lit a candle. That is what I have done on every visit there. That is what Catholics do. It was tasteless garbage. But then I had brought it all upon myself.

26

UNDIPLOMATIC SERVICE

After the World Cup in France, the BBC began receiving requests for my reading of 'If'. And so the music department decided to ask me to make a recording of it for sale. But as single records of poetry are rare, it was suggested I record a poetry 'album'. This came as a big surprise to me. I had thought that this was really the territory of actors, not humble sports hacks.

The producer involved, Mike Cobb, had asked me if I was a poetry fan and I had told him that I had no knowledge of the Romantic poets but that I liked the works of Kipling, John Betjeman, and particularly W. H. Auden. Together we selected a number of poems for me to read. We even included one I had written myself called 'Silly Isles' about the Falklands war. The record sold well at Christmas time and at one stage was in the top forty album sales. I was now getting reviews in the papers, not for my sports broadcasting, but for my poetry recording. One critic, however, thought there were too many melancholy pieces, but my view was that poetry should be thought-provoking. I wasn't trying to amuse people with my offerings.

238

While we were in France, the British Ambassador kindly invited members of the BBC Television team to the embassy in the rue de Faubourg St Honoré for lunch. This was indeed a thrill. The building was originally bought by the first ambassador to France, the Duke of Wellington. Its magnificent furnishings had been sent to the Loire Valley for protection during the German occupation of Paris during the Second World War, along with the stock from its wine cellar. For many years they had both been back in their rightful place, in all their glorious opulence. It was on the front steps of the building that Margaret Thatcher had told a startled John Sergeant, the BBC's then political correspondent, that she was in fact standing down as Prime Minister.

The ambassador, Michael (later Sir Michael) Jay, had to cope with that plus the death of Princess Diana, which also happened on his patch. I was lucky enough to have encountered the Princess twice. On the first occasion I was lunching in the well-known London restaurant San Lorenzo with three representatives of a company who wanted me to become involved as an ambassador for their products. In walked Diana and strode on those marvellous legs towards our table. 'And how are you today, Mr Lynam?' she enquired. I nearly fell off the chair before stuttering, 'Very well, thank you, Ma'am.' I had never met her before. My stock with my companions rocketed. A while later I was in The Ivy, where Diana was dining with the Canadian musician Bryan Adams, *à deux*. They arrived and left separately, of course. This time I just got a nod.

Michael Jay had been a busy man in recent years. But he was a most pleasant individual and over lunch Jimmy Hill and I mentioned that, while in Paris, we had managed to play a couple of games of tennis. Mr Jay turned out to be a keen player himself and invited Jimmy and me, along with our producer Paul McNamara, to join him for a game of doubles on the embassy's pristine grass court. We turned up a few days later, having persuaded Macca to go out and buy some 'whites'. 'You can't play tennis at the British Embassy in that multi-coloured rubbish you normally wear,' I'd told him. We tossed up for teams: Jimmy and I would face Mr Jay and his new partner, Paul.

The match was going along nicely, pretty evenly poised, with the Ambassador proving to be no mean player. Then it was Paul to serve. He hit his hardest one of the day; not quite Andy Roddick pace, but hellish fast. Unfortunately it did not go over the net, or indeed into the net. It hit Her Majesty's Ambassador, and 35th successor to the Iron Duke, fully in the nape of the neck and actually forced him to fall flat on his face. We rushed to his aid, but, stoic diplomat that he was, Mr Jay brushed himself down and quickly recovered his composure. 'No problem. It can happen to anyone,' he said. What he was actually thinking was consuming McNamara with embarrassment. But now there was still the second serve remaining. I was giving Macca the arched eyebrow from the other end of the court. He popped the ball just over the net with the pace of a balloon filled with water and Jimmy hammered it down the line. 'Wouldn't have minded being hit by that serve,' said Mr Jay. Macca never quite fully recovered. 'The Duke of Wellington would have had you shot,' I offered.

27

A BRIEFCASE FULL OF MONEY

I had found presenting the Wimbledon Championships of 1999 a bit of a slog.

If you have a proper job you are probably thinking this is baloney. What could be easier and more fun than sitting in a privileged position linking in and out of tennis matches and interviewing the stars? Put like that, it does seem a piece of cake; but the job is actually rather more difficult than it may appear. If you thought I made it look simple –and my successor, the delightful Sue Barker, certainly does – then that is a compliment to us.

First of all there is a fair bit of preparation for the day ahead. Then, at about 9 a.m., in conjunction with the programme editor, the presenter will normally write the opening to two programmes, one for the start of the day on BBC2 and then for the BBC1 programme that begins a couple of hours later. Autocue is not used, so it is a matter of knowing your lines and adapting to the visual images that are shown to highlight what is to come. After that, the day is largely off the cuff, depending on the length or state of matches, and of course the vagaries of the British summer.

There was one added complication that year. BBC Choice, one of the digital channels run by the Corporation, also had rights to show some tennis, which meant that the presenter could find himself broadcasting on three separate outlets during the day. I had been less than happy with this additional burden, and said so. Who in their right mind would be watching a third-choice match on a channel where the audience figure was virtually unrecordable? The days were busy enough. They were just using an experienced broadcaster for free. Why didn't they get one of their children's broadcasters to record a couple of links for them? Anyway, having made my feelings clear, I still found myself with an increased workload. The presenter can be sitting in the same position for up to ten hours a day at Wimbledon. Commentators on tennis or golf usually get a break. The poor old presenter usually has to remain *in situ* all the time. Sometimes you even have to scurry for a comfort break. On many occasions I'd been hurried through my personal toilet because of a match ending abruptly, or the onset of a quick shower. If the sound engineer kept your personal 'mike' open, they could probably hear what you were up to anyway. Horrible thought for both parties.

In my experience, the Wimbledon Championships is the only major event in British television where play is broadcast on two – and for the first time that year, on three – separate channels at the same time. In golf or cricket on the BBC, for example, the coverage might change channels from time to time, but is never broadcast simultaneously on more than one. Wimbledon is the showpiece of BBC Sport and the hours given to it are extensive. Broadcasting on more than one channel at the same time demands the utmost concentration for the editor and the director – the experienced Martin Hopkins was a master of the technique – and the presenter had to remember what he had said on any given channel and which match or matches he had been dealing with.

And in 1999 it rained a good deal.

It is on rain days that the presenter really earns his money: linking in and out of recorded tennis, updating the live weather picture, and interviewing players, guests and officials, and all the time aware of the fact that you are disappointing the viewers who want to see some play. There was the famous time when Cliff Richard, a Wimbledon member and keen tennis player, was induced to sing to the assembled throng on Centre Court during a heavy downpour. I had linked over to him: 'With this weather, if he starts with "Summer Holiday", I shall not be best pleased.' He, of course, did not hear my introduction and off he went: 'We're all going on a summer holiday, no more worries …' The production crew fell about.

On another occasion, with the rain pouring down, the programme editor had persuaded me to bring my West Highland White Terrier Daisy into the studio. Apparently it was 'Take Your Dog to Work' day, and we put Daisy on camera. She behaved perfectly, even giving a little yelp to order. 'Des interviews his dog,' said the following day's papers. I received bones and cards from dog lovers for days. Someone even sent in a kennel.

I had not felt particularly well throughout the Championships of 1999. Nothing too specific, just a feeling of fatigue. Towards the end of the fortnight I had even telephoned the editor, Dave Gordon, to warn him that if I did not feel better I might have to have a day off. As it turned out, I kept going.

In my long career, I think I have missed just one programme

through ill health, and that was as a result of food poisoning, which must say something for my constitution. I have, though, done plenty of programmes when feeling below par both before and after the broadcast, whilst enjoying a remarkable temporary recovery when the red light came on. It was like Irene Handl's 'Dr Theatre', or in my case 'Dr Television'. It is almost certainly the adrenaline rush that makes the body and mind put their ills to one side temporarily. For the same reason, you will never hear a live broadcaster suffer from a sneezing fit or hiccups: adrenaline takes care of those little problems as well.

I have always felt that television companies are quite cavalier with broadcasters' health. I must have done thousands of live programmes for which there was no one to take my place if I had suddenly toppled over with some ailment. Luckily it had never happened.

At Wimbledon in 1999, though, the problem would have been taken care of. Sue Barker would have been ready, willing, and able to take over if I had taken to my sick-bed. A year later she would do so for another reason, but neither I nor she had an inkling then that it would happen.

The Championships ended with American victories in the singles. Pete Sampras claimed his sixth title – he would win one more – and Lindsay Davenport took the ladies' championship. Tim Henman had taken us through one of his emotional rollercoaster rides to the semis and given Sampras a mighty match before going out to probably the best ever exponent of grass-court tennis.

I took myself off to my little house in Sussex for a few days before going on holiday. I had been looking forward to playing a spot of golf or tennis. Unfortunately, on the Monday after Wimbledon I had been walking down a street in London when a person called out to me just to say hello. As I turned to acknowledge him, I tripped over the pavement and went down like a sack of coal. Had I had a few drinks I would probably have fallen better. But to save myself, my left hand went out and took all my weight.

You know what it's like when you do something like that. You get up quickly, hoping that no one has seen your stupidity. But as I did so, I felt a shooting pain in my hand. Subsequently I found I had broken a small bone. Result: hand in plaster for a few weeks. No tennis. No golf.

I was feeling somewhat low when I received a call from my agent to say that Brian Barwick, my old friend and colleague at the BBC who had left the previous year to take over as Controller of Sport at ITV, had been in touch with her saying he wanted to have a meeting with me.

'What on earth about? I asked Jane.

'He won't tell me' she replied, 'but he wants to talk to you along with his boss David Liddiment, the Controller of Programmes over there.'

I knew Liddiment as well. He was also ex-BBC and his department had supervised *How Do They Do That?* which I'd presented.

'Can you come up to London in the next few days to meet them?'

'Look,' I said. 'I can't imagine what they want. I'm knackered at the moment. My hand is hurting like hell. There is no way they have got anything for me at ITV. If they think it's important get them to come down here.'

A couple of days later a large car pulled up outside my house. Out of it stepped Liddiment and Barwick, duly suited and booted. They were both carrying briefcases. I greeted them, remarking, 'I hope those cases are full of money.' Liddiment replied. 'It's funny you should say that.'

They beat about the bush for a while as a neighbour was present who, not realising that we were about to conduct a business meeting, duly hung on, enjoying Barwick's wit. Brian has always been one of the funniest people I have known in the business, and he proceeded to tell a story about a recent trip to India. My neighbour had to be removed almost forcibly – he was enjoying himself so much. He had not met people like these two sharpies before.

We eventually got down to it. They wanted me to leave the BBC and come and join them in their adventure of making ITV Sport more authoritative and more appreciated. I was staggered. Barwick came out with a line that resonated with me: 'At the age you now are,' he said, 'you will prolong your career and be much better for being more lightly raced.' I would be fifty-seven in two months' time.

I was listening. The job would entail the presentation of the Champions League and the FA Cup, the two football contracts that ITV had. I would not be involved in the broad range of sport that I enjoyed at the BBC. In fact, the only other contract of note that ITV had on a regular basis was the Formula One motor racing series, not a specific interest of mine anyway. And of course they had a share of the European Championship and World Cup finals, which would also be my responsibility.

It was July. They wanted me to start with them a few weeks later in September for the first Champions League match of the season. I told them that it was impossible – my contract at the BBC had some time left to run. 'That can be overcome,' Barwick said. 'We've taken legal advice on the detail of how it's constructed.'

I was beginning to realise they meant business.

They then shocked me to my boots. The money they were talking about was not ten or twenty per cent, or even fifty per cent more than I was getting. They were offering me a veritable fortune: a huge sum which, they assured me, would be the most lucrative contract for a performer in television at the time. 'Forget Cilla or Parkinson or Barrymore, or indeed anyone else,' said Liddiment.

'We know we have to pay top dollar to get you, and believe me, this is top dollar, but everyone at ITV is up for this. We want you to come.' They also mentioned that included in any contract would be extra payments for one-off shows that may or may not come about.

When they got back into their car and headed to London they left a now very unsettled broadcaster behind. Here was the chance to secure my financial future. Tons of money for about a quarter of the work. No recorded highlights either. All live football to work on. A new start. No more battles to fight on behalf of a BBC whose management seemed to be losing their grip, and even their desire to maintain their sporting presence. It had been stimulating to hear real enthusiasm. I had not heard anybody at the BBC speak in such a positive way for years. Nonetheless, Liddiment and Barwick would have travelled north very unsure of whether their message had got across. I learned later that Brian thought he had probably sold me on the deal; David had been much more circumspect.

I had also raised the subject of Bob Wilson. Bob was the sitting tenant, as it were, of the programmes I was being asked to take over. I had already been Bob's nemesis at least once. When *Match of the Day* had returned to the BBC some years before after a gap, I had been asked to present the show. That had been a big disappointment for Bob. In *Match of the Day*'s previous existence he had been the sidekick to the all-powerful Jimmy Hill and would have expected to succeed him eventually. But he'd been overlooked and had finally found his way to ITV, where he had presided over Euro 96 and the 1998 World Cup in direct opposition to me at the BBC. Bob had never received a very good press professionally, although he was extremely competent and of course had played football at the highest level as Arsenal's goalkeeper in the double-winning side of the early Seventies. As a presenter he was usually described, unfairly in my view, being someone who knows how difficult a job it sometimes is, as predictable or stiff.

We had been colleagues for a long time in the past. We had always got on pretty well and had even socialised once or twice. I had nothing against him and was now extremely concerned that I would be damaging his position, his pride, indeed his life once again. The man had just suffered the awful loss of his beloved daughter, who had put up a brave fight against a rare cancer before finally succumbing; and this was different from the *Match of the Day* situation. Then, I had merely been selected ahead of him and owed him no apology. Now he was the man in position.

I had raised this point with Liddiment and Barwick early in our conversation. They told me it was not a worry. Bob would be looked after. Indeed, he was to be offered a new contract and would continue to do some of the programmes. At the time I took this to be programmes of the same standing. I subsequently learned he would be relegated to highlights shows or programmes on the newly-formed ONdigital, the ill-conceived and in the end disastrous ITV digital channel.

I went to bed that night fantasising about the money but fairly clear in my mind that, despite the attractions, I would stay where I was at the BBC. I would simply cut down my workload, give up the radio show I had been doing on Friday evenings, and consolidate my position. Yes, this approach had simply focused my mind, underlining that I should concentrate on the bigger picture with the Corporation and calm down a bit. Liddiment and Barwick had been thought provoking and had made me a most attractive proposition, but it would be too difficult to make such a dramatic career change. 'Even if you really wanted to,' I kept telling myself, 'you're not brave enough to go through with it.' I didn't think I would have the guts to climb out of my comfort zone.

Before going on a couple of weeks' holiday to Spain, during which time I would have to make my decision, I went to visit my old friend Jimmy Hill.

Jimmy and I had worked on BBC football programmes for some years. I often teased him on air. I once told him at the end of a programme that if he didn't stop talking, the 'Nine o'Clock News would become the Ten o'Clock News'. But Jim was more than capable of giving as good as he got. 'Let them wait,' he said. 'This is important.' I had to scramble off air. Once, I introduced Terry Venables as the man who knows about managing in Europe, Alan Hansen as a man who knows about playing in Europe, and Jimmy Hill as a man who just knows. It was a gentle tease and Jimmy took it in good heart.

Once Jimmy had referred to a time when he was 'playing just a minor role at the BBC'. 'You're still playing a minor role,' I responded and, as ever, Jimmy took it as it was intended. During one Comic Relief he, Alan Hansen and I were involved in a sketch in which we had blown Jimmy up for talking too much. Alan had pressed the button and there was a big puff of smoke and a loud bang. Jimmy was off to make-up to have that 'just blown up' look applied, and the punch-line was that he would still be talking even after the explosion. He actually was, even during the elaborate make-up. He was definitely type-cast. Hansen and I were in stitches.

Jimmy Hill is exactly the same on- and off-screen, but some people successfully conceal their real personalities from the public very well. Bob Monkhouse was one person who, until his latter years, seemed to me to do it the other way round. On television, doing those innumerable game shows, I always thought he came over as a bit too smooth, even smarmy. But when I got to know him, I found Bob to be a most kind, modest and charming man.

I had just read his autobiography, one story in which had made me laugh out loud. It went like this. Bob as a young man was appearing in variety and there was a popular song of the time, the lyric of which, normally went 'A. You're adorable. B. You're so beautiful' and so on. Bob, a good looking guy, had adapted it to himself. 'A. I'm adorable B. I'm so beautiful,' he sang and was about to deliver the next line of the song when a bloke in the second row filled it in for him 'and C you're a c**t!' he called out. Bob never quite recovered from the humiliation that night.

I was walking through the BBC Television Centre reception one day when I spotted Bob, who had his back to me talking to the receptionist. As I went by I sang, 'A. You're adorable ...'

He turned round. 'Des, you read the book!'

I bumped into Bob on a few other occasions. He was always very friendly, and then it came about that we were to work together on a series of shows for a large brewery concern. I was to present the conferences. Bob would be the 'after lunch turn'. I was amazed at how much work he put into it. He researched all the main characters in the company and had a gag to relate to each one. For the boss, he would say 'Bill Bloggs, a difficult man to ignore [pause] ... but well worth the effort'. He always brought the house down. We dined a few times together with our respective ladies and Bob was amazed by my recollections of the great comics of yesteryear whom he knew personally. Bob was a very clever writer and much more than a game-show host, though that is how people mostly remember him. I remember him as a great companion and a genuine guy.

I'd first come across Jimmy Hill years before when he was already a huge name, not just from his television appearances but as a result of his previous career as a footballer and Chairman of the Professional Footballers' Association, when he was largely responsible for getting rid of the maximum wage that had existed in the British game to prevent players switching clubs for more money (imagine that rule applying today). He was also a former football manager who had taken Coventry City from the bottom division of the Football League to the top one. In recent years I had taken over from Jimmy as host of *Match of the Day*, with his blessing. He'd had a wonderful run on the show in its heyday.

The purpose of my visit to his charming home in the Sussex countryside was to hear what he had to say about my dilemma. He'd offered me a very broad pair of shoulders for me to cry on the previous year when my private life had become very public for a while; his common sense and good nature had helped me through a difficult time. Jimmy's television persona is extremely positive. He appears to be a man of little self-doubt with strident opinions, not all of them popular, and this does not make him universally liked. But I have found him to be one of the most generous and warm-hearted people I have ever met. I trust him absolutely, and now I needed his wise counsel again.

I told Jimmy how lucrative the offer from ITV was, without being specific about the money, and the limited amount of work it entailed. He told me I would be demented not to take it.

'The BBC does not work on sentiment,' he said. 'They could easily tire of you in the next year or so. Look after yourself and your well-being.'

Jimmy had left the BBC the previous year after the World Cup in France and had been bitter in the extreme about how the Corporation had simply let him walk away. He had not even received a letter from anyone to say a simple 'Thank you' for the years of service. In my mind I tempered his advice with the knowledge that he held no brief for the Corporation. But I had listened very carefully to what he had to say.

He also felt that BBC Sport was on a downward spiral. Only the previous year, the Corporation had been attacked by a select committee of MPs for being 'lazy and arrogant'. David Faber, a Conservative member, had accused John Birt, the Director General, and Sir Christopher Bland, the Chairman, of 'throwing in the towel' as far as sport was concerned. 'Channel 4 stole the cricket from under your noses,' he said, 'and you have also lost the Cup Final.' I had been quoted by him as saying that the BBC should and could have found the money to keep both if they'd had the desire. He had not quoted me incorrectly.

All this was now swimming around in my mind. 'If they don't care, why should you?' said Jimmy. 'Look after yourself.'

I'd had a bit of a run-in with Bland the previous year when, with what I'd thought was considerable bad timing, he'd written a memo to the sports department in the middle of the Wimbledon

Championships suggesting that they 'needed to develop fresh and compelling coverage better reflecting the needs and wishes of the audience'. Here we were working flat out on a tennis tournament, the television coverage of which was the envy of the broadcasting world. The tone of his letter created much displeasure amongst the ranks. The feeling was he had made us seem like 'second-raters'.

Not for the first time, I told the troops I would respond on their behalf. I wrote as follows.

Dear Sir Christopher,

I and my colleagues in the sports department, having just rejoiced in the renewing of a long-term contract with Wimbledon, were dismayed to read remarks made in the board of governors' assessment that our sports coverage needs to develop 'fresh and compelling coverage' to reflect the needs of audiences and sports authorities.

I can tell you that everywhere I go, viewers constantly tell me that the BBC's coverage of sport is unrivalled. Indeed at this moment we are in a broadcast centre at Wimbledon where other broadcasters compliment our coverage and at times envy it.

We are a highly self-critical bunch and endeavour to review continually our approach and editorial and technical expertise, but in the view of most of my colleagues, and it is certainly mine, the only times we are undermined is when the BBC decides it will not compete financially for contracts or we are damaged by unsympathetic and at times crass scheduling. I could quote a lot of examples.

It would be nice from time to time if we heard a little more positive reaction to our endeavours from within. Heaven knows we have enough critics elsewhere in the media, often with vested interests.

Sir Christopher wrote back saying that the viewers who constantly told me that the BBC's coverage of sport was unrivalled were entirely wrong. He pointed out that the BBC had financially powerful rivals who were increasingly creative and that to see them off, the BBC would not only have to match their money but better their creativity.

But it had not been so much the content of Bland's original missive that had annoyed those of us at the coal face so much: it had been the timing of it.

The day after my meeting with Jimmy, we shot off to southern Spain, renting a villa with our friends, including Phil and Mary King. Phil and I had had a few scrapes round the world, following Muhammad Ali in particular. He was and is one of my closest friends. I was best man when he married Mary (second time round for both of them), and in my speech I'd told the guests that I was well equipped for the job, having lived with both the bride and the groom – they'd both shared a flat with me in their time. Phil had gone on to be a programme editor for Thames Television and ITV Sport but when Thames lost their franchise to Carlton Television, for no good reason that any impartial observer in the broadcasting business could work out at the time, he had been out on his ear. But now he was back in business with an independent production company. Phil laughs better than anyone I know. He eats all the wrong food, drinks huge amounts of red wine, and smokes forty a day; but he continues to enjoy rude good health – and I pray it will long continue. He helped me through one of my lowest periods, as I have already described; he's a true friend in need, and excellent company on holiday. This would be the fourth year running that we would set out for the Costa del Sol and our resting place in the hills behind the town of San Pedro del Alcantara. Mary had been the long-time senior programme assistant with ITV Sport. And here was the irony. If I were to take up the offer just presented to me, I would be working directly with her. I knew that if I told them about it, they would be all for it. Phil was no great fan of the BBC and Mary, I knew, had always said that she would like to have worked with me. There would be little objectivity in their counsel, and so for two weeks I kept my problem to myself. Up and down the swimming pool I would go, one hand in light plaster from my fall, mulling over the pros and cons of this potential career move.

Brian Barwick had called me once or twice on my mobile phone to underline the seriousness of the offer and why it was perfectly right for me. Towards the end of the fortnight, I was expecting another call from him – he needed to know one way or the other which way my mind was leaning. We arranged a time for the call but, just before it was due, somebody else phoned me. My friends, all having enjoyed a little lunchtime attitude adjuster, decided that now was the time to snatch my phone from me and change the 'dull' ringing tone, to the 'Match of the Day' theme. Knowing that they would instantly recognise Barwick's voice, I had a slight hissy fit about reclaiming the cellphone from them. Des had had a sense of humour failure. They could not understand why I had got so tense over something so trivial. How were they to know?

I had finally come to the conclusion that time was becoming more precious; that I should now consider myself before my so-called status as a BBC stalwart; that I should protect my health more, take some of the heat out of my existence and work less.

During those few heady days of wine and sun on the Costa del Sol, I decided I would accept the ITV offer. I told Barwick, that subject to the contractual complications being sorted out, we would have a final meeting the day after my return; but I was pretty certain in my mind that I would be joining them. Jack Arlidge's words, 'Fortune favours the brave, Des,' which had first spurred me to follow my dream into broadcasting, resonated more now than ever before.

Mary King, or 'Hutch' as she is known, was one of the first people I called after my resignation from the BBC. She could not believe that I had kept the impending deal to myself during our Spanish trip, especially when the wine went down. 'You should be in MI5,' she said.

An hour or so after I telephoned ITV from their managing director's car to tell them that I had resigned from the BBC, Bob Wilson had been called in to an urgent meeting with Barwick and Jeff Farmer, the ITV Head of Football Production who was party to my being signed up.

Bob was told about their 'coup', as they saw it, and immediately threw a complete fit. 'You're not signing him ... You must be joking, he's past it,' screamed Bob, who is actually slightly older than me. That was one of the kinder things he said about me. Bob also drew attention to the fact that in his contract he was described as ITV's 'main football presenter'. It came as a shock to Barwick and Farmer: that little detail had for some reason passed them by. Bob could have sued them on that point or resigned. He threatened to do both, vehemently, but in the end did neither. I know in my heart that if the tables had been turned I would not have been able to take what was being done to him. But Bob took advice from his friends in ITV, who placated him and told him there was enough work for everyone and that it would be much more sensible to eat a bit of humble pie and benefit from the new and improved financial deal being offered to him. Bob took this course. I would not have done so. In his autobiography, Bob mentioned that he withdrew the insults he had levelled against me and recorded that, in due course, he'd telephoned me to wish me well. I have no recollection of such a call, but more recently, when I chose not to renew my contract with ITV, Bob wrote me a most charming and flattering letter. I replied to the effect that normal friendship, I supposed, had been resumed.

I felt – and still feel – bad about treading on Bob Wilson's toes, but I had at least made my stipulations about his continued employment. I honestly felt at the time that ITV were actually minded simply to let him go. In broadcasting, there is always someone ready to take your place. When I left the BBC, the pawing of the sand by my potential successors was positively earth shattering.

Bob remained at ITV in a secondary role for four of my five years there. But our paths rarely crossed. He seemed at no time a happy man; but in the long run the death of his lovely daughter, not to mention a couple of hip operations he had to undergo, probably had much more to do with his demeanour than my arrival in the hot seat. That, after all, was only television.

28

'USE YOUR SENSE OF HUMOUR'

It was the second of August 1999, my son Patrick's birthday. I called with my best wishes. It would be the only non-stressful activity of the day.

From my agent's office I dialled the familiar number of the BBC and asked to be put through to the office of the Managing Director of Television, Will Wyatt. The telephonist recognised my voice and connected me to his office. The familiar voice of Will's secretary answered. I had spoken to her on many occasions and she greeted me with her usual charm and consideration. After some brief pleasantries – I think she remarked on how much she had enjoyed the Wimbledon coverage – I told her that I needed to come and see Will as soon as possible as a matter of urgency.

The Managing Director himself came on the phone. I repeated that I needed to see him as quickly as possible. I would have been surprised if he had not detected some nervousness in my voice. To my utter surprise he did not ask me what the urgency was all about. He simply said that if I could get to Broadcasting

House for ten o'clock sharp, we could meet. I thanked him and put down the phone. 'That's the easy bit,' I said to Jane.

I subsequently learned that Will had straight away telephoned Bob Shennan, the BBC Head of Sport, to ask him what he thought might be behind my request for an urgent meeting. 'Has he got himself in the tabloids again?' he'd asked, referring to my embarrassment of the previous year. But Shennan had been unable to cast any light on why I was coming to see Wyatt.

At my disposal for the dreaded task ahead was the limousine and driver of Richard Eyre, ITV's Chief Executive. Jane and I clambered in the back and spoke little as we headed for Broadcasting House. Jane stayed in the car while I went through the back door in Portland Place, showed my ID, had a joke with the doormen, and got in the lift to the third floor.

I went through the door of the Managing Director's office. His secretary, to whom I'd spoken earlier, greeted me with a smile. I tried to smile back – she probably saw before her the kind of shaky quivering lip that Herbert Lom had perfected in the Pink Panther films (he was supposed to be mad at the time, mind you).

'Will is just finishing a meeting,' she said. 'He'll be with you in a moment. Tea or coffee?' 'Nothing for me thanks,' I gulped.

The door to Will's inner office opened and out popped a couple of executives I knew to say hello to, which I duly did.

Will invited me in. 'What's the problem? he said.

'Will, we've been friends and colleagues for a long time and you've always treated me fairly. But in the list of most difficult conversations I have had in my life, this is definitely in the top five. I'm quitting the BBC as of now. No turning back. I'll be an ITV person by this afternoon.'

Will staggered back and clutched the desk behind him in the

manner of a silent movie star conveying shock without words. I thought my old friend was about to have a heart attack. I was beginning to realise just what I was letting myself in for.

It was still only five past ten. It was going to be a very long day.

When Will eventually recovered, to find he still had the power of speech, he told me that he could not understand my decision. As I expected, he did not compare ITV Sport favourably with its BBC counterpart. He felt ITV flirted with sports. They had no real commitment.

I emphasised how sorry I was to have to tell him I was leaving and that my decision was irreversible. He told me that it could not have come at a worse time for the BBC and would further dent their reputation. The recent loss of cricket and football contracts had damaged the BBC sports department. He mentioned that the lawyers would have to get involved and it may be that I would find myself on a considerable period of 'gardening leave' before I could take up any new appointment. I knew of course that ITV had taken Counsel's advice on my contractual position and that this would be unlikely, but I did not respond.

Once again I told him that I could not be budged but said I hoped that when the dust settled our friendship would resume. He showed little enthusiasm for that prospect and found it difficult to shake hands as I left his office. I fully understood.

I threw myself into the back of the ITV limousine and could barely speak as Jane asked me how the meeting had gone. 'Done,' I said.

We made haste for the ITV headquarters building at Gray's Inn Road and were driven straight to the underground car park.

Upstairs, Richard Eyre, David Liddiment, Brian Barwick, ITV's lawyer Simon Johnson, and Head of Football Jeff Farmer arrived. We had phoned ahead to say the deed had been done.

There were handshakes and pats on the back all round, but I felt less than self-congratulatory, just anxious about what I had done, the manner of it, and what I was letting myself in for. Now they wanted to sit me down and put me through my paces with the questions I would be likely to face from a hastily arranged press conference at one o'clock. But first, they said, you will no doubt have some calls to make. They gave me an office. First of all I called Bob Shennan, who had already been made aware of the news. The conversation was brief: I thanked him for his kindness and consideration to me during his fairly brief tenure of the job and emphasised, probably sounding rather like a Mafia don, that it was nothing personal, just business. I had a more difficult few moments with Niall Sloane, the charismatic tough Ulsterman who ran the football programmes at the BBC. We had worked together on Euro 96 and the World Cup of 1998. Both series were hugely successful for the BBC, and for me. We had received much critical acclaim and won several broadcasting awards. Niall had made a touching speech on my behalf at one of the BAFTA ceremonies. We were pals. He listened to what I had to say. His sole response was an 'OK mate'. It would be a long time before Niall and I resumed our friendship. In a way it was hugely complimentary that my soon-to-be-former colleagues were taking my departure so hard. If they had been pleased to see the back of me they would have been rather less aggrieved. Then I rang 'Motty', John Motson, the BBC's legendary commentator, with whom I had started in BBC network radio thirty years before. I caught him on his mobile. 'John, I have some news that you had better hear from me first hand. This morning, I resigned from the BBC and am taking up a role as football presenter for ITV.' There was a moment's silence on the other end. Then, 'Oh come on Lyne, this is another one of your dopey jokes,' he said. A few months earlier I had rung Motty at home, pretending to be Ian Wright, the former Arsenal and England footballer, and had him going with the impersonation for a while before I collapsed in laughter. Motty was used to my gags. 'No joke this time, old friend,' I said. 'I'm deadly serious.' I learned later that John immediately ordered his driver to stop at the nearest pub, where he downed a very large gin and tonic.

I spoke to a few other old colleagues and friends and then made myself available to my new associates. They'd worked out ten of the most likely and difficult questions that the press might ask me about my decision.

In truth I could not imagine that a sports hack leaving one organisation for another was a suitable subject for a press conference. I thought the TV columnists might have a few lines about it, and that one or two sports writers would give me a mention. I had that notion completely wrong. As Niall Sloane wrote in his letter to me shortly afterwards, 'I was not surprised at the furore you caused. I felt you always underestimated public and critical perception of yourself.'

As we walked towards the room at ITV where the press conference was being held, Brian Barwick nudged me. 'Listen,' he said. 'When you go in there, make it bright and breezy. Have a smile on your face and use your sense of humour.' For a long time afterwards I reminded Brian about that advice. As we opened the door of the press conference room we were greeted by the television cameras of all the news networks, not to mention a live Sky broadcast. The flashes of a battery of still cameras went off in our faces. There was a stack of reporters with their notebooks ready. I was apparently big news. I was shocked, and somewhat embarrassed. So much for 'bright and breezy'. I managed to compose myself enough to disarm the assembled throng slightly by saying that under no circumstance would I criticise or disparage the BBC, with whom I had enjoyed a long and happy career. That got rid of a good few potentially difficult questions straight away.

I was of course asked about the money. We had rehearsed that one. I told them only that my accountant and the Inland Revenue were party to any details on that score, but I did say that if any one present had changed jobs for a lower salary I would shake their hand. I told them that I was beginning to feel a little stale at the BBC, though that wasn't strictly true; and that I was looking forward to a new challenge, in particular to doing live games as opposed to recorded highlights.

I had often described working for the BBC as a cause rather than a job. Its public service remit had suited me. In sports broadcasting at the BBC, every decision was made on an editorial basis. Would it make a good programme? The potential audience figure was nearly always secondary. Once, when asked by a reporter why I thought the BBC did sport better than ITV, I had replied that the BBC was in the business of broadcasting, ITV was in the business of business. I would in due course find out if that rather flip remark had any real basis in truth.

I still could not believe the furore that my announcement had created. By now I was front page in the London *Evening Standard*, and had been the lead item on the BBC, ITV and Sky news programmes. Newsreaders like Martyn Lewis, Anna Ford and others had swapped channels with limited media attention, but for some reason I was big news. The papers were writing obituary-like notices. Rose had burst into tears reading one of them, a most sympathetic article in the *Sunday Times* written by Bryan Appleyard and entitled 'Des is gone and England with him'. 'Des Lynam', he wrote, 'is taking from the BBC to ITV a character he has perfected, the laconic but indomitable spirit of Middle England.' Moving stuff from Bryan, but rather over the top. I could not believe it. I had been lead item on the news ahead of a train crash in India that had killed hundreds. I later heard that people on holiday abroad had only one topic of conversation for a while: my move from the BBC to ITV. 'Unbelievable' was the common response. I was beginning to disbelieve it myself. Dawn French and Emma Chambers later discussed it in their *Vicar of Dibley* characters, apparently depressed by my decision. What had I done?

A few days after my switch I went to the funeral service for Helen Rollason, my former BBC colleague who had tragically succumbed to bowel cancer in her early forties after a most valiant fight against the disease. I drove to the little church in Essex near her home. It was going to be a difficult day, not only because of the emotion of the occasion; I would also have to face a host of BBC characters who had been colleagues until a couple of days before, often of twenty or thirty years' standing. I had been asked to read a psalm at the service and did so from the pulpit, scarcely able to look down at the faces before me. I just about got through it.

Afterwards in the churchyard, no one from the BBC approached me until Dave Gordon, my editor on Olympics and other big events, came and had a word. Dave is a rounded man, perfectly able to put my switch of channels well down the list of importance, bearing in mind why we were assembled. That broke the ice and soon I was in conversation with Brendan Foster and my old boss, Jonathan Martin, and Stuart Storey. We sloped off to the pub with one or two others and talked, mercifully not about me, but about Helen and her bravery.

Helen, a former teacher, had become a freelance broadcaster in the Eighties with ITV and had covered the Seoul Olympics for them as a reporter. She had done a good job. Jonathan Martin had been particularly impressed by her and had subsequently made her an offer to switch sides. She became a presenter but had a torrid time while covering Wimbledon in 1990, when she had found it all too difficult and had one or two embarrassing moments. I had missed those Championships because I was presenting the football World Cup.

She had asked me afterwards what she should do. I would have been sympathetic anyway but I was more understanding that year because I had made that almighty cock-up at the start of one of our broadcasts from Italy when I had completely 'dried up' in front of camera. Although I'd 'got straight back on the bicycle' for the remaining programmes of that World Cup, even receiving some excellent write-ups, my confidence had been severely shaken.

I told Helen, 'Look, your hiccups were positively minor compared to my catastrophe. If I can try to forget it and move on, you certainly should.' I know it boosted her confidence at the time. She pressed on with her career but always seemed a little shy on screen, which I found rather attractive. but she continued to have her critics within the BBC sports department.

After Helen had been diagnosed with cancer though, her diffi-dence seemed to disappear and she became quite tigerish in her battle against the illness. She started raising funds for her cancer charity, which is still going strong to this day, and continued to work on television, often wearing a wig to cover her hair loss from the harsh chemotherapy she had to endure. I was in total admiration of her courage. She behaved in the way that most of us would aspire to when the chips are down,

265

though I for one would struggle to show her kind of strength in adversity.

During Helen's illness we would occasionally lunch together at one or other smart restaurant in London. Because of her condition she was unable to take any alcohol, so I would join her on the mineral water and we would laugh and gossip and rumour monger, as BBC colleagues will do, becoming high as kites in the process. 'I'm going to give up drinking bloody expensive wine,' I said, 'I obviously don't need it.'

Round about that time I had made one of my occasional forays into the world of racehorse owning. John Motson, Judith Hann, the presenter of *Tomorrow's World*, myself and one or two others had bought a young gelding with visions of it one day becoming a 'Grand National' horse. John and I had wanted to call it 'Angus McKay', after our legendary first boss in BBC Radio. This did not appeal to our fellow owners so we decided to compromise with 'Out of the Blue', the signature tune of Angus' programme, *Sports Report*. Unfortunately this name had already been taken and we ended up for some reason with 'Out of the Deep'. The horse turned out to be some way short of a Grand National type. In fact it was a sickly animal. If it didn't have toothache it had a back spasm and spent most of its time under veterinary care, despite the good intentions of trainer Jim Old. 'Out of the Deep' raced only once and clearly did not take to the experience; but while our hopes were still high for the animal, we would occasionally drift down to the stables in Wiltshire to see the beast, who was a bit on the bad tempered side – temperament without talent, that unfortunate combination.

It was while at the stables that I was reminded of something Jenny Pitman, the famous Grand National-winning trainer and my sparring partner at several Grand National broadcasts, had

266

once told me. 'Horses,' she'd said, 'should be put on the National Health. You should see what good they do for the spirits of some sick people who visit our stables.'

Helen had often asked about the horse, so I put a proposition to my co-owners of 'Deep'. Could we make her an honorary owner and bring her down to the stables to see the horse? There was unanimous agreement, so I rang Helen the following day. 'Congratulations,' I said. 'You've become the joint owner of a pretty useless racehorse.' 'Oh, I can't really afford it,' she replied. 'Sorry, I forgot the word "honorary",' I said. 'The gang would just like you to be included and if you can make it, we're off to see the horse next week.'

Helen came down to the stables with us and there was an immediate rapport between her and this normally grumpy animal, who behaved impeccably with her. As usual it bared its teeth to the rest of us. Horse sense, I suppose.

Afterwards we adjourned to a local inn, where we lunched. Helen was beaming and seemed entirely happy, her problem put to one side for a few glorious hours. There was one moment when I caught her with her mouth full. 'Christ,' I said, 'you're eating for bloody England, you are.'

Half the food sprayed out as she and we wept with laughter. Not too long after that happy day, Helen's condition deteriorated, despite the efforts of her doctors, who had grown to love this gutsy girl, and she died.

On the day I received the news I took a lone walk along the sands near my home in Sussex. The waves were crashing in, and the skies were black and thunderous. And I was raging too; at the injustice of Helen's untimely death. Anyone who saw me would have seen me sobbing uncontrollably. I didn't give a damn. I was mourning my friend.

29

HELEN AND JILL

Helen's was not the only memorial service I went to in the late summer of 1999. In September there was a most moving thanksgiving service for the life of Jill Dando, who had been murdered on her own doorstep in April of that year. The event had shocked the nation.

Jill had been the most loved female on British television and to this day one can scarcely believe she met her death in such a violent way. Jill, like me, had begun her broadcasting career in local radio. We had never worked together at the BBC but had done a couple of 'earners' together elsewhere. We were friends.

The previous summer we had been invited, along with Carol Vorderman, to a meeting with Jaguar cars at Le Manoir aux Quat'Saisons, the famous restaurant by the Thames in Oxfordshire. Jill had called for me – she'd decided to drive because she had a programme in the evening and could not have a drink. She pulled up outside my house in a cream suit, silk scarf, *à la* Grace Kelly, looking stunning. She was so happy, having recently met Alan Farthing, the charming doctor whom she was planning to marry. I hopped into her convertible BMW and was driven down the motorway in fine style. The white van brigade gave us plenty of attention, and I guess we probably started a few rumours on the way. We had both just been voted the two people the nation would most like as next door neighbours. 'Not if we held one of our parties,' said Jill. We laughed all the way.

The news of her death and the manner of it will live with me forever. I had been getting out of my car at Wimbledon, where I was about to rehearse a presentation to the All England Club for the renewal of the Corporation's broadcasting contract with them. I was in one of my grumpy moods. I thought the whole procedure entirely superfluous. There were no serious rivals for the contract, and the Club knew exactly what they could expect from the BBC in terms of expertise. What they were really interested in was the money involved, but their media advisers had insisted on putting us through this charade.

One of the engineering riggers came up to me.

'Have you heard about that Jill Dando? he asked. I thought he was about to tell me a joke.

'What about her?' I replied.

'She's been knifed,' he said.

'You're joking. She's OK, isn't she?'

'No. Dead, I believe.'

I rushed inside to meet with my colleagues. They had all just heard the news too. There was utter shock and disbelief. Soon we learnt that the manner of Jill's horrible killing had not been by knife, but that she'd been shot.

We staggered through the rehearsal for the following day's presentation. To say we did it half-heartedly would be an utter exaggeration of our enthusiasm. I thought that with any decency the BBC and the All England Club would have called the whole thing off.

In the late afternoon I received a phone call from Jane Lush, a BBC executive and former producer who had worked closely with Jill and who had also been a personal friend.

'We are mounting a tribute programme to Jill this evening,' she said. 'I've spoken to both the Director General and the Managing Director and they both agree with me that you should front it.' I was surprised to be asked but of course I immediately agreed to do it, if that was what the Corporation wanted. I sped off to Television Centre in Wood Lane where Jane and her staff, many still in tears, were waiting for me. We began to look through the clips of dear Jill at her most sparkling. It was surreal. She had only died a few hours before and the circumstances of her killing were not yet totally clear. Now I was struggling to retain my composure too. With Jane's help I wrote what I hoped would be an appropriate script, underlining both the tragedy and the affection in which she was held, a difficult balance.

Then, extraordinarily, with air time approaching, the computer ate the script. We could not retrieve, it whatever we did. They managed to find a manual typewriter and I was about to start all over again when a rather lethargic computer buff came to our rescue and rediscovered the words just in time.

I am immensely proud of the programme that went out, but I would have given anything for it never to have been necessary.

It was a long time before the police found someone to charge with Jill's murder but eventually Barry George was duly convicted. Later he appealed against the conviction but it was upheld.

The more I read about Barry George, the more he seemed to me to be the local loser; yet the manner of Jill's murder was highly professional. I cannot tie the two things together, but of course the police, a jury, and the Court of Appeal were satisfied they had the right man.

There were rumours that Jill might have been killed by a Serbian gang unhappy with her appeal on television for Kosovan refugees during the Balkan troubles. Critics of that theory say the executioners would have claimed the hit, which would be true if it had been organised; but what if an individual, who might have lost a loved one in that conflict, was taking a very personal revenge? It seemed to be a military-style killing, by someone who really knew what they were doing.

Not long before the murder, the Belgrade Television Centre had been hit by Allied bombing, an act outrageously defended as a legitimate target by the British government. Secretaries, make-up girls, as well as broadcasters, had been killed in the bombing. Imagine that happening here. Did somebody take personal revenge on poor innocent Jill, or did Barry George really commit the crime? The jury in my mind is still out.

Oh, by the way. Jill did the Kosovan appeal after I had been asked to. I turned it down.

Jane Lush wrote me a charming note after the programme. But during the memorial service for Jill, some of my now ex-BBC colleagues were still giving me the cold shoulder following my resignation. Matthew Bannister, rising high in the Corporation at the time, who had been an outside tip to become the new Director General, turned to me just before the proceedings began. 'That's the last time I take you fucking racing,' he whispered. I had been his guest at Royal Ascot in the summer.

At least he spoke to me.

Soon I got into my ITV stride and after the first programme at Chelsea was out of the way, began to feel more comfortable

271

with my decision, and was generally made very welcome by my new colleagues.

There were a couple of nice surprises. ITV were paying for my car and there was medical insurance, benefits never made available to performers at the BBC. Of course I was 'on the road' for the programmes that I presented. I rarely went to the office and more or less did my preparation and script writing from home. I had not exactly been a five-day week man at the BBC, except when big events came round, but I missed having an office and a secretary to do my mail. I was missing the stout services of Karen Williamson, who had looked after me at the BBC, and came to rely more on Jane Morgan's office to deal with my day-to-day business.

Of all the people at ITV that I worked with, the coolest towards me was Ron Atkinson. We'd had a minor spat some years before about something I'd said, which I had intended as a joke, but about which he had taken offence. Maybe there was a little hangover from it. Also, he had been a pal of Bob Wilson and probably felt defensive on his behalf. I didn't blame him. But neither did I especially court his approval. Not my style. I was actually an admirer of the man as a football manager and now broadcaster. His 'Ronglish' language, as it became known, was not to everyone's taste or understanding, but he certainly knew the game and read it better than any other co-commentator in the business.

In due course we became friends and much later I would influence a hugely successful change of direction for him before his world caved in.

30

SATURDAY NIGHTS AGAIN

It has quite often been written in the press that I left the BBC to do its replacement programme, *The Premiership*. This is not the case. When I joined ITV in the summer of 1999 it was to present live football, not highlights. At that time ITV had no ambition to compete with the BBC for the Saturday night football show. I was hired to present the FA Cup and the Champions League matches. This involved just twenty-three shows, plus any Cup replays, and of course in addition there would be the major finals of the World Cup and European Championship every two years. It was hardly a demanding schedule and the rate of pay per programme was huge, almost embarrassing, but I hadn't asked for it. The offer had come to me. I hadn't negotiated a penny more than ITV had decided to pay me.

Few people at ITV were party to the actual amount I was being paid, and I dare say there would have been a great deal of resentment had it become common knowledge. The figure remained the guesswork of the tabloid press.

Although I had joined ITV in early August, my first programme for them was not until the middle of September, a Champions League match between Chelsea and AC Milan at Stamford Bridge.

On the night, I thought I might have been a little nervous, but I was working with my old sparring partner Terry Venables and felt very comfortable. People kept wishing me good luck as though it was my first ever television broadcast. I had a good few thousand of those behind me. All that had changed was the channel and the rate for the job. And of course I now had to get in and out of the adverts.

I had always been critical of commercial television presenters 'welcoming me back' after a break. It was they who had been away, not me. I thought the phrase entirely superfluous. And if a presenter tells me 'Don't go away' as they lead to a break, I usually want to kick the screen in. It is patronising, and even bad manners in my view. I resolved I would ignore the adverts in the sense that I would not especially mention the breaks at all. Just carry on around them, so to speak. No one at ITV carped about this, and they let me do it my way.

There was obviously less time to chat on screen than there had been in a similar programme at the BBC – one journalist even worked out how much I was actually being paid per minute. He had guessed my salary though and was consequently way out.

I was now a fully fledged ITV presenter. The programme went well, although the teams could not produce a goal for us on the night.

On another Champions League evening, before one of our programmes from Old Trafford, Sven Goran Eriksson, newly appointed as England manager, arrived for an interview live on the show. He was early and we sat together for fully half an hour before the start of the programme.

He is a difficult man to make small talk with but for some reason I mentioned the British tabloid press and warned him that unlike Italy, where he had been a club manager and where the press will slaughter you for losing a match, in Britain they are more interested in your private life. 'Watch out for that,' I said.

Recently Sven did a radio interview with me and I reminded him of the conversation. 'You were right,' he said.

At the end of my first season at ITV, I presented my four-teenth FA Cup Final from Wembley. My first had been the 1985 match between Manchester United and Everton for the BBC. The Corporation had lost the contract to cover the national event to my current employers a couple of seasons before. Now it was my pleasure once again to play host to the nation for what had formerly been the biggest day in the football calendar but which was now a lesser event in the public's consciousness, due, of course, to the amount of live football available to view-ers. It no longer had quite that special appeal and the 2000 Final between Chelsea and Aston Villa did little to further the cause. Between them they produced a monotonous spectacle that would have bored the pants off even the most ardent supporter. We did our best to enliven the broadcast with the build-up, only for the match to let us down. It had happened quite often over the years. One of our guests on this day was the violinist Nigel Kennedy, an ardent Villa fan, who waltzed into the studio late but did a charismatic interview and displayed a little of his musical genius with a touch of Vivaldi as well.

Then it was off to Belgium to shoot some trailers for the forthcoming Euro 2000 Championship. In Brussels I found a very grumpy looking, rather overweight policewoman whom I persuaded to be filmed. In one of the trailers I was seen to say 'Everyone here is brimming with excitement at the fabulous

275

event to come, aren't you?' Camera cut to face of my stooge, looking suitably pissed off. It worked like a dream. She didn't speak a word of English. I hope she never saw the end product of her television debut. But it was very funny.

We had a good squad of people covering the Championship itself. Venables and McCoist were old friends from the BBC, as was Clive Tyldesley, who had become ITV's number one commentator after the retirement of the veteran Brian Moore.

As in all these major football championships there was an opening ceremony, which on this occasion I had volunteered to voice-over. I had always thought the commentary on these often over–produced extravaganzas had been far too worthy. This one turned out to be a very arty affair, which had little to do with the substance of the forthcoming event; you know, men on stilts, boys in tights flying through the air on trapezes, all supposed to mean something but nobody knowing quite what, except for the balletomaniac whose concept it was. It was sort of Cirque du Soleil without the talent. I decided to take the piss out of it all, a bit like Wogan does with the Eurovision Song Contest. I don't think my bosses were entirely convinced by, or even understood my irony, but afterwards, the *Guardian* loved it.

ITV, as usual at these events, was sharing coverage with the BBC, but we had England's first match against Portugal. England, largely outplayed, extraordinarily went two goals up. Then Figo really got into his stride and England were beaten 3–2. David Beckham had to endure some horrific taunting from the England fans that had nothing to do with his performance but were personal slurs about him and his wife. I can still see the anger and frustration on his face as he left the pitch, powerless to defend Victoria's honour.

I was ashamed of some of the hooligans who were following

Even on a tough day, this cartoon made me laugh.

The *Sports Personality* presenters down the years. Barker, Lynam, Dimmock, Carpenter, Rider, Bough and Lineker.

Co-owners of a slow and somewhat temperamental racehorse, Judith Hann, self, John Motson and honorary owner, Helen Rollason.

Launching the 1998 Poppy Appeal with Arsene Wenger and Tony and Cherie Blair at Downing Street.

My 'Danny DeVito' photo.

What have I done –
I've left the Beeb.

With Shearer and Owen before Euro 2000.

Rose and I with the Linekers.

With two lovely 'avengers', Honor Blackman and Joanna Lumley at the BAFTAs in 2000.

With HRH and Gaby Roslin at a Bowel Cancer charity event: 'Prunes every morning does the trick,' he told me.

Laugh till you cry
with McCoist.

With legendary jockey
Frankie Dettori and Jane
Morgan my long-time
agent and friend.

With Mary Nightingale on 'Millionaire': we won £32,000 but they gave us £64,000.

With Ron Atkinson and Terry Venables – my ITV chums.

With Gazza, who always needs an arm around him.

England in Belgium and Holland. Scenes of them being washed down the street by water cannon in the centre of Brussels after terrorising that historic city are difficult to erase from the mind. They were obscene and frightening.

And for England's second match, with Germany, the little town of Charleroi was like a fortress. Barbed wire, armed police everywhere, dog handlers. A veritable war zone. This was supposed to be sport.

We had our lighter moments of course. At one venue, it was so hot in our cramped little makeshift studio that the pundits and I had to be kept cool with ice-packs. They failed to control the body temperature of Mr Venables, who must have lost half a stone during the broadcast. McCoist and I dubbed him the World's Hottest Man.

Belgium and Holland are small countries and we were able to travel on a daily basis to each stadium. For this, ITV provided a luxury coach that became known as the Desmobile. Journeys after the games usually involved a good few glasses of Chablis, hotly contested quizzes, not by any means confined to sport, and plenty of laughter.

Kevin Keegan was the England manager for the Championships and he agreed to give me a one-to-one interview. I travelled to the team headquarters and found him as charming as ever and amazingly honest. Criticisms had been levelled at him for his lack of tactical awareness and I put the point to him. He admitted certain limitations and said that if in the end he wasn't good enough he would quit. Although England failed to qualify from their group, Portugal and Romania got through while Germany, like England, were eliminated, Kevin stayed on in the job for another few months, but the damage had been done and he resigned his position in October 2000.

During one of our broadcasts I created an absolute first. It was the first time the BBC had ever been trailed on ITV.

ITV2 had been in existence for about a couple of years. Broadcasting on it at the time was the height of privacy. It was not readily available to all viewers. To watch it you needed either a satellite dish or to be on a cable network. It was made up mostly of repeats of soaps and had a small budget. But during this Championship, the highlights of some matches would be shown on this channel as well. The phrase ITV2 might have been in the Lynam brain, but the words that came out, referring to a forthcoming attraction, were of course the well-imprinted BBC2.

My studio colleagues and at least seven people in the mobile control room heard this slip-up. Not one of them had the gumption to mention it in my earpiece. Had they done so, I could have made a joke about it and recovered. They left me with egg on my face.

I completed the programme, reasonably pleased with the show, only to be confronted by the ashen faces of Brian Barwick and Jeff Farmer. You would have thought I had defamed the Queen, complete with four letter words.

I was disturbed by my *faux pas* but in the great scheme of things all it did was give a laugh to my ex-BBC colleagues and a line for a couple of the tabloids. Nobody died.

Before we had left for Belgium that summer, I had been part of a team from ITV who went to the Mandarin Oriental Hotel in Knightsbridge to make a presentation to the Football Association for the right to retain the contract to cover the FA Cup. Adam Crozier was the top man at the FA at the time, and ITV were fairly confident that they would retain the rights. However, I felt they would be getting the short end of the deal if the contract was renewed on the same basis as before, which gave Sky, who had the major share of the rights, first choice of FA Cup ties and live coverage of England matches, with ITV getting only the highlights.

While we were in Belgium, ITV learned that the FA were leaning towards a combined BBC/Sky deal which, if it went through, would mean the exclusion of ITV from all worthwhile domestic football, the BBC and Sky already having the Premiership between them.

The powers that be decided to do something about it. David Liddiment somehow found the money to make a shock late bid for the Premiership highlights, for a show that would replace *Match of the Day*. He had always had a fancy for bringing Saturday night football to ITV. The bid was huge: some £180 million for three years, and it was accepted. ITV had lost live coverage of the FA Cup, for which I had specifically joined them to cover, and won the rights for Saturday night highlights, which I had not been disappointed to relinquish. Football on terrestrial television had once again been turned upside down.

Now I had to look pleased about it.

After the details of the bid for football broadcasting rights became common knowledge, all hell broke loose. Greg Dyke, whose record in football negotiations was on the negative side, slammed into ITV for paying an extortionate amount for highlights football. He said he wasn't prepared to pay that kind of money. 'It would be bad business for the licence-fee payer.'

What had actually happened was that Dyke had been beaten to the punch. He had been cocksure that the BBC would retain the contract and nick the FA Cup deal from ITV too. He had been greedy and had not kept his eye entirely on the ball, indeed had underestimated ITV's desire to stay in the domestic game. In the end he would pay a much higher rate per match to conclude the FA Cup contract. How good a deal was that for the licence-fee payer?

Gary Lineker opened one of the BBC's programmes at Euro 2000 like a funeral director, talking about the sad news of the loss of the contract. He made it sound like the loss of a life. Knowing him well, I suspect he was encouraged to toe this party line, but it was a mawkish broadcast. This was an in-house inconvenience, hardly a tragedy. The viewer would have been entirely unmoved. The press, as always, wrote the story on a 'winners and losers' basis. ITV were the winners for a change.

But now I had a decision to make. It wasn't urgent. I would still be out and about for one more season presenting the FA Cup and the Champions League. The new contract would not cut in for over a year.

David Liddiment rang me. 'I know this isn't exactly what you had in mind,' he said. 'But keep a smile on for the press, won't you?' I promised I would. The *Daily Mirror*, who were coming to do an interview with me anyway on the day the news was breaking, got a scoop. 'Des gets his boots back', they head-lined, somewhat embarrassingly.

The morning after the story broke, Alan Hansen, who was staying in a hotel over the road from the ITV base in Brussels, came rushing over to see me. 'The only thing that put a smile on my face last night,' he said, 'was the thought of you having to go back on the Saturday night treadmill.'

'How do you know I'll be on it?' I countered.

'You will,' he said. 'You won't want anyone else elbowing past you.'

On the Sunday, Lineker wrote a piece in the *Sunday Tele-graph*, the body of which was uncontroversial, but it could have been read into the headline that he was criticising me. I had seen it and had not been unduly bothered, but one or two of my colleagues had been offended on my behalf. Friends are always more keen to defend you than you are for yourself. The following day a handwritten note arrived from Gary apologising profusely and underlining that he had the greatest respect for me. He said he had complained bitterly to the sports editor of the paper for the headline over which he had no control. I phoned him and thanked him and told him not to worry about it. Gary and I have always got along well, and still do. When I left the BBC, I opened the door for him and he has taken the opportunity like he took his goals, unhesitatingly.

Occasionally I am asked to say a few words about him. 'He's the luckiest bloke alive,' I say. 'Brilliant footballer, good broadcaster, a multi-millionaire with a beautiful wife, four wonderful kids, single-figure handicap at golf. Thank you, God, for giving him those ears.' It goes down pretty well. When I first joined ITV, a journalist asked me if, bearing in mind all his caps for England, I was worried about competing with Gary Lineker. 'Only if I have to play football against him,' I replied.

I once turned up in one of those Walkers Crisps adverts with Gary, the one where he pinches the crisps from a nun. They did a variation on the theme in which a rather large nun pinches them back off him. On the day of the filming in Regent's Park, Gary and I had got changed in a caravan some distance away from the shoot. Into the back of a limo we got and at a traffic light the driver pulled up next to an elderly cyclist, who looked into the back of the car and saw Gary Lineker. He was delighted. Then he looked across to the figure next to Gary. It was a nun. With a moustache. He nearly fell off his bike.

31

'F*** IT, WE'LL GO AT SEVEN'

While I was doing *Match of the Day* I was always nagging the management at the BBC about the 'on air' time. In the Seventies, when Jimmy Hill was the presenter, the show went out at ten o'clock and commanded audiences of ten million plus. In my time, audiences for football highlights were diminishing. There was plenty of live football on the box as an alternative attraction.

However, I was convinced that, despite the fact the BBC had paid a huge sum for the rights, they were marginalising the product by showing the programme later and later. They were doing the same thing with Barry Norman's film programme. He and his producer finally left for Sky in disgust. That programme, now presented by Jonathan Ross, has become minority viewing. It goes out way past most people's bedtimes.

The 'on air' time for *Match of the Day* was supposed to be 10.30, but almost every week, for one reason or another, I would find myself opening the show at a quarter to eleven or even eleven o'clock. The starting time wasn't so bad. It was the finishing time. I knew the viewing figures were tailing off badly the later we were. Plus my postbag was full of letters from parents who complained that the show was much too late for their children to see. It was decided eventually to produce a Sunday morning repeat for the youngsters, but time and again I complained. In November 1995 I wrote to the Managing Director, Will Wyatt:

Dear Will,

After considerable thought, I felt I had to write to you personally about the scheduling of Match of the Day. Everywhere I go, I am under considerable pressure to defend the BBC's position on sport. 'Sky has it all now' is the common cry, fed of course by the Murdoch press. As you might imagine, I defend well but what consistently undermines our competitive edge is the continued 'marginalisation' of BBC Sport in the eyes of the viewer.

Here we are with an acknowledged excellent product yet time and time again I find I have to defend its 'on air' time. Just when we need all the back-up we can get, I feel we are being let down. At the moment, football nostalgia programmes get a better airing than football of the moment. This is absurd.

What about young viewers? Is it reasonable to expect them to stay up till around about midnight to watch their teams? Their viewing habits are beginning to move away from us.

Even on nights in midweek, when we have international matches to show, we cannot get an 'on air' time before 10.30 p.m.

I have always fought the BBC corner strongly, but it is getting very wearing and my fellow broadcasters feel the same, having not only to take on the competition externally, but continually losing the internal battle as well.

Will wrote back saying that scheduling was a complicated business and earlier did not always mean a better slot on Saturday nights. He sent me a raft of notes from a document called 'The BBC1 Broadcast Analysis', which purported to suggest that the programme was in a good slot. I was not convinced.

I knew also that when the contract came round for renewal, the lateness of the programme and its 'reach' would be levelled against us. I had also heard that if ITV got their hands on the product they would show their version much earlier.

The view at the BBC was that it would be impossible to finish editing the matches down to size and present a stylish pro-gramme in the early evening. There simply wouldn't be enough time to complete the job. And besides, *Match of the Day* had always been on later on Saturday nights.

I suggested to the editor that we attempt a trial 7 o'clock programme. We would write, edit, and do a show at that time, but we would simply record it and put it out to the viewers at our usual late hour. It would be a self-examination to see if it was feasible. If it was, then maybe we might think about mak-ing *Match of the Day* a 7 p.m. programme. We actually man-aged to do the exercise comfortably, but nothing came of it. It just proved that in television, as in other fields, each task takes as long as the time allowed for it.

But now that ITV had their hands on the product, the specu-lation resumed about an early evening show. David Liddiment had always been in favour of it. 'Football and *Blind Date*, a magic early evening popular television formula,' he used to say. 'We'll clean up.'

As the months went by to the first *Premiership* show on ITV, there was much discussion about the idea. I was in favour of it but I knew that it would have to be really early not to get in the way of the 'entertainment' strand on Saturday nights and that it would then have to be repeated later for those who missed the early show. After all, the fans that went to matches might very well not be home in time to see the early version. I was all for a six o'clock start. That way the matches would seem almost live. More people might not actually know the results or might avoid them, making the product that much more exciting.

The later show would have to be late enough not to hit the audience figure for the six o'clock version.

There was a body of opinion at ITV that we would be breaking the mould for highlights football, that it was too risky, and that a 10 p.m. start was ideal. As it turned out, neither of the proposed times was delivered. Sky's contract with the Premiership blocked a six o'clock start and ten o'clock would hamper whatever 'entertainment' ITV usually put out at that time on a Saturday night.

At the ITV summer party in June of 2001, two months before our first show, David Liddiment eased up to me. 'Fuck it,' he said, 'we'll go at 7 p.m.' 'That's very brave,' I said, 'but it's great, mind you. I think it will take a few months but it will eventually catch on.'

Down the years I had always thought that if ITV got hold of a sport, they ended up simply trying too hard to make the coverage 'different'. I constantly reminded my colleagues that *Match of the Day* wasn't broken and they shouldn't try to fix it. I came up against a stone wall here and there. One executive told me, 'What we don't want this to be is *Match of the Day* with adverts.' 'But that is exactly what it is,' I replied. 'Let's not be gimmicky. Let's just get it right and impose our own style as it evolves. What we don't want to do is alienate the millions who've grown up with *Match of the Day* and probably resent its moving until we prove ourselves. We're already testing them with a new time.'

The Premiership began its three-year run on 18 August 2001. I had been contemplating how to open it. Paul McNamara, who had been my director on *Match of the Day*, had joined the ITV team to bring his considerable expertise and know-how to the new show. 'New show, new time, new channel. Old hand [referring to myself]' had been my choice. Macca said: 'Why not add "Better for you, better for me, better for all of us"', referring to the earlier timing. I adapted my opening accordingly. I was to remind him of his contribution for the next three years. It became a standing joke whenever he offered any new idea I didn't fancy. Seven weeks later the memory of that opening actually made me wince.

ITV had come up with a couple of 'ideas' to give *The Premiership* a different look from *Match of the Day*. Both failed miserably.

The first was that one of our pundits, Andy Townsend, the former captain of the Republic of Ireland and a top ex-player, would position himself in a video truck at the ground where the match he was covering had taken place and from there reprise the talking points of the game with his comments. It became known as Andy's 'tactics truck', and it took him a long time to shake off the tag.

The idea had been prompted by Channel 4 using a similar device on Test cricket. The difference, however, was that the cricket was on-going when they used it. We were trying to simulate it after the action had finished. The pundits on the rest of the day's matches were ensconced in the studio with me. It begged the question: what possible benefit did the tactics truck give the programme? On occasions Andy was able to persuade a player to join him to go through the replayed clips, but the idea mostly brought us ridicule, despite Andy's ability.

ITV also came up with the idea of using a device called 'Prozone' (not to be confused with Prozac, I said on one of the programmes) where computerised figures could be put on screen to show formations, number of runs by a player, etc. Now this was a useful tool for coaches on the Mondays after matches, but on Saturday nights it took up valuable time when you could be actually watching more of the play itself. Also Terry Venables, who had to cope with it, was constantly being hustled along and found it difficult to match his thoughts to the diagrams being shown in the time allowed. It was not a device for a quick fix.

There was also a theory, which I found quite ridiculous, that because the audience figure was likely to be higher towards the end of the programme, simply because on past records more people watched after half-past seven than before that time, we should turn accepted news values upside down and not lead the programme with our best match but save it till later in the show. This is like *News at Ten* starting with a 'cat up a tree' story and saving Blair's resignation till the last item. It was madness, but I kept being told that at this time of the evening we were in showbiz rather than news. The idea did not work and made us a laughing stock in the eyes of our critics.

All in all, with these added complications, plus the number of advertisement breaks, the actual amount of football shown in the one-hour programme was very restricted. Remarkably, after the first show, the Sunday tabloids gave us a big tick. The *News of the World*, in particular, was very positive. But by the time the audience figures came out on Monday, they had turned against us, when some of them began working out just how little match action had actually been available to the viewers.

I received a note from David Liddiment. 'Take no notice of the press,' he wrote. 'The show is great, hold your nerve.'

As it turned out. it wasn't my nerve that needed holding. Some of my old BBC colleagues, who quite understandably were perfectly happy for ITV to get a hammering, bet me that the show wouldn't last long in its seven o'clock slot. I took a few of the bets, assuming that, whatever happened, ITV would keep faith for at least a season.

There was a huge lobby from within ITV against the early timing. Cilla Black's *Blind Date*, a waning show, had been moved and, as it turned out, was in due course dumped. But she and her people were making a hell of a fuss that her new timing was damaging her audience figure. Actually when it reverted to its former time, it still died on its arse.

Paul O'Grady, alias Lily Savage, made a loud plea on one of his programmes (actually on ITV) 'to get rid of that bloomin' football. I don't want to watch that on Saturday nights at 7 o'clock,' he screamed. Paul's a talented guy with whom I've worked once or twice, but I thought he was bang out of order. I took umbrage with this fellow ITV performer putting the knife into us on an ITV programme, but my complaints fell on deaf ears.

After six weeks of busting our guts to get the programme out live by seven o'clock I was hauled into the office of David Liddiment. With him was the Controller of Sport, Brian Barwick, the same duo who just over two years previously had pitched their offer to me to join ITV – an offer that had changed my broadcasting life. They both looked pale and fidgety. They made a little small talk for a while, before I got to the point for them. 'I take it you are going to change the time of the programme,' I said. 'That's what this meeting is all about.'

They were having extreme pressure both from within ITV and from the advertisers, who were being charged prime-time rates but were not getting the audience figures they required. They had tried their best to stem the flow of criticism but could not resist the onslaught any longer. I was not unduly shocked by the news – I had heard rumours for a couple of weeks – but decided not to give them an easy ride on this occasion, even though they were, and still are, good friends of mine.

I reminded David about his 'hold your nerve' letter. He seemed embarrassed. The seven o'clock start had been his idea and his decision. Brian Barwick looked shell-shocked. He was very proud of his position as Controller of Sport and had given the department more status and standing than it had previously enjoyed. He knew that the BBC would be laughing up their sleeves at this unusual setback for one of the most bullish people in the business.

I pointed out that we were still in October, still in British Summer Time. The football audiences for Saturday nights never built to their maximum till the clocks went back and winter set in. They were being hasty and lacking courage. 'Keep it going until at least the end of December,' I suggested. 'It's catching on, the audience will build.'

It was all to no avail, the lobby against them was simply too strong. 'It's not too bad for you.' I said. 'You'll make page four of *Broadcast* [the trade magazine]. I'll be on the front page of the tabloids. You watch them find a picture of Des looking depressed.'

'What will you do?' asked Barwick.

'I'll let you know,' I said.

I had already decided, of course. I wasn't going to let internal politics in ITV deprive me of my living. There was not much wrong with the programmes that a little tinkering wouldn't improve. I would stay on. I hadn't become a better or worse broadcaster overnight.

The following day's *Sun* had a banner headline bigger than if Osama Bin Laden had been found running a butcher's shop in Fulham. 'Cilla 1, Des 0', it screamed. In the piece I was described as a 'flop'. Did that hurt? You bet your life it did, and I was angry as well.

On the last seven o'clock show I invited the viewers to join us next week at 'our new improved' time of ten-thirty.

After the change of time, *The Premiership* settled down into what it was always going to be: *Match of the Day* with adverts. Terry Venables was the number one pundit on the show, while Ally McCoist and Andy Townsend were bringing more recent playing experience to the analysis, as was Robbie Earle.

They all put a great deal of work into it and we constantly endeavoured to underline to the viewer something that wasn't patently obvious at first sight. We wanted to set the agenda for those football discussions on Sunday mornings. The easiest thing in the world is to show the goals again and say they were great. I notice since the BBC regained the contract for Saturday night football, the expertise going into the analysis doesn't seem to be as sharp as it used to be. Despite the outstanding talents of Alan Hansen and the thoughtful style of Mark Lawrenson, the programme would appear to be less penetrating and not as crisp as it was on *The Premiership*, or indeed as it was on *Match of the Day* in the past.

As our run of *The Premiership* continued, the newspapers more or less left us alone, a sure sign that we were getting it right; but the tabloids never completely get a negative story out of their systems and from time to time we were dubbed 'ITV's Premiership flop', despite the fact they could level no up-to-date criticism at us. It was annoying, but not life threatening.

While I had not been overly delighted at getting back to a live programme every Saturday night, once I got stuck into it I began to love the Saturday routine all over again. Into the office for midday to catch the early Saturday match – there was invariably one on Sky or pay per view – then a plate of eggs, chips and beans with the boys, to hell with the cholesterol, then settling down in front of eight screens to watch the afternoon's games. There was plenty of betting, much banter, and great laughs as the goals went in all over the place.

Towards the end of the games, the editor would confirm to the commentators down the line who we needed for interviews. Then we would discuss the talking points for the show and the pundits would duly set off for the videotape suites to find visual evidence to underline them.

I would write the links after we had decided the running order for the show. Most of the work was done by about eight o'clock and we would then hang around until it was time to change, ready for the studio rehearsal about half an hour before the 10.30 air time.

We had of course proved that we could get everything ready to go on air at seven o'clock. Why were we hanging around till 10.30 with an off-air time of midnight? We could have been done and dusted by 8.30 if we had recorded the show, allowing us all to get on with our Saturday evenings, but the powers that be were worried that a story might break in the time between recording and broadcast. In all my years of doing football highlights on Saturdays, on both major networks, it had never happened. Managers don't get sacked on Saturday evenings. Club chairmen are usually just sharpening their knives over dinner at that time. If the argument about a story breaking on a Saturday night stood up, then what about the repeat of the programme that went out on Sunday mornings? That was recorded on

Saturdays before the live show. Somehow the argument broke down then. It might have been something to do with the costs of mounting a studio production on Sundays.

The main positive in doing the show live was that you had to be on your toes. Something happens in your brain when you know you can have a second chance by recording, and invariably you need one.

Anyway we all loved doing the programme and it was no hardship.

In December, Terry Venables was asked by the Middlesbrough manager Bryan Robson to give him a helping hand at the club. 'Boro' were struggling at the time. Venables decided that he fancied the idea of helping his old friend and putting his coaching experience on the front line again and he asked for leave of absence from the show.

On a flight to Athens for a Champions League match, I had found myself sitting next to Ron Atkinson and I had casually mentioned to him that I thought he would be excellent on *The Premiership* if an opportunity ever became available. He said he would jump at it. Ron had always been used by ITV as a co-commentator, out of vision. When I heard the Venables news, I went to see Brian Barwick and suggested Ron as Terry's substitute, informing Brian of the conversation I'd had with Ron. In my opinion, having a former manager or coach is an asset to the programme. He can speak from the kind of experience that ex-players, for all their brilliance on the field, cannot. My suggestion was not received with enthusiasm, but Brian put the idea to the programme's editorial team, headed by the excellent Tony Pastor, another ex-BBC man, but they were even less enthusiastic. They thought Ron might be a bit old hat. My view was that he held strong opinions, would not be shy in voicing them, and had great charisma. I won through. Ron joined the team and was a huge success. He remained on the show when Terry, who hadn't got the managerial bug quite out of his system, eventually took the job at Leeds, which ended for him in bitter disappointment.

On the day of another flight to Athens, my morning had begun in a leisurely fashion. I was collected from home at around 10.30 a.m. to make the midday flight to Athens for the following night's Champions League match between Olympiakos and Manchester United.

My old friend and colleague, John Philips, was on the plane. We had worked on two Olympic Games and many other major events together at the BBC, me presenting, him editing. He was one of the best I had ever worked with, but was now freelance and finding himself with ITV to produce a series involving Terry Venables for their digital channel. We had a splendid flight together laughing all the way, recalling old times. How could we know that across the world, much more sinister flights were taking place at exactly the same time?

I always brought just hand luggage on these trips, but it was while waiting for the bags of other members of our group in Athens airport that a Mr Simon Davies, a London-based representative of an American company, approached me. He looked ashen. 'Mr Lynam,' he said, 'Have you heard about New York?' 'No', I replied. 'It's believed terrorists have flown airplanes into the World Trade Centre towers and killed thousands. I have just heard on the phone.'

I could scarcely comprehend what this stranger was telling me, but I could tell from his demeanour that this was deadly serious. I quickly passed the horrific news to my colleagues, one of whom was in the middle of a call home and corroborated the enormity of the tragedy. His wife was distraught having watched live as the second plane hit tower number two of the Centre. It was a picture that would remain indelibly printed in our minds for evermore as later we watched it repeated over and over.

My immediate reaction was that sport now moved into a minor key and that all football matches would be postponed as a mark of respect. To my amazement, UEFA could not get its act together in time and that night's, Tuesday's, games were played, preceded by a minute's silence. I thought this a huge mistake but one or two of my colleagues felt otherwise on the basis that these criminals should not be allowed to disrupt normal life worldwide. My view was that sport is a pastime, an occasion for enjoyment and pleasure. My pleasure could happily take a step back in respect to those who had lost their lives in this most horrifying way. Alex Ferguson, like me, thought the games should be postponed, and in due course the Wednesday night matches were.

The rest of that day was spent in subdued manner. Along with the rest of the world, we could talk of nothing else. Back in our hotel rooms we watched the horrible detail of this apocalypse. We were stunned and moved to tears by the bravery of some of the rescue workers, mostly New York's valiant firefighters. We saw those mind-numbing pictures of people actually jumping from the buildings to their certain death. It was as if the world was coming to an end. President Bush seemed unable to handle the enormity of the tragedy, referring to the perpetrators as 'folks'. 'Folks,' for God's sake! The speech writers had made him a little more articulate by the following day. The man obviously could not think on his feet.

Then, I suddenly realised that the wife of one of my closest friends, Malcolm McDonald, had flown to New York a couple of days before for a short break. It was her first trip to the US and I knew she had planned to visit the World Trade Centre. I hurriedly called Malcolm. Luckily, she had managed to phone him just before all the lines were cut. She was safe but in shock. She had booked to visit the Centre that night.

We re-arranged our flights home from Athens for the following morning. Football could wait. In terms of importance it was now way down the scale. The date, of course, was the 11th September, 2001.

A few weeks later, having taken a short break in Cyprus, Rose and I were flying home with Cyprus Airways. Most people on the flight were asleep, but I noticed two Middle-Eastern-looking men suddenly get up from their seats and move towards the front of the plane. They then did something that passengers never do. They moved past those curtains that shield the cabin crew from the public and swiftly pulled the curtains, which had not been closed, tightly behind them. Who were these two? I had to know. Without thinking what on earth I would do if they were up to no good, I got up from my seat and moved forward as they had done. No other passenger took a blind bit of notice of them or of me. 'Where did those two men go?' I asked a stewardess. 'They went onto the flight deck,' she replied, and then moved off calmly towards the back of the plane. I furtively tried the door to the cockpit, it was unlocked. I could see the two dark-skinned men standing behind the pilot and co-pilot. And then the captain turned round.

'Mr Lynam,' he said. 'I heard you were on board. Allow me to introduce my co-pilot and two of my colleagues who are travelling to London to pick up one of our other aircraft.'

9/11 had obviously got to me.

*

While *The Premiership* had become a consistent programme and had bedded in very nicely, one kept hearing from the commercial arm that the programme wasn't 'washing its face'. ITV had paid so much for the product that they were never able to sell enough advertising space to get their money back. I was reminded of my comment of a few years before about ITV being in the business of business rather than the business of broadcasting. Their record of flirting with sports only to discard them when they didn't pay their way produced a long list. Athletics, snooker, darts, ice skating, boxing and racing, not to mention the Olympic Games, had all at one time been on ITV. Now they were down to a share of football, Grand Prix motor racing, and every four years the Rugby World Cup, although recently they have renewed some interest in boxing on the back of Olympic hero Amir Khan. I was fairly sure that when the highlights contract came round again ITV would go through the motions of bidding and then be delighted when they lost. The people in the sports department, some of the best I had worked with, desperately wanted ITV to retain the football highlights and were talking a good fight, but in the long run their jobs were put in jeopardy when ITV's bid, as I suspected it would, fell short. BBC got *Match of the Day* back at a knockdown price, in comparison to what ITV had paid for the three years of *The Premiership*. Greg Dyke had won a football contract at last and he was crowing.

Jeff Farmer, the Head of Football, rang me to tell me the news. All the boys and girls who had worked on the shows were bitterly disappointed. I was not in the least surprised. Later, Charles Allen, who had become the supremo of the newly amalgamated ITV company, was quoted in the newspapers, when talking about the company's financial state, as saying: 'Well, we won't have to pay for *The Premiership* next year.' I thought it insulting to all those who has sweated blood for the programme.

I had already told ITV that I would not seek renewal of my contract after the European Championships of 2004. Five years with ITV, having originally only agreed a three-year deal, was just about right. I didn't want to outstay my welcome.

I continued to do the job to the best of my ability as I presented the final season of *The Premiership*, the live Champions League matches and Euro 2004.

Both Chelsea and Arsenal had a great chance of winning the Champions League that season. Unfortunately for English football, they were drawn together at the quarter-final stage with Chelsea running out the surprise winners over the two legs. They then had to play Monaco, the first match in the Principality. Chelsea played well until Claudio Ranieri 'tinkered' a bit too much with the team and they were eventually beaten, leaving them too much to do in the second leg.

That night, as always, we discussed the match over a few drinks till the small hours, often the best part of the football away trips. Ron Atkinson was seething about the poor performance of Chelsea's famous French international defender Marcel Desailly, whom he thought had been culpable in the extreme for Chelsea's loss. But Ron being Ron, his opinions were all couched in good humour. Ron was in high spirits as he'd planned to stay on in the South of France for another day.

Then calamity.

The following day, shortly after I arrived home in London, I received a call from Brian Barwick. 'Ron Atkinson has resigned,' he told me. I was shaken. 'Don't tell me the BBC has picked him up,' I said. 'No, I haven't finished,' said Brian. 'We've been forced to ask Ron to resign and he has agreed to do so.'

Ron had used the word 'nigger' when talking about Desailly. Now if Ron had said the word on our broadcast, believe me I would already have known. What transpired was that after finishing his commentary, Ron had laid down his lip-mike and had been vehement in his disgust about Desailly's display, using the offending word in the process. The sound engineer had failed to switch off the mike and Ron's tirade had been picked up in a Middle Eastern country, who – irony of ironies – had been taking the commentary without permission.

Ron unquestionably used a word that is highly offensive to black people. But to say he is a racist is laughable. Ron started the careers of so many black players and treated them the same as any white player. That is to say he would praise them, bawl them out, take the mickey out of them, and they would become his friends. To my mind, he used an old-fashioned and out-of-date term, meaning little by it. Had he not been decent enough to resign when asked, he may well have had a case against ITV for allowing his words to go to an illegal source. Ron's misdemeanour has dramatically affected his life. I cannot believe that the punishment fitted the crime.

The day after it all happened, I was walking in central London when two black guys came up and said 'Hello'. They were painters and decorators in their twenties. 'What about old Ron?' they said. 'I'm more interested in what you have to say about it,' I told them. 'Well we don't like the word, although we use it about each other in fun,' they said, 'but being sacked for that, that's crazy.'

32

SIR ALEX IS UNHAPPY

As I write, *Match of the Day* has completed its first season back on the BBC after the Corporation beat ITV for the rights and ended their three-year run of the Saturday evening football highlights show. The audience is diminishing for football highlights and a flaw in the contract allows Sky to broadcast extended highlights of the Premiership at an earlier time, which has not helped the BBC. Apparently, when the deals with the Premiership were struck, not only did the BBC miss this loophole, but Sky themselves had initially been unaware of it.

Since *Match of the Day*'s peak years, the programme has had to undergo numerous attacks of one sort or another. Back in 1978, ITV, after negotiating secretly with the Football League, announced a deal to take over the Saturday night highlights. The press called it 'Snatch of the Day'. Instigator and negotiator for ITV was the current chairman of the BBC, Michael Grade. But the Office of Fair Trading ruled it out and a compromise was reached for sharing the contract with the BBC for the next four seasons. The two broadcasters alternated between

Saturdays and Sundays, switching their air-time each season. The BBC show could have been re-titled 'Match of One Day or Another'. It was 'confuse the viewer' time.

In 1983–4, live coverage, commonplace today, was introduced for the first time, with the BBC being allowed seven games a season. In the second year of the contract, football was beset by disasters: at Bradford, where a fire in the grandstand resulted in many deaths; and the Heysel Stadium tragedy in Belgium, where the warring fans of Liverpool and Juventus created mayhem, again resulting in loss of life.

The following season there was a deadlock in negotiations, which meant there was no football on screen until the January and it was the last season when highlights were shown for seven years. People tend to think that *Match of the Day* had an un-broken run until the Premiership went to ITV in 2001. Nothing could be further from the truth.

ITV had bought the Football League rights back in 1988, leaving the BBC with the FA Cup, highlights on Saturdays, and live ties on Sundays. This was the season when I took over the presenting role from Jimmy Hill, who continued on the show as a pundit.

He and I had travelled to Hillsborough, Sheffield, on a Friday night in order to cover the following day's semi-final between Liverpool and Nottingham Forest. We were there merely to record an opening for the highlights show. This we duly did on the Saturday afternoon and then settled back to watch the match, which we had been looking forward to immensely.

But things were obviously not right. Fans began spilling on to the pitch. The situation was chaotic. Some of the Forest fans, thinking the Scousers were spoiling for a fight, began running on to the pitch at the other end. Alan Hansen told me later that he had collared a few of the Liverpool fans and told them to get back off the pitch or the game would be abandoned. It was then he was astonished to hear from one of them: 'Al, you don't understand, there are people dying in there.' And there were – almost a hundred of them.

Of course the match was abandoned, and the cost in human life immense and horrifying. Our bosses at the BBC wanted Jimmy and me back in London that evening to mount a special programme about the disaster. I drove back down the motorway like a madman, shocked by what I had seen, anxious to do the programme justice. We received much acclaim for the broadcast, but I will never forget the agonised look on some of the faces of the fans who had seen death on a day out at a football match on a sunny day in Yorkshire.

In 1992, the BBC, in partnership with Sky, contracted a five-year deal with the new Premier League and the FA Cup, squeezing out ITV in the process. We were now back in business every Saturday, plus some midweek games and Sunday live FA Cup ties. Alan Hansen and Trevor Brooking were the regular pundits, with Mark Lawrenson making appearances as well.

I continued with the show until 1999 and my departure for ITV. Gary Lineker took over as presenter for a couple of seasons until the BBC lost the contract, and now he's back fronting the programme once again. But if football highlights wasn't a diminishing product in 1988, it certainly is today.

During my time on *Match of the Day* we quite often seemed to upset Alex Ferguson. Firstly, he always complained that the picture behind my presenter's seat had images of players but none from Manchester United, who were now the masters of English football. He saw this as an insult. On one show, Alan

Hansen and I had talked about Ryan Giggs, who was fast becoming an outstanding player. 'I wonder what he sounds like?' I asked. 'We never seem to be allowed to speak to him.'

Alex went into a rage. 'When I want you to tell me how to run my football club, I'll tell you,' he wrote.

Quite rightly he had been protecting the young and, at the time, fairly inarticulate Giggs from the media and he'd thought my remarks were critical of his care for his young star. I actually thought he was handling Giggs perfectly. I had merely compared footballers to young stars in other sports who have no fears about facing the microphones and cameras at an early age, and had mentioned by comparison the seventeen-year-old Spanish tennis player Arantxa Sanchez-Vicario giving interviews live in three languages after having just won the French Open Championship. A question of education, of course.

After one Saturday match, when Roy Keane had been sent off for Manchester United for particularly aggressive behaviour, we sent a message down the line to the commentator at the match, John Motson, to question Ferguson on his reaction to the sending off and any disciplinary measures he might take against the player. Motson approached the manager after the game and perfectly politely put the appropriate question. We are not talking Jeremy Paxman here; Motty was quite gentle in his enquiry and perfectly within his rights to pose the question. Fergie went into a blue funk, threatening to ban Motson from the ground, his tirade liberally spiced with bad language. We were witnessing all this from the comfort of our offices in London. There was a view was that it had been perfectly right and proper to ask the question, which had been couched with the utmost respect and good manners, and that the response was totally out of order. 'Right,' we thought. 'Let's put it out like it is. We can bleep the swear words.' Any newspaper would have reported that kind of behaviour. The consideration was that the viewers would expect us to put such a question to Ferguson and we were against censoring his behaviour. The editor of the show and I felt this way, but eventually it was decided that, to protect Motson from embarrassment and avoid a major and perhaps permanent row with Ferguson, the confrontation would not be shown. I have great admiration for Alex Ferguson, the outstanding manager of his time; and, for the most part, he has been helpful and considerate to me. But on that occasion he was out of line.

Our relationship with Manchester United wasn't helped by a question from me to Alan Hansen on the opening day of the season in 1995. United had had a clear-out of some of their most established players, such as Mark Hughes and Paul Ince, and they lost their opening game 3–1 to Aston Villa, their only goal coming from the 21-year-old David Beckham. I said to big Al, 'United were scarcely recognisable from the team we've known over the last couple of seasons. What's going on, do you think?'

Hansen replied: 'You can't win anything with kids … He's got to buy players, it's as simple as that …'

Alan has never been allowed to forget his quote, which he quite rightly blames me for leading him into. United ended up winning the double with their 'kids', and T-shirts with Alan's infamous forecast sold like hot cakes at the Club's shop for months.

During this run of *Match of the Day* we televised the infamous 'karate kick' incident when Eric Cantona, having been sent off at Selhurst Park in a midweek match, attacked a fan who had been goading him. Cantona, of course, received a lengthy ban for his action, but just as he was coming back into the game he agreed to do a face-to-face interview with me at a hotel in Lancashire. My editor Niall Sloane and I drove north and waited for the arrival of our man. We waited and waited, both of us looking out anxiously from the hotel reception down the long drive that led to the entrance. We thought Cantona would be arriving in a Mercedes or Ferrari, the kind of wheels most modern highly paid footballers drive. Fully half an hour after the appointed time, when we had resigned ourselves to the great man not turning up, we looked out to see a battered old Peugeot approaching the entrance. Cantona popped out of it and proceeded to charm the living daylights out of all of us, apologising profusely for his tardiness. He shook hands with the whole crew. The female programme assistant got a severe attack of the vapours and went all unnecessary, no doubt committed to undying love. Then this Gallic charmer settled down to do an impeccable interview. Bearing in mind the Selhurst Park incident had cost him months out of the game and considerable criticism, I wanted to know if he regretted it all. Cantona thought for a moment and just when I was expecting one of his 'When the seagulls follow the trawler' type of quotes, he said: 'Non, I would like to kick him again.'

When I began presenting *Match of the Day* in 1988, I doubled it up with *Grandstand*. This was hardly arduous because, at the time, the BBC only had the FA Cup and England matches – ITV had signed a four year contract with the old First Division.

I began the first show with. 'Come on. It hasn't been that long – you know it – course you do – one, two, three ...' And the opening titles ran with the familiar theme tune.

Jimmy Hill was now one of the regular pundits, alongside Terry Venables. They rarely agreed about anything on the show, which made for good television. There had never been any kind of instruction to either of them to be contentious. It just worked out that way. I used to tease them along and sit back and enjoy every moment of it.

Terry reckons that he couldn't get in a London cab in those days without the driver referring to his relationship with Jimmy. 'You hate that Jimmy Hill, don't you Tel?'

'No I don't,' he'd reply. 'Actually, we're good friends.' 'Come on, Tel, you really hate him, don't you?' And on the conversation would go until Terry gave up. 'You're right, I hate him, I hate him.'

Venables and I loved working with Jimmy and we both think of him with the highest regard, but he continually made us laugh over the years.

One day I was walking round the pitch with them at the City Ground in Nottingham before a live FA Cup tie and the crowd, as one, began a chant: 'Jimmy Hill's a wanker. Jimmy Hill's a wanker...'

'How on earth do you put up with that,' I asked him.

'That's fame for you,' he replied.

Another time, after a match at Bramall Lane, we'd finished the broadcast and the crowd was long gone. As we neared the tunnel, a tall good-looking young man approached Jimmy. 'Mr Hill,' he said. 'What was your view of the goal that we conceded?' 'Well,' began Jimmy, 'you see, the keeper made a right Horlicks of it, should never have come for the ball ...', etc., etc. To my horror, Jimmy hadn't realised he was actually talking to the goalkeeper. I nudged him and whispered the young man's identity to him. Totally unfazed, Jimmy continued, 'But obviously it wasn't entirely your fault ...'

As we started presenting more games – the following season

we had twenty editions of the programme – it became more difficult for me to retain the *Grandstand* chair as well, especially as some of the football, including replays, would be shown on *Sportsnight*, the regular and long-running midweek sports programme. So it was decided that Steve Rider and I would do a swap and that he would take over *Grandstand*. Both of us were perfectly happy with the arrangement. So after around five hundred programmes I became the ex-*Grandstand* presenter on a regular basis but continued to do the programme on Grand National day and at Wimbledon until 1999.

In 1992, with the formation of the new Premier League, the BBC was back in league football and the show was back every Saturday in the season. Now Alan Hansen and Trevor Brooking were my new regular partners. I began the first show: 'Good evening. I suppose it's back to the future.'

We had the FA Cup as well, in partnership with Sky, football's new paymaster. ITV were out in the cold. It seems to be a pattern.

And so *Match of the Day* and *Sportsnight* became my regular shows, plus all the other major events like Wimbledon, the Grand National, World Cups, and the Olympics. I was a busy boy, and very happy with my lot.

It was a consistent pattern for the next seven years.

33

THE D.G.s AND ME

The role of the Director General of the BBC is the most powerful job in British broadcasting. The incumbent is the figurehead of a great British institution, loved by most, but criticised by all.

'Whither the BBC?' is the constant cry in the press, often from vested interests.

The licence fee system, which made perfect sense when the BBC was the only broadcaster, is now under continual review as the audience becomes more arbitrary in these days of multi-choice radio and television. So far, few have been able to come up with a viable alternative to the broadcast licence, despite its limitations and inadequacies. If the BBC goes 'commercial', the pot of advertising revenue would be dramatically split to the cost of those broadcasters who rely on it so heavily, like ITV and Channels Four and Five.

Also, the nature of the BBC's funding allows the Corporation, in theory anyway, to rise above the simple criterion of audience figures alone as the barometer of success.

Having said that, if the BBC's audience drops too low, if their programmes become marginalised, then how do they justify their unique revenue system if people are not watching or listening to their output?

All this is the province of the D.G. It is a continual conundrum, not to mention keeping a broadly-talented staff of some twenty-five thousand people happy.

Oh, and maintaining the organisation's independence from government, which it quite often has a duty to disagree with. What sort of person can possibly cope with this gargantuan task?

The country may well have had a female Prime Minister, but the office of D.G. has yet to fall to a woman and in my time at the Corporation, no fewer than six different gentlemen held the position.

In my local radio days, Hugh Carleton Greene was in office. He was a former newspaper correspondent. He was succeeded by Charles Curran who had joined the Corporation as a 'Talks Producer' and risen through the ranks. I had something in common with him: he was born in the west of Ireland. He was genial and very complimentary about my broadcasting on the *Today* programme in the early Seventies. Next came Ian Trethowan, another former newspaper man who had been a news presenter on ITN. He was a big racing fan and indeed liked sport in general and I got to know him fairly well.

Alasdair Milne followed him. He had joined the BBC as a general trainee from Oxbridge and had risen to be an editor on television current affairs programmes. He found himself in the middle of a crisis about a programme concerning the troubles in Northern Ireland, which was banned. BBC journalists were united in their criticism of that decision. Curiously, I found myself in a picture used in a *Times* leader column where Milne,

Home Secretary Leon Brittan, Michael Grade, the new Controller of BBC1, Lord Young, the BBC Chairman and the very first D.G., Lord Reith, were pictured with me and The Two Ronnies. Extraordinary combination, but it was yet another of those 'Whither the BBC?' pieces.

Milne resigned just over a year later.

His successor was Michael Checkland, a most personable man and a great supporter of sport and indeed of me. Michael had been Deputy D.G. responsible largely for the funding of various aspects of the Corporation. He was an accountant by training. On his first day in the job he gave a press conference in the Council Chamber of the BBC at Broadcasting House. 'How can you be right for this job?' came the attack from one critic, 'You're not a journalist,' as if that was the qualification for all things. Michael simply turned to the portrait of the glowering father of the BBC, J.W.C. Reith. 'Neither was he,' he said simply and cleverly.

John Birt came next. He had been an ITV producer and eventually Programme Controller. Michael Grade, the BBC1 boss now found himself under a former colleague who had been junior to him at ITV, could not put up with the thought of it and left for pastures new, namely Channel Four. This was a loss. Michael had a great showbiz intuition and little self-doubt and was great to work with.

I wish I could say the same about Birt. He was a man with limited personality or charm, but a considerable ego. Although, to all intents and purposes, a sports fan, he did little to inspire any confidence in the BBC's future as a major sports broadcaster. He was instrumental in changing management structures which simply confused us and had us screaming against the bureaucracy of it all.

I had a conversation with the next D.G., Greg Dyke, before he actually took up the job and told him that if he didn't back the sports department, the BBC were 'looking into the abyss'.

Then I left. Then he took over as D.G., and he lost the Premiership football contract to ITV.

By February 2002, our Premiership programme had recovered from its 'timing' crisis and had settled down into a programme every bit as good and in some ways better than *Match of the Day*. One morning, I had opened my *Daily Mail* over breakfast to find a picture of myself on page three and a headline which said 'Des is off his game on ITV says Dyke'. At a Broadcasting Press Guild lunch, Dyke had described me as 'looking tired and as though he doesn't care'. I subsequently found out this was said 'off the record' but said anyway, and as I have learnt over the years, and Dyke should surely have known, there is no such thing as 'off the record' with some reporters.

I noticed that the *Daily Telegraph* was also carrying the story. I spoke to Jane who gave me the unhappy news that the other papers were reporting his statement as well. I was bitterly hurt and angry. I thought it grossly unfair. As any of my colleagues would have vouched, I was putting as much into the programme as possible. I never skimped anything. I was harshly critical of everything unless I was satisfied we were doing the job to the very highest standards in broadcasting. Now Dyke, sponsor of Roland Rat, who had once tried to tempt me to ITV from the BBC, had made these damaging remarks, fuelled no doubt by his chagrin at losing the football since his arrival at the BBC, when he had set himself the goal of being the saviour of BBC Sport.

But, that morning, I had to regain my composure and go off to cut the ribbon at the re-opening of a hospice charity shop and try to be charming and amusing to the volunteers and members of the public who would be there. As it turned out, they were a wonderful bunch of people but, of course, several had seen the morning papers and were ready to storm the barricades of Television Centre on my behalf. Or so they implied. I kept smiling with my mind elsewhere when a tiny elderly lady approached me. 'We last met when you were sixteen,' she said. 'I am Mrs Greenwood. I used to be Head of Social Services in Brighton and worked with your father. He was the most decent man I ever met. He taught me more about psychiatry than any doctor'. She nearly brought a tear to my eye. Mrs. Greenwood had balanced my morning.

I waited for a call or a note from Dyke. It never came. We did receive a copy of an e-mail where he announced he would be advising senior BBC staff to turn down any future invitation from the Guild unless everyone connected understood the difference between 'on the record' and 'off the record' remarks. It went on 'This morning's stories implying that I made certain 'on the record' comments about Des Lynam, an old friend and respected broadcaster, came as a surprise to most people who were there, including me.' The trouble was, only the Broadcasting Press Guild and one or two others ever saw that. The rest of the nation read about me being insulted.

Greg and I have built bridges since and I, for one, was sorry to see him having to resign, in my view, wholly unnecessarily as D.G. He was beginning to put BBC Sport back on the map and he had the confidence of the staff and public. But a simple note from him at the time would have been more than welcome. And now I find myself back working for the BBC from time to time, with a radio series and the occasional appearance on television. Recently I was in Television Centre and a tall chap approached me with a smile. I knew him of course. I had worked close to him in the late Seventies on *Nationwide*. 'Welcome back,' he said. He was the new D.G. of the BBC – Mark Thompson.

34

GOOD COP, BAD COP

The influence of BSkyB on television sport has been immense.

They changed the face of English football, paying billions for the rights to show live action. Without football it is highly possible that the whole satellite venture might have failed. Football is the company's 'dish driver'. Other sports are covered extensively too, but football is the mainstay of the business. Once upon a time, the premise adhered to by both television companies and the football authorities was that you would kill the game if it were exposed to too much live coverage. The fans would stay away from the grounds and the sport would subsequently wither. It's not so many years since the only live domestic club game on television was the FA Cup Final. No wonder the audience figure represented almost half the population. Now the event is comparatively small beer, just another match on the live football merry-go-round. There is a live match on television usually five days a week in the season, yet still the crowds keep turning up, for the time being anyway.

The money pouring into the game at the highest level has

seen the quality of stadia improve dramatically, with many clubs building brand new ones. But the main beneficiaries have been the players. The top stars are now earning the kind of money that means they will have no need ever to work again when their playing days are over.

In my view many of them are grossly overpaid, and while foreign imports have improved the quality of skills on show, many clubs have been lumbered with expensive foreign signings who do not quite live up to their promise. Even well-run football clubs like Ipswich Town have fallen into the trap of signing expensive foreign imports who fail to keep them in the Premiership and who are then virtually unsaleable. After relegation, the Club found itself with huge debts and for a time had to go into administration. Their story is not unique.

Down the leagues, football is run much as it always was, on a shoestring. There is hardly a club in the Football League that is financially viable. They nearly all depend on handouts from any wealthy individual who may come along to foot the bills, and they are all looking for a player to sell to one of the major teams. But with the introduction of so many foreign players into the British game, that market has more or less dried up. The incidence of a player from the lower divisions moving to the Premiership for a sizeable fee is nowadays rare. It's easier to bring in a player from abroad whose contract has ended elsewhere as no fee is involved – at least not to the club: there will always be an agent around with his hand out and he and the player will be the beneficiaries of the deal. But the days of the big clubs helping the minnows to survive have more or less gone.

When it comes to major international football competitions like the World Cup and the European Championship, then terrestrial television still dominates. The government rules state

314

that this must be the case; but week after week in the football season, terrestrial channels are largely reduced to bit part players, only showing highlights.

ITV have retained less than half the overall coverage of the Champions League, the premier European competition, and the BBC broadcasts the FA Cup live; but Sky are football's main paymasters and while that continues will remain in a dominant position.

Sky Television is an ideal place for a young sports presenter to hone their televisual skills without being in the full glare of the spotlight. Many of them are a sight better at the job than I was when I was thrust on to *Grandstand* and just about survived in the late Seventies. Many years later *The Mail on Sunday* quoted me as saying, 'I would never work for Sky. If they offered me four times my salary I wouldn't even listen.' I don't ever remember giving this exact quote, but it certainly came over as an arrogant thing to have said. It prompted the then Head of Sport at BSkyB, David Hill, to send a letter to my boss at the BBC, Jonathan Martin. 'Dear Jonathan,' he wrote. 'Do me a favour, tell Des it's a problem he'll never have to worry about.' Jonathan penned a note on the top of the letter, which he passed to me. 'Methinks he doth protest, etc. ... struck a nerve, I feel. I'm not going to respond.'

I did respond to Hill. 'I suppose three times the salary and a company car is out of the question then. Keep smiling,' I wrote.

Actually Hill was quite wrong because a while later I was approached by a gentleman called Sam Chisholm, who had become the Managing Director of BSkyB. An uncompromising New Zealander hired by Rupert Murdoch, he asked me to name my price to come to the channel 'that mattered' in sports broadcasting. One minute he was telling me I was a genius, and then next minute using some industrial language to criticise my lack of courage if I failed to take up his offer. I took an instant dislike to this uncouth little man playing 'good cop, bad cop' with me, and made up my mind instantly to stay precisely where I was.

There was an embarrassment later when a old journalist friend of mine, Norman Giller, having heard from a BBC source that I had been offered a deal with BSkyB, doubted the whole thing, in print. I rang him up and told him that unfortunately, despite our friendship, I was now going to have to sue him. I said it in jest, but he printed a retraction. Had I let it stand, it could have seemed that I was making the story up to curry favour with my existing employers, which I was not.

The problem had occurred because apparently Chisholm had never discussed the possibility of my working for his organisation with his own Head of Sport, Vic Wakeling. Giller had received his information from Wakeling and had reasonably assumed that he would know about any offer to me. Extraordinarily, he did not. Chisholm had worked through Wakeling's number two, Trevor East.

Years before, Giller had actually given me my first write-up after my early television broadcasts. 'This man will become the face and voice of television sport in the Eighties,' he wrote. I thought I was struggling at the time and he gave my confidence a huge boost. When we last met, Norman reminded me of that piece. 'Yes but you never mentioned the Nineties and the 2000s,' I said. 'No vision at all.'

In the early Nineties I received a telephone call from a lady called Liz Howell. She had a broadcasting proposition to put to me. I checked up on her credentials which were sound: Liz was an experienced producer who at the time was working for Sky Television.

When we met, I liked her immediately. She was quite direct, no beating about the bush from Liz. She explained to me that she was part of a consortium that would be bidding for the franchise for breakfast television. It was at the time held by TV-am but was up for grabs.

Liz told me that she and her associates had thought that I would be the ideal kind of person to front their shows if they were successful in winning the contract. I told her that I was pretty happy doing sports, that the Barcelona Olympics were in sight and that no matter who they were and how big their budget, they would never have enough money to reward me for getting up at 3 a.m. in the morning to go to work. I pointed out that nearly twenty years before, when I was a young man, I had worked on Radio 4's early morning *Today* programme and the experience had nearly killed me then. 'And that was radio,' I said. 'With all the paraphernalia of television, it would be even more exacting. No. Thanks for the compliment, but not for me.'

In fact, I had often thought that I would have liked a news and magazine type of programme to present, rather like the old *Nationwide*. My interests had always been broader than just sport, but not in the early mornings.

A few days went by and Liz contacted me again. 'Well, we would like to put your name in our bid document as the kind of presenter we would hope to have front our programmes,' she said. I told her that there was still no chance of my doing early morning television, but that I obviously could not prevent them mentioning me in the way she described. 'We would like to pay you a fee for the privilege,' she said and I trousered a nice few quid for allowing my name to go forward as the 'type' of broadcaster they had in mind.

Liz and her associates had no need to pay me, but they did and I thought it was more than fair of them.

Then, after some weeks, I turned on the radio to hear that GMTV had been successful in their franchise bid to take over the morning breakfast slot from TV-am, it was only a matter of hours before Liz was on to me again. 'We got it,' she said. 'And with the help of your name. Now can we talk seriously about you carving out a whole new career for yourself?'

Once again, I was adamant that it was not for me. They were paying me this huge compliment but I was happy with my job at the BBC and those early mornings were still not for me. 'Who do you think would be a good broadcaster for our show?' I was asked. They wanted someone who could deal with the heavy items but who also would have a lightness of touch.

'Well, there's a chap who does mid-morning television out of Manchester for the BBC,' I said. 'I think he's excellent. Might be right up your street.'

'What's his name?' asked Liz.

'Eamonn Holmes,' I said.

Whenever I see Eamonn these days, we often have a laugh about my sponsorship of his career. I had also recommended him for *How Do they Do That?* after I had had enough of the show, and also for the *Holiday* programme when my sports commitments prevented me continuing. Eamonn makes live television look easy. He must owe me an absolute fortune, but he was welcome to those years of early rising.

If you are in the television business you are never going to please everyone, and should not expect to do so. Overall, I've been very lucky to have received a positive press reaction to my broadcasting down the years. All the broadsheet newspapers

have written glowing profiles of me, often to my embarrassment, and the tabloids have nearly always been supportive; but
of course here and there I've received a barb or two, which
never upset me. Everyone is entitled to an opinion about you if
you stick your ugly mug in their living-rooms uninvited.

You have to understand that the description 'television critic'
is really a misnomer. If you've seen a programme, you can make
your own mind up about its value. Why would you need someone else's opinion? If you haven't seen it, you don't care. Theatre
critics serve a more valid purpose. Find one you like, and he or
she will provide a good guide as to whether or not you should
go to see a particular performance.

No. TV critics are really in existence to amuse. They write
entertaining essays, using television and its performers as subject matter. There are several clever and witty exponents of the
art. Clive James made his name in the trade with some brilliant
writing. Of the current crop, A. A. Gill, Martin Kelner, Giles
Smith, and Brian Viner come to mind as some of the best.

One or two are just mean spirited and see little good in anything coming out of the box. You wonder why they do it. Writing about something that rarely gives you pleasure would be a
bore, and so they get their satisfaction out of others' pain. One
individual, an unattractive specimen called Victor Lewis-Smith,
has a writing style which is often cruel and hurtful. I think his
vitriolic style emanates from the fact that he himself has had a
stab at both radio and television and has been rather less than a
hit at both.

His critiques are made up of insults and what he perceives to
be funny lines. Some years ago when I was presenting *How Do
They Do That?* he came up with the headline, 'How Do They
Get Away With It?' That was OK: the title lent itself to an easy

variation – indeed we used to call it 'Why Did We Do That? ourselves. However, this was a show achieving an audience figure of up to twelve million at the time. Audience numbers are not the sole criterion of a good show, and it certainly had its faults, but a very large number of people liked it. I would not have turned a hair about his remarks normally but he had been particularly cruel about my co-host, Jenny Hull. The article had made her burst into tears and she was inconsolable. Her confidence, already fragile, was shattered.

I broke the habit of a lifetime and responded to his article.

'I read your recent criticism of our programme' I wrote, 'and I would like you to know that I recently watched your so-called comedy series [he had been involved in an unsuccessful little programme late on BBC 2]. I didn't laugh at the time, but I have been laughing about it ever since.' I guess he didn't like it. The biter had been bit. Critics are always the most fragile souls when they hear a home truth. He has been taking pot-shots at me ever since, even when a programme has nothing to do with me.

When Michael Parkinson jumped ship to do what I did, leaving the BBC for ITV, this person wrote a damning article about his first show. 'It's lazy,' he wrote. 'It reminds me of Des Lynam.' Now if he'd written that it reminded him of my style of broadcasting, or that my programmes had been lazy in style, he would have been entitled to his opinion. I wouldn't necessarily have like it, but he would have had every right to say that. He did not, and it was drawn to my attention that he'd written that I was a lazy person.

I was advised this was defamatory and through my lawyer I complained to the paper. I have many faults, but laziness is not one of them. To their shame, the paper defended the article, claiming that the perpetrator had a 'quirky' style of writing.

I wanted to sue the individual and the newspaper, but my barrister advised me against. Even if I'd won, I would probably only have received minimal damages. If I lost, the costs could have been astronomic. And so I was encouraged not to commit myself to the vagaries of the British libel laws. While the paper, frightened obviously of this so-called talent in their employ, would not apologise, they indicated the truth of the matter by paying all my legal costs, and a clarification was put on their databases.

Let me give you an example of the kind of writing of which this man is an exponent.

He was reviewing *Nigella Bites*, the cookery programme presented by Nigella Lawson. Her husband, John Diamond, who really was a talented writer, had died just a short while previously from throat cancer after a valiant and very public fight against the disease.

'A few months ago,' this critic wrote, 'when it transpired that diamonds do not last forever, the papers were full of tributes after her husband John finally croaked (I think that's the appropriate word); but truth be told I never cared much for him or his cancer diary and his passing simply fuelled an idle fantasy that perhaps his widow might appreciate a little no nonsense comfort and consolation from a physiognomically-challenged TV critic ... glad of a partner who could actually taste her creations, rather than simply passing them in puréed form through a hole in his neck.' His employers obviously saw that as 'quirky'.

Once again, Mr 'Quirky' wrote about the late entertainer Leslie Crowther: 'The grim reaper also ended the television career of Leslie Crowther ... [he] moved to Radio 2 and stayed there until his motor accident, at which point the erstwhile presenter of *Stars in their Eyes* began seeing stars in his own eyes (due to smashing his head against the roof of his car) and he not only became a hit on the radio but also on the dashboard, the windscreen and finally the pavement.'

Now, Leslie Crowther wasn't everyone's cup of tea as a broadcaster, but his memory did not deserve this kind of abuse, which must have been extremely painful for his family to read. Not long ago he wrote: 'Poor Jill Dando (or was it Jan Dildo. How quickly we forget). Like George Best, the travel presenter failed to survive the Danny Baker doorstep challenge.' These bad taste insults masquerading as television critiques would no doubt be defended by the newspaper printing them, the London *Evening Standard*, as 'witty'.

35

'HEROGRAMS'

I have been fortunate to have picked up a few broadcasting 'gongs' over the years. They mean nothing outside the business, but they are very useful in underlining one's worth to employers, who tend to take much more notice of them than the recipients. There are exceptions, of course. I know at least one broadcaster who has picked up an award or two and it has given him awful delusions. There are also some famous names whose work over the years has been top-notch but they have never had to worry about an acceptance speech. Mostly it depends on who sits on the panel of judges for these awards: I always think there should be a panel to judge the credibility of the judges.

The awards given by the Television and Radio Industries Club are interesting. This is a club for people who make televisions, as opposed to people who make television, and you find yourself sitting on the table of Mr Hitachi or Mr Panasonic. The Royal Television Society makes annual awards for sports broadcasting, and here again it is a wonderful night out, mixing with friends, competitors, not to mention a few enemies. I recently presented the Awards and took the mickey out of everyone.

In 1996, a BBC producer called Beatrice Ballard called me and asked me if I would be interested in presenting an awards show.

It was going to be called *Auntie's Favourites*, and the viewing public would be asked to vote for their favourites in various categories. I decided that it wasn't quite for me at the time for one reason or another and Michael Parkinson, who had not returned to his famous chat-show at the time, presented it instead.

As it turned out, I did take part in the programme because, to my amazement and delight, I was voted the nation's favourite BBC presenter. Even Sue Barker told me that she and her mum had voted for me.

And so I found myself receiving the award from Caroline Aherne, on whose *Mrs Merton Show* I had recently been a guest. Caroline was in one of her extrovert moods on the night, and in giving me the award she threw herself at me, wrapping her legs around my waist. That threw me, and the few words I had prepared left my mind and I mumbled my thanks. 'Looking at all the famous people here tonight,' I said, 'I'm the only one here I've never heard of.' It was an old stand-by of mine which I had used in my radio days but it didn't quite work anymore. People apparently had heard of me now.

Parkinson did a super job in presenting the programme and it was shortly after this that Beatrice Ballard and he reformed his old chat show. Parky was back, if not from the cold, then certainly from the cool.

The very best thing about winning an award is that you have deprived a competitor from so doing. When a friend wins something, it's great too. Gore Vidal said that, 'When a friend succeeds, a little something inside me dies.' I know what he meant, but I reserve that feeling for enemies, of which I luckily have precious few. Just before my last season with ITV, the RTS very kindly gave me a 'Lifetime Achievement' award. Before I received it, Gary Lineker, also a recipient that night, made a nice speech in which he gave me much credit for helping him with his television career. It was an exaggeration, but very flattering. When I got up I said, 'I knew he was going to be good. If I'd realised how good, I'd have told him to piss off!' It got me off to a great start with my few words.

The most important broadcasting awards, as far as television is concerned, are the BAFTAs, and in 1994 I received the Richard Dimbleby Award for 'The Most Important Personal Contribution on Screen in Factual Television'. That did turn my head a bit. I received the award in Glasgow from Ally McCoist, who in due course would become a friend and colleague. In my acceptance speech I mentioned that I could not be more pleased with the honour, because it was in the name of my broadcasting hero. I had been brought up on Richard Dimbleby's voice on the radio and, later, his television broadcasts. The memory of his moving description of Churchill's funeral was a perfect example of broadcasting at its very highest quality. I learned afterwards that his sons, David and Jonathan, who, of course, have both taken up the baton as first-rate communicators, were delighted with what I had to say. Indeed, when David was to receive the same award a few years later, I was asked if I could present it to him. Sadly, I had to decline because of a previous commitment.

I received a very complimentary personal note from John Birt; and, as he had done after every success I had been deemed to have, Marmaduke Hussey, the chairman of the BBC, also wrote a very kind note of congratulations. The bosses loved it when their people picked up these awards. It was great publicity for the BBC. 'Dukie', as Hussey was known, came over like an old buffer, but behind the façade was a very acute mind. He was also a great lifter of spirits and we were always delighted when he decided to visit the sports department.

He mentioned to me once that he had never been in to see *Grandstand* go out on air. 'We'll fix that,' I said, and a few weeks later the Chairman arrived in the studio to watch me go through the presentational role. An hour or so into the broadcast, we received a bomb warning. It was taken seriously enough for us to have to evacuate the studio. I handed over to Peter O'Sullevan at the race meeting we were covering, and he was instructed to hold the fort until we could resume – or to cover the 'blowing-up' of Television Centre if that was how it turned out.

I put my notes together before I strolled out into the car park. Waiting there ahead of all of us was 'Dukey'. 'You didn't hang about,' I remarked. 'I lost one leg in the bloody war,' he said, 'I can't afford to lose another one.'

After a while we returned to the studio, minus the Chairman. He had seen enough.

Occasionally I was asked to hand out an award at the annual BAFTA show. One year, Dale Winton presented the award in front of the one I was set to do and for some reason he gave out the current score of a football match being played that evening. When I came out, I said, 'It comes to something when Dale Winton starts giving the football scores. Don't think I couldn't have done *Supermarket Sweep* [pause] if I'd had to.' It got a great laugh but when I returned to my table, Dale came wafting by. 'That was unnecessary,' he said, and drifted away. I was concerned that I had bruised his rather fragile ego. I was only having a bit of fun at his expense. Had it been a joke the other way round, I would have laughed as much as everyone else. I dropped Dale a note afterwards apologising for hurting his feelings. He obviously forgot about it, because a while later he was on my radio show and it was never mentioned. I like Dale but during my *Match of the Day* run he was usually also in Television Centre for the lottery programme. I used to be concerned about bumping into him because Dale would always insist on giving me a couple of big smackers on the cheek. I didn't particularly mind it, but I was terrified that Alan Hansen would see it. There would have been no recovery from that.

In my first year at ITV, when there was constant talk of them coming up with some 'other ideas' for me, I was asked to be the presenter for the television BAFTAs. This was a big test for me. I had never done such a show, although I'd always felt I could give a reasonable account of myself.

I enjoyed the experience tremendously. I'd written most of the script myself and enjoyed delivering a few gentle barbs: 'BBC Director General, Greg Dyke, is here with twenty people around his table … fighting for the ten places available …' etc. Not least, I enjoyed having my arms round Honor Blackman and Joanna Lumley; but it was Carol Vorderman who stole the show with a turquoise dress she was very nearly wearing that night. She was sex on legs.

I got a wonderful letter of thanks from BAFTA afterwards. But that was the beginning and the end of my non-sports broadcasting for ITV.

More recently, in April 2005, I had the pleasure of presenting Paul Gascoigne with the 'Sports Book of the Year' award at the Grosvenor House Hotel in London. Paul rightly received the award for his compelling autobiography, on which he had collaborated with the talented writer Hunter Davies. Many years before, Hunter had written a book called *The Glory Game*. He'd somehow managed to gain almost total access to the Tottenham Hotspur team of the time, a fact that must have helped him to pen one of the best sports books ever written.

As I handed over the trophy to Gazza, he wept. He had been through so much.

I first met him when he was at the peak of his powers at England's training camp in Sardinia, just before the 1990 World Cup. I'd arranged a one-to-one interview for BBC Television and he led me a merry chase before I caught up with him. As he approached our camera position I could see he was wearing a T-shirt emblazoned with all sorts of tasteless words and phrases. Clearly, I did not want to put this in front of our viewers.

I said, 'Look, the British public already think you're nutty. Why don't you give yourself a chance to show everybody you're a decent young guy and try to prove them wrong? Go and put your tracksuit on.' My words must have had their effect because, good as gold, he went and changed and did a super interview.

The next time I saw him face to face was at the Spurs training ground a couple of days before the 1991 FA Cup Final. By now Gascoigne was mega-famous after his exploits and tears of the year before, and once again he messed me around for a couple of hours before he settled down to do an interview. He spoke very well again and two days later, on Cup Final day, I introduced the interview by describing him as 'much misunderstood' and said that viewers would see a seemingly level-headed young man. Well, he came over as that in the interview, but then promptly went out on the pitch like a lunatic, threw himself into tackles, kicked the Nottingham Forest player Gary Charles up in the air, and injured his own cruciate ligament in the process so badly that it put him into hospital and out of the game for a year. So much for 'level-headed young man'. Not one of my better links.

By 2002, the life of Paul Gascoigne and its spectacular ups and downs had been well documented, but ITV had decided that he would be a useful addition to our panel of experts for the World Cup finals, for which England were one of the favourites. I had enquired if anyone knew whether or not he could actually do the job. I had never seen him on television commenting on matches except those in which he had played himself. Some of those earning a living as football pundits aren't exactly paragons of English grammar usage, but they get their opinions across, However, I doubted Gazza could do the job. But the producers told me he would be an excellent 'face' to have for the big occasion. The trouble is, television producers never have to cope with the actual interviews. I was also told we were in competition with the BBC for his services. As it turned out, ITV won the bidding war but it was a pyrrhic victory. Gazza was wracked with nerves and found it difficult to speak on camera. He was also trying too hard, and was keeping notes during the match which he then had difficulty in reading. On the first programme, in which France failed to score against Senegal, Gascoigne said he didn't know where Senegal was. 'I think you'll find it's been part of Africa for some time,' I said. But as I said it, I knew it was a little too sharp a response for him and his face reddened. I could have bitten my tongue off.

Gascoigne had been in good hands. Apart from my one rather tart remark, I was helping him as much as I could. Andy Townsend, Ally McCoist, Bobby Robson and Terry Venables all love him and were doing their level best to steer him through, but in the end ITV used him for one or two filmed reports in which he met the public, which was much more successful.

During his time with ITV, Gazza seemed to be going though hellish problems. He was still drinking and popping pills and arrived at the studios most mornings in a pretty emotional state, not helped if he read a bad review of his performance in the papers, which he often did. Lately he has got himself together. As I write, he is off the booze, and has been for over two years, and seems to be exorcising his demons. He did a moving radio interview for me when he went through all his addictions and terrors. 'I'm even an addict of Alcoholics Anonymous,' he said. 'I want to go to more meetings than they have.'

Paul Gascoigne has been one of English football's greatest ever players. He's also a generous and emotional person. I hope he manages to find a niche in life that makes up for not being able to play his beloved game at the very highest level.

36

ORCHESTRA OR CHORUS?

In the last couple of years I have managed to pick up no less than £58,000 for charity by appearing on a couple of television programmes.

The first was *Who Wants to be a Millionaire?* Every now and again they have a 'celebrity' version of the show, and I was invited on to one of these. I was also allowed to choose who I would like to be my partner on the programme: I invited Mary Nightingale, the ITN newsreader, whom I had got to know a few years earlier when we did a travel awards show together.

I felt that Mary and I might blend together nicely on the quiz show and, of course, there was no harm in bringing a little glamour to the proceedings. As it turned out, Mary was only a few weeks away from giving birth to her first child, but she still looked gorgeous. My fear was that I would get a sports question to which I would not know the answer. If that happened, I knew that Ally McCoist was waiting for me. He had been on the show himself and won just a paltry £1,000 and I had given him some dreadful stick at the time. As anyone who has been on the show will tell you, it is quite a nerve-wracking experience and the fact that you have four options creates strange seeds of doubt in one's mind. However, Mary and I were doing well and had got £32,000 in the bag. Up came the £64,000 question, which was: 'Which word, with a theatrical connection, derives from the Greek meaning 'to dance'?' The alternatives were: *chorus, orchestra, apron* and *proscenium*. Mary thought it was probably *chorus*. I felt that was almost too obvious, and edged towards the word *orchestra*. But we had no real problem because one of our 'phone-a-friends' was nothing more or less than a classics scholar. We were home and dry. Mary spoke to him and we were surprised to hear him quite doubtful. He hummed and hawed but, just before the thirty seconds were up, he plumped for *chorus*. I still felt doubtful, but I would have looked a complete fool if I'd gone against him and he'd been right. So it was *chorus*. Final answer. The right answer was *orchestra*. We were surprised. Our classicist had got it wrong. But we were happy to have got as far as we did: £16,000 for each of our respective charities. Mary then got on the phone to her friend. He immediately asked how much we had won and was shocked to hear his answer had been wrong. He had prevaricated on the phone only because he knew that both the word *chorus* and the word *orchestra* came from the same derivative with more or less the same meaning. The recording was still going on with another pair of contestants but we decided to have a word with the producer of the show. Out came the reference books and they realised there may have been a bit of confusion. We were not allowed back on the show but very sportingly the programme gave us the £64,000 anyway. Mary and I have always wondered how far we might have gone had we been allowed to resume. The story made the main evening news.

More recently, I was asked to appear on the BBC Saturday night Lottery show with a few other television faces. The programme was celebrating some anniversary or another. Again, there was a lump of charity money up for grabs. This time, though, seven of the contestants would get just £1,000. The ultimate winner would walk away with a charity cheque for £26,000.

It was a long process. We had to take part in all four lottery games as presented in turn by Ian Wright, Eamonn Holmes, Dale Winton and, finally, Phillip Schofield. I had never watched any of the shows, having nearly always been working on Saturday nights myself, but I just about crept through the first two versions, did well in the third, and found myself going solo in the fourth. Another nice cheque, to be split between the Bobby Moore Fund for Cancer Research and the Brain and Spine Foundation. The programme was recorded in front of a studio audience. During a pause, Dale Winton, now sporting a little goatee beard, asked me if I liked it. 'Not particularly,' I replied. 'That's not what you said in bed on Friday night,' he said. The audience laughed, but you always worry that there might be just one person among several hundred who will go away thinking he wasn't joking.

If you are a broadcaster, a lovely way to make a few bob is to do a commercial. Voice-overs pay quite well, but if you are asked to be 'in vision', the fee goes up substantially. The beauty of it is that it usually only involves one day's, or even half a day's, filming. I have earned two hundred times more in one day than I did in the whole of my first year of employment by the Midland Bank Executor and Trustee Company.

At one time, the BBC was very sniffy about allowing their talent to do commercials. The rules eased a bit in my time there, but newsreaders and the like are still prohibited from putting their names to any product lest it inhibits their journalistic impartiality.

A few years ago I was asked by the Gillette Company to do an advertisement for their men's deodorant called Right Guard. The agency involved was quite honest with me. They told me that the idea had been written for Charlton Heston but he'd pulled out at the last minute. The gag was to be that Heston, in his Moses role, would part the Red Sea – relating that to reducing one's underarm perspiration. I found myself doing the acting instead of the Hollywood star and, because it was obviously ridiculous for me to be doing it, I hammed it up with the full agreement of the director, John Lloyd, whose track record includes *Blackadder* and many other hit comedies. Whether or not it sold much Right Guard, I never learned. But it did become something of a cult, with university students in particular.

Another product I got involved in was a plant food, or fertiliser. Here was indeed a lucky break, because I was signed up for five years, with an option on the company's side for another five. The filming of the first advert was to take place in Miami, where you could rely on the sunshine and where the rear garden of a magnificent house was being altered to try to get it to look as English as possible. I arrived at the set and was astonished at what I saw: there were about eight trucks, three caravans, a huge catering wagon and about a hundred technicians. All for me to deliver a couple of lines.

I was introduced to Horace. Horace Hagdown was in his eighties and was originally an advertising man himself. When he was young, he ran into someone called Martin Small, said to have been the inventor of the roll-on deodorant, who told him that the way to make a million dollars was to find a need 'and fill it'.

Then a nursery man called Otto Stern came to see Hagdown for advice about marketing. He complained that his trees and shrubs were arriving in poor condition: the two men became partners and discussed the idea of producing a fertiliser. They took on a technical consultant and produced a water-soluble plant food. Hagdown's wife, Peggy, came up with the name: Miracle Gro. By the time I got involved with the company, it was already selling about £15 million a year of the stuff in Britain alone. The advertising agency involved wanted to do something quirky with the new ads, but dear old Horace definitely had an irony deficiency and our best work was done in trying to keep him amused off-set. He spent most of his time sellotaping English-style flowers on to the indigenous American plants in the garden.

Horace had more money than he could possibly know what to do with and, thanks to his product, I trousered a good few quid as well. Not all went smoothly, though. An intermediary company had been hired by the advertising agency to find the talent for the job – in this case, me. I kept hearing that Miracle Gro thought my fees were a bit over the top. It was only when I found out that the intermediaries were taking round about 45 per cent of the gross that I understood. I had a long protracted legal battle with them, which ended nicely for me when they went into administration and I dealt directly with the Miracle Gro organisation myself. They didn't take up the option of the second five years, because they changed their advertising style to make it more pan-European. I have been replaced by computer imagery, which at least has cut short the continual jibes from my friends, who knew that the only thing I ever do in my garden is sit in it.

I've drawn the line over the years with products I don't agree with. My pet hate is those moneylenders who purport to solve people's problems when in fact they are often getting them into even more debt.

The old moustache has involved me in one or two campaigns as well, in particular for Woolworths and Marks & Spencer, both times involving a decent spot of self-deprecation. Well, if you can part the Red Sea …!

People always ask me about when I went on the *Friday Night with Jonathan Ross* show. He more or less built the interview round my moustache. I wear it simply out of habit. I have a perfectly formed upper lip. At least, I had the last time I saw it. I have shaved it off on holiday once or twice over the years and on each occasion I cannot wait for it to grow again. I feel positively anaemic without it.

I first grew facial hair in the early Seventies. In fact, I grew a 'full set' but after a couple of months I tired of it. While I was shaving off the beard, though, I left a Zapata-style moustache, which was reasonably fashionable then. I know, I know, it isn't now.

Over the years I have occasionally been mistaken for Dickie Davies, the one-time presenter of ITV's *World of Sport* in the days when they had a Saturday afternoon sports programme. Grey hair, moustache, sports presenter, and the same height sitting down: I suppose I can understand why.

In 1984, when the BBC had the Olympics, ITV were battling against us with some of those spurious sports that filled their programme. One lunchtime, their show was starting a while before our own. We were looking forward to the big clash on the track between Zola Budd and Mary Decker, which would end in controversy as both runners fell and Budd was accused of tripping her rival. Dickie went on air with his programme and I listened to his opening words. 'Well, we may not have Mary Decker,' he said, 'but we certainly have double deckers.' They had bus racing. Fair play to him for a clever line at the time.

I was driving back through France one day some years ago and stopped at a filling station for petrol somewhere in the Dordogne. I noticed that there were several haulage vehicles parked alongside – British trucks, clearly identifiable as such. As I looked towards the shop, which had a small refreshment bar, I saw that the drivers were sitting there enjoying a coffee. They were gesturing towards me and eventually, just as I was finishing refuelling, one of them approached me. 'Excuse me,' he said, 'I was just having a bet with my mates inside that you are the television sports presenter. You are, aren't you?' 'I suppose I am,' I replied. He rushed back inside and as I went in to pay for my petrol, the three others were handing over bundles of francs to him. 'Well done,' I said. 'No, all thanks to you, Dickie,' he said.

37

ANYONE FOR TENNIS?

I am hugely privileged to have been invited to enjoy a game of tennis at the All England Lawn Tennis and Croquet Club, Wimbledon. My hosts have usually been my old friend Jimmy Hill, Christine Truman-Janes, or Bill Threlfall, one of the best tennis commentators around and much underrated. Bill was actually ranked World Number One player for his age group – seventy or over. In his youth he might well have been a top player had he had more time free from flying aircraft on and off aircraft carriers with the Navy's Fleet Air Arm. 'It's about time you became a member,' he said. 'The easiest way to get a membership at Wimbledon,' I said, 'is to win the Championship.' Anyway, Bill, his fellow commentator and another former colleague, John Barrett, ex-star player Mark Cox, and Barry Wetherill, whom I also knew quite well, proposed me and gave me the appropriate references. That was six years ago, as I write. I am not holding my breath.

It may be apocryphal, but the story goes that the Chairman of an Irish tennis club was meeting his opposite number at

Wimbledon for lunch. 'How many members have you?' asked the Irishman. He was told there were just a few hundred male members and even fewer ladies. 'Have you thought about advertising?' enquired your man.

Anyway, Wimbledon did afford me a nice gesture in recent years, when I was invited to watch the tennis from the Royal Box. It was a pleasant surprise. I was at ITV at the time.

On another occasion, after my tenure as a Wimbledon presenter came to an end, my good friend Christine invited me to watch play from a very privileged position on Centre Court. I was right in the front row of the stand where the overhanging roof doesn't quite protect you when the rain starts to come down, and so when that happened I put up an umbrella to protect myself. I didn't even realise at the time which umbrella I was using until I saw a picture of myself with the said piece of apparatus on the front page of one of the following day's papers. Some hack even had the temerity to suggest that I was probably being paid to advertise the company's name on the brolly. This was outrageous, but it prompted me to play a joke on my close friend Brian Bedson, the Chief Executive of the company involved, Wyndeham Press plc. I sent him a bill:

To: Presenting your company worldwide at a major sporting event on live television and full press coverage: £50,000

Brian wrote back quick as a flash with his riposte:

To: Supplying umbrella for use at public occasion: £50,000 + VAT @ 17.5%

While we were sitting with Christine, a mobile phone went off during a match, almost a hanging offence at Wimbledon. 'How rude,' she said and then, to her horror, realised that the offending noise was emanating from her own handbag. She was mortified. At the time she was on the Club committee.

The Championships are two of the best weeks in the sporting calendar and so when Bob Shennan, the Controller of BBC Radio 5 Live, recently asked me if I would be interested in presenting a show each evening, I jumped at the chance. I had travelled full circle, queuing up for hours to watch play on the outside courts as a teenager, to my radio commentary days, through 'The Des and Gerry Show', being the presenter of the live television coverage, and, now, radio once again. It was so great to be back at the BBC at a big event. For me, it was like coming home.

38

ANYONE FOR TABLE TENNIS?

On 24 October 2003 I stood on the balcony of my house by the Thames and watched as the last three Concordes flew towards Heathrow, the end of one of the most controversial, but magnificent, periods in British aviation. I have to admit I got rather emotional and shed a tear at the passing of this wonderful machine. It seemed to me that, instead of progress, we were regressing. Supersonic flight for passengers was at an end for the foreseeable future. I first flew on Concorde in the Seventies, not long after the plane was commissioned. The experience was completely exhilarating. Just three and a half hours to Washington DC. The trip was made compliments of BBC Radio, for whom I was presenting a programme called *Going Places*. As the title would imply, it was a show about transport and travel and was aired at 6.30 on Friday evenings on Radio 4. Actually, I was a stand-in because Barry Norman, the regular presenter, had some television commitments that clashed, and I was brought in by the producer, Roger McDonald, to take his place for a few weeks.

As it turned out, Barry missed out on a fantastic experience. Concorde to the States, and back, first class, on the *QE2*, reporting on transatlantic travel as we went and transport systems within the USA while we were there.

At the start of our return journey, as the *QE2* was steaming slowly out of New York harbour, with the Statue of Liberty in our sights, McDonald and I were in the privileged position of being on the bridge of the ship. During the four-day voyage, we dined at the Captain's table and had access to all parts of the vessel, including the engine room, a vast cavern of pipes and boilers, with muscle-bound, sweating men hard at it as the passengers enjoyed the finest wine and cuisine above them. Not the sort of working environment I would have chosen. In the mid Atlantic the weather deteriorated and we watched as a line of elderly passengers queued up for anti-seasickness jabs. Luckily, we remained untroubled.

One morning, I heard an announcement about a table tennis competition and, with a bit of spare time on my hands, I thought I would have a crack at it. I had noticed a rather nice little cup, which would make a pleasant souvenir of the trip. I duly entered and found myself playing a couple of elderly gentlemen, whom I managed to ease past. I was now in the Final to be played the next day in front of an audience.

I arrived and picked up one of the rather ragged bats that were supplied, with a percentage of the pimples missing, and looked up to find my opponent, whom I had not met up to this point. He was dressed in green polo shirt and green shorts, and under his arm he was carrying three table tennis bats, and the bats had covers on them. I was in trouble. In the knock-up, I spent most of my time picking the ball off the floor as another shot sped past me.

342

In this match, I was overwhelmed 21–3, 21–4.

This guy was good. It was just after we had shaken hands that his wife approached me. 'Hope you didn't mind my husband playing left-handed,' she said. 'Isn't he left-handed, then?' I stuttered. 'No,' she said, 'but he thought he would make it a bit fairer by playing that way.' My opponent turned out to be a member of the South African table tennis team. I hope the victory gave him some pleasure.

I was back on Concorde some years later, flying once again to Washington to do an interview with the American boxer Riddick Bowe, who held a version of the World heavyweight title at the time. We obviously needed the interview in a hurry. We arrived at around five in the evening, having set off from London around the same time, conducted the interview, had dinner, a few hours' sleep, and then back on the very same plane. I had been away from home for just around twenty-four hours.

My last trip on the great plane was in March 1999 when returning from the first Lennox Lewis–Evander Holyfield World heavyweight title fight, the one in which Lewis was disgracefully judged to have drawn when he won almost every round. He avenged that piece of nonsense, of course, when he and Holyfield met for the second time.

After the fight I met up with the comedian and actor Lee Evans, and together we watched in amazement as Jack Nicholson got involved in a discussion about the fight with a few London 'heavies'. They were, of course, in awe of him. Eventually, Jack tired of the company. 'It's been great talking to you guys,' he drawled. 'Listening to you has been a little more tricky. Goodnight.'

In the Concorde lounge in New York, I spotted Chris Eubank

and went and sat with him. Chris chatted for a few moments and then went back to his book. 'What are you reading?' I enquired. 'I am reading *Thayings*,' he said. 'Great things that people have thaid.' 'You want to get hold of some Oscar Wilde or George Bernard Shaw,' I told him, 'they were a right pair of clever dicks.' 'Shaw? Yeth, I think I have heard of him,' replied Chris. 'How are you thpelling that?'

Talking of a right pair, I bumped into Jordan at a comedy awards show one night. ''Ere,' she said, "we've got something in common. We both come from Brighton.' 'Well, I lived there for a long time,' I said, 'but I'm delighted to meet you because I think you have absolutely made the most of yourself and done brilliantly. By the way, do I call you Jordan or Katie?' 'Call me Katie,' she said, 'Jordan's the business.'

We were chatting away when Katie spotted the newly crowned Miss World, who had just arrived and was also there to present an award. She was Rosanna, the daughter of Chris de Burgh, who was with her. I had met Chris a few times and he had written me a perfectly charming letter when I'd had my problems with the tabloid press. Chris, too, had been on the receiving end of the 'love rat' type of disclosure. I had met Rosanna a couple of years before when she and her Dad had been to a Liverpool match. She was just about sixteen, and I remarked to Chris then how stunningly beautiful she was. 'Must get it from the mother's side,' I'd joked. Chris agreed. Now, representing Ireland, this willowy girl had just won the Miss World crown.

Jordan was keen to meet her, and so I introduced them. They chatted for a bit, and after Rosanna had moved away, Jordan remarked how gorgeous she was. 'You're a beautiful girl your-self,' I offered. 'Nah,' she said, 'I'm just all make-up and false tits.' When it comes to sex appeal, though, I can tell you, Jordan beat Miss World hands down – or is that tits up?

The actor Leslie Phillips was also there. He and Jordan went out on stage, hand in hand, to present their award. Leslie was doing his 'ding-dong' bit, with good reason this time. I was next. I complained to host Jonathan Ross that, just when I was trying to pull Jordan, Phillips had stepped in. 'I'm obviously too young for her,' I said.

It may sound a strange thing to say for someone who has spent a good many hours of his life with a television camera up his snout but, quite unlike the highly photogenic Miss Price, or even Mr Eubank (a man who could hardly be described as camera shy), I am one of those people who hates having his photograph taken. My face actually downplays my inner feelings. When I feel average, I look despondent. When I'm happy, I look bored. When I'm elated, I look barely content, until I actually laugh. I do that rather well. But many times in my life I've been told by passing strangers to 'cheer up'.

There have been so many occasions where I have been required to sit in front of a photographer to have my picture taken for mug shots to publicise programmes. I've spent even more time making excuses to try and get out of having to do so.

Most photographers say 'smile' when they want you to smile. Nothing is more certain to induce *rigor mortis* in my face, which becomes paralysed with hate for the person imparting the instruction. David Bailey once said to me: 'Give us a touch of hope, Des.' It made me laugh out loud. Again 'A crumb, anything', and it made me laugh again. We bonded. And he took a great photograph.

The best photographers take the fewest pictures, sure in their ability to get the best out of you. The hopeless ones take thousands of shots to cover their backsides. And they're always the ones who say 'smile'.

Patrick Lichfield, like Bailey, takes the minimum of time and has been a pleasure to work with. I once also had my photo taken by Antony Armstrong-Jones for the front page of the *Radio Times*. He was very fussy. You can judge for yourself the quality of his picture: it's in this book. I call it my 'Danny DeVito' cover. When he was taking it, I suggested that I would look like a very short person standing up because you cannot see that I am actually sitting. Of the group, I am easily the tallest person there, but you would never know it. He assured me that it would be all right. I'll leave you to make up your own mind.

Those in the picture are: John Thaw, Julie Goodyear, Bruce Forsyth, Michael Palin, Amanda Burton and David Jason.

39

RETIRING? ME?

In my time at ITV I presented *The Premiership* for three seasons, the FA Cup (including two finals) for two seasons, and the Champions League for all five seasons I was there. Of these the Champions League produced the best quality football and found me travelling all over Europe in the process to cover the games.

The year before I joined ITV, Manchester United became the European champions and the year after I left, Liverpool won it. Unfortunately, in my five seasons, the nearest a British club got to winning were semi-final appearances by Manchester United, Leeds, and Chelsea.

I thoroughly enjoyed my time at ITV. My senior editor, Rick Waumsley, John Watts, whom I had known at the BBC in the Seventies, Paul McNamara, Tony Pastor and David Moss were able and charming colleagues; Brian Barwick, now chief executive of the Football Association, was a tremendous Head of Sport and the man mainly responsible for my move to ITV. We had a lot of fun.

The European Football Championships in Portugal in the summer of 2004 was to be my last big live event as a television sports presenter. England had qualified and looked to have a great chance of winning. The stadia in Portugal were modern and beautifully prepared. I was keen as mustard to do the job as well as I could. I wanted to leave the business at the top of my form.

On my first day I'd arranged to do an interview with David Beckham at the England team headquarters. I'd first met Beckham when he was about nineteen years of age. He had just won the Northern Young Sports Personality of the Year Award and I had been asked to present the awards in Manchester at an untelevised event. Beckham was already making his mark in the Manchester United team and he came over as a pleasant young man with a good sense of humour.

In more recent years I'd bumped into him occasionally at a Champions League or England match and although we'd never had time for anything approaching a conversation, he nearly always took time to say hello. Then, in the summer of 2002, along came the famous Beckham party to which I found myself invited. 'It'll be some sort of bun fight,' I said to Jane Morgan. 'I think I'll be washing my hair on that day.' On my behalf she turned the invitation down. But over the next few days, I kept hearing that the occasion was the hottest ticket in town and, to my shame, I got Jane to 'get me back in again'.

It was a spectacular party, held in aid of charity. Beckham was just getting over his metatarsal injury, which would hamper him in the forthcoming World Cup finals in the Far East. Nonetheless, he and Victoria found time to commit themselves to the occasion wholeheartedly.

They warmly welcomed everyone personally and then, after

dinner, Beckham found himself making a speech in aid of the charity involved. He was reading the speech from cards, and not doing it terribly well. Then he used his marbles: he admitted he wasn't very good at speeches, got rid of the cards, and spoke from the heart. He delighted everyone present. Many thousands were raised for the charity.

Now in Portugal in 2004 I was about to interview him. My producer managed to find the oldest and hottest taxi in Lisbon for the journey, driven by a homicidal maniac who seemed to be doing his level best to kill us. I am a nervous car passenger at the best of times and was not pleased. As it turned out, Beckham had got confused about the timing and had kept me waiting for several hours, having gone off to see his wife. When he returned he was full of apologies and the interview took place.

I also told him that in the next few months, after I left ITV, I would be starting an interview series on Radio 5 Live and asked him if he would be one of the guests. 'It will bring you untold riches, of course,' I said. He promised he would, and in due course on a trip back to England he turned up to fulfil the promise.

I interviewed him for nearly an hour. He was articulate and honest, and never ducked a question. I even asked him about the dreadful tattoo on the back of his neck. 'You'll regret that when you're my age,' I said. 'Luckily no one will care about me then,' he said.

But of course David Beckham will never be anonymous. In my view he will achieve much in life beyond football. As Muhammad Ali might have said to him: 'He's not as dumb as he looks.'

England's first match was against France and they seemed to be home and dry until Monsieur Zidane changed the course of the game. Gareth Southgate had joined our team of pundits and brought a special insight to the proceedings. He was articulate and bright and has a future in the media if he so desires. Everyone thought that despite the setback, England would still qualify for the later stages.

The following day, my ITV bosses were whooping and hollering about the audience figure for the broadcast, around twenty million, not including the pub audiences. It was the biggest since David v. Goliath, etc. Such things bother TV executives, but I just wanted to do the broadcast.

A couple of days later, Sir Bobby Robson enjoyed one of his 'firsts' on the trip. He had his first glass of beer in his seventy-one years. I suggested he must have had a few pints as a young lad. He insisted not. Bobby rarely took any alcohol, unlike the rest of us on such tours, who were usually gagging for it after the shows.

We travelled round Portugal in the Desmobile, a luxury coach usually used by pop groups and the like, as we had done four years before in Belgium and Holland. Bobby told me that his secretary had mentioned that only the Pope and I had 'mobiles'. 'Bet His Holiness doesn't have a loo on his,' I offered. Bobby's second 'first' came a night or two later in an Indian restaurant, one of the few in Portugal. After his beer experience, now it was the first ever curry for our football knight. 'At the rate he's going on new experiences,' said Ally McCoist, 'he's only a week away from his first crack cocaine.' We cracked up. I miss nights like that.

England got through to meet Portugal, the hosts, in the quarter-final but the match was a BBC exclusive, so Terry Venables, the Head of Sport, Brian Barwick, myself and one or two others were given what were supposed to be VIP tickets to go to the game. The seats turned out to be in Row U up in the sky amongst assorted fans of both countries. Venables and I ended up having our photographs taken more times than Naomi Campbell on an average week. Venables was exhausted after climbing to our position – he was just a couple of weeks away from a replacement hip operation. Beckham missed a penalty in the shootout, and England were out.

Sunday 4 July was my last day. I noted it was Independence Day. Ron Atkinson phoned from home to wish me luck – a big gesture from a man who was missing out on his first major championship for years and going through his own particular nightmare at the time.

There were messages from other friends and colleagues, but I remained strangely dispassionate and unemotional about the whole thing. Just another major event coming to an end. I knew I would be more likely to miss it all in August when there would be no *Premiership* programme to do, and that is how it turned out. I have missed the banter and the laughs with a group of fabulous people, but now I am on to the next chapter in life's little adventure.

Wherever I go, I often still hear the opinion that ITV do not cover sport as well as the BBC. It was a view I held myself until I went to work for them. Actually, they cover football equally well, despite the constraints of a commercial station, and they will never get the lion's share of any audience when they go head to head with the BBC on major events, simply because they have to show the adverts. They are, after all, what pay the bills.

Early in 2005, ITV proved they could broadcast the Boat Race equally as well, if not better, than the BBC, despite its seeming an unlikely event for them. Peter Drury did a masterly commentary, but unfortunately ITV's reputation of going in and out of sports is not a good one. I have listed elsewhere those sports with which they have flirted and then abandoned. ITV need to amend their strategy for sport and show some long-term commitment without looking immediately to the profitability or otherwise of the event. The new head of the sports department, Mark Sharman, will no doubt have this in mind, but will the money men allow him to follow his broadcasting and journalistic instincts?

At the time of writing, BBC Sport seems to be in a pretty healthy state, although it is now sometimes hard to find any continuity in its presenter personnel. They seem to have a great number of faces, many of whom have yet to capture the public's confidence or appreciation, although Steve Rider, Sue Barker, Gary Lineker and Clare Balding remain top notch.

And Sky goes from strength to strength, although once again, apart from one or two names, they cover so many events that it is difficult for the viewer to become familiar with those broadcasting them. In football commentary these days, the average football fan could be forgiven for thinking that there's John Motson and then a host of others, all of them competent but comparatively less well known. With multi-channel broadcasting, the days seem to be over when individual football commentators like David Coleman and Brian Moore became nationally famous. Much the same may well apply to sports presenters.

After taking a breather and thinking my broadcasting days were possibly over, I have found myself busy again. I've done several programmes for the BBC, including a VE Day special and a third appearance as host of *Have I Got News For You*, plus another prime-time show *Are You Younger Than You Think?* – and without the silly moustache, I probably would be. I've also presented a sports legends series for Sky with Sir

David Frost and a radio interview series, plus a Wimbledon show for Radio 5 Live, as well as penning these reminiscences. As Shakespeare wrote, 'If all the year were playing holidays, to sport would be as tedious as to work.' I've realised that I still like to be busy.

Despite all that, it is still not a proper job and I continue to have the distinct feeling that, really and truly, I should have been at work.

LIST OF CREDITS

BBC Radio
Sports Report
Sport on 2
Today
After Seven
Treble Chance Quiz
Forces Chance
The Des Lynam Show
They Think It's All Over
The Queen's Silver Jubilee
Going Places
Des Meets
Des at Wimbledon
Boxing, tennis and golf commentator

BBC Television
Grandstand
Sportsnight
Match of the Day
Sportswide
It's My Pleasure

Points of View
Sports Personality of the Year
Hillsborough Memorial Service
A Tribute to Jill Dando
How Do They Do That?
The Holiday Programme
The Travel Show
VE Day Special: *We'll Meet Again*
Have I Got News for You
Are You Younger Than You Think?
Football and boxing commentator

ITV
The Premiership
The Champions League
The FA Cup Finals
The BAFTA Awards

SKY
The World's Greatest Sporting Legend

Major Events Presented
World Cups
European Championships
The Olympics
FA Cup Finals
Winter Olympics
Grand Nationals
Wimbledon Championships
World Athletics Championships
World Skating Championships

Commonwealth Games
World Boxing Titles
Open Golf and Ryder Cups

INDEX

DL refers to Desmond Lynam.